TEXAS
~ EDITION ~

I Didn't Know That
ALMANAC

2007

COOL SPRINGS PRESS
A Division of Thomas Nelson Publishers
Since 1798

www.thomasnelson.com

Published by Cool Springs Press, a Division of Thomas Nelson Inc., P.O. Box 141000, Nashville, Tennessee, 37214

First printing 2006
Printed in the United States of America
10 9 8 7 6 5 4 3 2 1

Cover Design: Bruce Gore, Gore Studios
Interior Design & Layout: Drew Pope

Cool Springs Press books may be purchased in bulk for educational, business, fundraising, or sales promotional use.

For information, please email **SpecialMarkets@ThomasNelson.com**.
Visit the Cool Springs Press website at **www.coolspringspress.net**.

Table of Contents

Howdy, Folks!

There's no doubt that Texas is a unique state. The name alone evokes images of larger-than-life icons, bold flavors, unforgettable sights, and a sense of pride that non-Texans just won't understand.

With this edition, we continue to provide "did you know" facts and conjecture about the many aspects of Texas life. Whether you're new to Texas or a native, there's something here for you.

Warning: While doing our research for this book, we found that often a kernel of information would surface that we couldn't resist investigating further. As a result you'll find small-to-tiny gems of trivia among the bigger stories. Once you've read it to the end, we suggest you give it a second pass to catch what you might have missed.

Join us again as we celebrate life in Texas!

WHAT IN THE SAM HOUSTON?

Texans are rightly proud of Sam Houston! Not only was he president of the Republic of Texas (twice) and a member of both the U.S. House of Representatives and the Senate, he was also the only person in history to be a governor of two states (Tennessee and Texas)! During the Texas Revolution, Houston won the Battle of San Jacinto, defeating Mexican general Santa Anna and winning independence for the Republic of Texas.

Born in Virginia in 1793, Houston led a full—and tempestuous—life. After his father died suddenly when Sam was fourteen, his mother took the family to Tennessee, where Houston spent most of his time with the Cherokee Indians, learning their language and customs.

His political career began while he served under Andrew Jackson during the campaign against the Creek Indians. Later he studied law and became an attorney in Nashville, Tennessee, where he was elected to Congress twice before becoming governor of Tennessee. During his reelection campaign, he and his first wife separated and later divorced.

Houston moved to Arkansas, married a Cherokee woman, ran a trading post, and drank so heavily that his nickname became the "drunken raven." This period nearly destroyed his reputation, and after a high-profile arrest for assaulting a man with a hickory cane, he moved to Texas to make a fresh start.

He became involved in the movement for Texas independence, and in 1835 he was named a major general of the Texas army. He stayed active in Texas politics even after it was annexed by the United States.

With his third wife, Margaret, Houston raised eight children. When he died in 1863, his last words were, "Texas. Texas. Margaret." ⊕

Did You Know?

With our puritanical ancestry, Americans are pretty darn good at euphemisms for, uh, swearing. The words Sam Hill (as in "What in the Sam Hill—?") are just an early nineteenth-century euphemism for "hell" used as an oath . . . and in Texas, the larger-than-life Sam Houston is often substituted!

Who was the father of Texas?

Stephen Fuller Austin was born in Virginia in 1793. When he was five years old, he moved with his family to Pitosi, Missouri, a town established by his father Moses. As a young man, Austin took over the family's store after returning from college, eventually managing the family mining business, and serving in the legislature.

When the family business failed, Stephen moved to Arkansas territory, engaging in trading and land speculation. While there, the governor appointed him circuit judge, but after serving one month, Austin moved to Louisiana, studying law while staying with his friend Joseph Hawkins.

Meanwhile, Austin's father, newly bankrupt, traveled to San Antonio, gaining a land grant for 300 families in the Spanish territory of Tejas. Although unwilling to join his father, Austin obtained a loan from Hawkins for the venture. Upon his father's death in 1821, Stephen left a newspaper position, traveling to San Antonio to reauthorize the grant, forming the only Texas colony approved by Mexico's national government.

Finding the best location for the colony, Austin advertised land along the Brazos and Colorado rivers. Eager to relocate to the rich bottomland, colonists quickly grabbed the 300 grants. Obtaining contracts for more families over the next few years, Austin maintained authority over the settlers but made little money from colonists unwilling to pay for his services and unhappy with his cautious leadership.

When Mexico tried to stop further immigration, Austin's diplomacy gained exemption for the colony, but trying to appease the Mexican government, Austin was charged with insurrection in 1834 and imprisoned until 1835. Returning to Texas, he still favored alliance with Mexico, but the outbreak of the Texas Revolution in October forced him to press for independence, achieved in 1836 with the establishment of The Republic of Texas. Thus Stephen Austin would become known as "The Father of Texas." ⊕

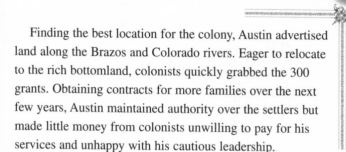

The Old 300

The settlers of Austin's first colony were called **"The Old Three 300."** The majority hailed from the South—most from Louisiana, followed by Alabama, Arkansas, Tennessee, and Missouri. Most were successful farmers, some quite affluent, and all but four were literate. The 300 families, most of British ancestry, were required to renounce U.S. citizenship and become citizens of Spain.

Oil Barons, Roughnecks, Roustabouts, and Wildcatters

How did a one-armed mechanic and self-educated geologist named Patillo Higgins get others to believe in the future of Texas oil? Higgins spent over a decade convincing others and raising capital to drill a discovery well on a site named Gladys Hill. Higgins collaborated with George O'Brien, George Carrol, Emma John, and J. F. Lanier in the Gladys City Oil, Gas, and Manufacturing Company. Their shallow wells failed. Frustrating years passed before Higgins ran an advertisement in a local newspaper. Only one man replied.

That man was Captain Anthony F. Lucas. A Czech engineer who had served in the Austrian navy, Lucas also had experience as a salt miner. The local press and geologists, skeptical of Higgins, did not think Lucas would change their minds. His first few attempts were failures, and the money ran out. Lucas took James Guffey and John Galey, the same two who had left the area three years earlier, as partners. Something made them change their minds.

On October 27, 1900, Galey picked a spot and Lucas and his crew began drilling. The process was plagued by problems. Wildcatters had to drill through hundreds of feet of sand. Holes caved in, drill bits broke— until one of Lucas's drillers reasoned that water flushing the drill hole was not the best solution. Mud was. Instead of pumping water into the hole, they used mud. It helped retrieve the cuttings and kept the sides of the drill hole from caving in. Exhausted after two months of back-breaking drilling, the crew took a week-long holiday for Christmas. They were at a depth of 880 feet when they stopped.

ROUSTABOUT- Does general maintenance and construction work at oil fields.

ROUGHNECK- Carries out the drilling operation under the direction of the Driller. A promotion from Roustabout.

DRILLER- Operates and monitors all drilling systems and equipment and supervises all drill crew work. Drillers also control the power-driven derrick that raises and lowers the drilling bit into the well bore.

WILDCATTER- Engages in speculative mining or well drilling in areas not known to be productive.

THAT HISTORIC DAY IN JANUARY

Revived by their break, within a week the crew had drilled down to 1,021 feet. The date was January 9, 1901. The drill bit broke and the crew needed to replace it. Seventeen hours later, they lowered the drill back into the hole and heard a pop. Mud started bubbling up and the drill pipe came back up with a great force. Then nothing happened. Frustrated, the drillers started to clean up the mess when an immense cannon sound scared the group back from the hole. Mud spouted out of the hole, natural gas rushed out, and then greenish-black oil gushed into the air.

The gusher was twice the size of the derrick and reached 150 feet in the air. The Lucas I **flowed at an initial rate of** 100,000 barrels a day. It was more than **all the other oil-producing wells in America combined.** The world had never seen such a gusher. Spindletop Hill was quickly covered with over 100 oil companies. **The gusher at Spindletop** was responsible for several oil company giants: Gulf Oil, Amoco, and Humble Oil Company, which later became part of Exxon. Nothing in the oil industry was ever the same **after that day in January.**⊕

TEXAS-SIZED OIL COMPANIES

Company Name	Revenue in Millions	Profit
Exxon Mobil Corporation	$288,189.0	$25,330.0
Chevron Texaco	$147,967.0	$13,328.0
Conoco Phillips	$121,663.0	$8,129.0
Valero Energy	$53,918.6	$1,803.8
Marathon	$45,444.0	$1,261.0
Tesoro	$12,139.2	$327.9
Frontier Oil	$2,861.7	$69.8
Holly	$2,246.4	$83.9

"The King of the Wildcatters"

Glenn McCarthy—a barroom-brawling, hard-drinking, fast-talking quintessential Texas oilman—discovered eleven oil fields and helped expand many others. Born in 1907 on Christmas Day, McCarthy was working as a water boy in the Beaumont oil fields by the age of eight. He first discovered oil in Anahuac, near Trinity Bay on the Gulf Coast, and between 1932 and 1942, McCarthy struck oil thirty-eight times! Besides wildcatting, McCarthy spent $21 million to build the famous Shamrock Hotel in Houston, reinforcing the perception that Houston—and Texas—were larger than life. "Diamond Glenn" spent his downtime engaging in fistfights at the hotel's private Cork Club. Edna Ferber's 1952 novel, *Giant*, contains a character, oilman Jett Rink, modeled after McCarthy. His flamboyant life ended quietly, in a two-story house near La Porte in 1988. ✪

TEXAS SPEAK

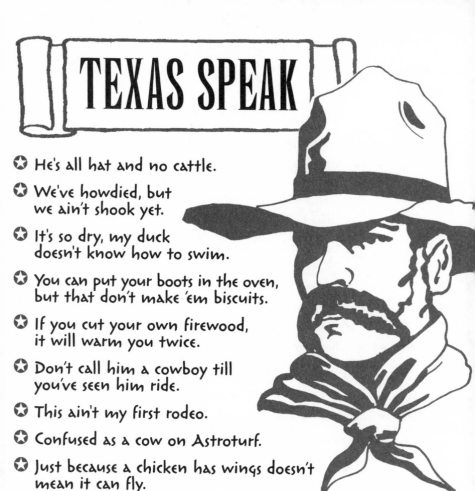

- ✪ He's all hat and no cattle.
- ✪ We've howdied, but we ain't shook yet.
- ✪ It's so dry, my duck doesn't know how to swim.
- ✪ You can put your boots in the oven, but that don't make 'em biscuits.
- ✪ If you cut your own firewood, it will warm you twice.
- ✪ Don't call him a cowboy till you've seen him ride.
- ✪ This ain't my first rodeo.
- ✪ Confused as a cow on Astroturf.
- ✪ Just because a chicken has wings doesn't mean it can fly.
- ✪ I'm so broke, I can't pay attention.
- ✪ The wind's blowing like perfume through a prom.
- ✪ If I felt any better, I'd drop my harp plumb through the cloud.
- ✪ She's thin as a bar of soap after a hard day's washing.
- ✪ As bad off as a rubber-nosed woodpecker in a petrified forest.
- ✪ Don't worry 'bout the mule, son, just load the wagon.
- ✪ Time to paint your butt white and run like an antelope.
- ✪ It's so dry, the trees are bribin' the dogs.

December 29, 1845
TEXAS STATEHOOD

AFTER GAINING INDEPENDENCE from Mexico in the spring of 1836, Texans overwhelmingly voted for annexation with the United States in September 1836—but U.S. President Martin Van Buren opposed the proposition, claiming fear of war with Mexico, although antislavery sentiment probably influenced his decision too. This began almost ten years of a political Texas Two-Step!

President Mirabeau Lamar (1838–1841) opposed annexation, so the offer was withdrawn by the Republic of Texas in 1838. Sam Houston tried to revisit the idea early in his second term as president of the Republic (1841–1844). U.S. President John Tyler proposed annexation in 1844 to keep Texas from forging ties to Great Britain, but this treaty of annexation was rejected.

In the national campaign for president that year, James K. Polk pledged Texas statehood, and once elected, he vigorously pursued that goal. At long last, on December 29, 1845, the U.S. Congress accepted Texas's constitution and Texas officially became a state in the United States of America.

The formal transfer of authority from the Republic of Texas to the United States took place on February 19, 1846. On that date, Republic President Anson Jones declared, "The final act in this great drama is now performed; the Republic of Texas is no more."

Texas Counties

★ 254 Counties

★ 254 Names

★ 254 Stories

Did You Know?

- Texas has more counties than any other state in the union.

- Forty-one of those counties are larger than the state of Rhode Island.

- Brewster, the largest county, is 6,169 square miles. Connecticut (5,018 square miles), Delaware (1,982 square miles), and Rhode Island (1,045 square miles) can each fit inside this county. Connecticut and Rhode Island can fit inside Brewster County together!

- The first 23 counties in Texas were created on March 17, 1836.

- *Panola* (Panola County) is the Native American word for cotton.

- At one time, all county courthouses were required to be centrally located so that voters could travel there and back in one day.

- Today most county seats are within five miles of their county's center.

- *Lampasas* (Lampasas County) is the Spanish word for lily.

- The tallest mountain in Texas stands in Culberson County.

- San Jacinto and Val Verde Counties are named after battles.

- Freestone County is named after a peach.

- Harris County has the most people with 3,087,153. It is also the fifth most-populated county in the nation.

- Loving County has only 96 residents.

- There are 200 county auditors in Texas.

- Ten counties in Texas honor colonizers such as Stephen F. Austin.

- Live Oak County and Orange County are named for trees.

- The last county in Texas, Kenedy, was created in 1921.

POTUS

★ ★ ★ ★ ★ ★ ★ ★ ★ ★

PRESIDENT OF THE UNITED STATES

Four U.S. presidents can be considered Texans:

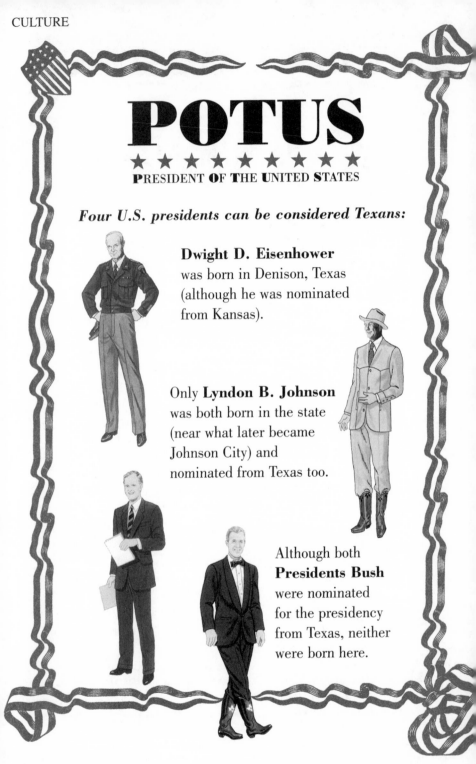

Dwight D. Eisenhower was born in Denison, Texas (although he was nominated from Kansas).

Only **Lyndon B. Johnson** was both born in the state (near what later became Johnson City) and nominated from Texas too.

Although both **Presidents Bush** were nominated for the presidency from Texas, neither were born here.

Largest  Texas Cities

The People

Population 2004
(State Data Center estimate) ... 22,490,022

Population 2000
(U.S. Census count) 20,851,820

Population 1990
(U.S. Census count) 16,986,510

Population increase 1990–2004 ...... 24.5%

Notable Nicknames

"Architect of Annexation"
Anson Jones (1798–1858)

"Betsy Ross of Texas"
Joanna Troutman (1818–1879)

"Father of Texas"
Stephen F. Austin (1793–1836)

"First Native Governor"
James Stephen Hogg (1851–1906)

"Mother of Texas"
Jane Long (1798–1880)

"Father of Texas Education"
Mirabeau B. Lamar (1798–1859)

"Father of Texas Journalism"
Charles DeMorse (1816–1887)

"Father of the Texas Navy"
Samuel May Williams (1795–1858)

"Poet President of Texas"
Mirabeau B. Lamar (1798–1859)

"Raven"
Sam Houston (1793–1863)

"Savior of the Alamo"
Clara Driscoll (1881–1945)

Population 2000 census	City
1,953,631	Houston
1,188,580	Dallas
1,144,646	San Antonio
656,562	Austin
563,662	El Paso
534,694	Fort Worth
332,969	Arlington
277,454	Corpus Christi
222,030	Plano
215,768	Garland
199,564	Lubbock
191,615	Irving
176,576	Laredo
173,627	Amarillo
141,674	Pasadena
139,722	Brownsville
127,427	Grand Prairie
124,523	Mesquite
115,930	Abilene
113,866	Beaumont
113,726	Waco
109,576	Carrollton
106,414	McAllen
104,197	Wichita Falls
94,996	Midland

THE OFFICIAL TEXAS STATE HOLIDAY

★

JANUARY 19 Confederate Heroes Day

Several states in the South have set aside days to memorialize men and women who gave their life for the Confederate States of America. In Texas, Confederate Heroes Day celebrates the birthdays of Robert E. Lee (January 19) and Jefferson Davis (June 3).

Even Arlington National Cemetery in Virginia has a memorial dedicated to Confederate soldiers. In fact, the history of Arlington begins with the Civil War. The United States's national struggle created the need for a cemetery to bury the war dead. Although hundreds of Confederate soldiers were buried there, it was considered a Union cemetery until after the Spanish-American War when the wounds of separation began to heal.

Jefferson Davis

A monument to the Confederate soldiers interred in Arlington was dedicated on June 4, 1914.

Robert E. Lee

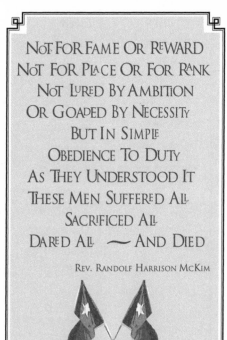

NOT FOR FAME OR REWARD
NOT FOR PLACE OR FOR RANK
NOT LURED BY AMBITION
OR GOADED BY NECESSITY
BUT IN SIMPLE
OBEDIENCE TO DUTY
AS THEY UNDERSTOOD IT
THESE MEN SUFFERED ALL
SACRIFICED ALL
DARED ALL — AND DIED

REV. RANDOLF HARRISON MCKIM

The Blizzard State
& Other Nicknames for the State of Texas

- **The Lone Star State**—This name comes from the symbol of the one star on the state flag.

- **The Beef State**—Often called this because of the importance of ranching and beef production in Texas.

- **The Banner State**—A political nickname given to a front-runner or someone in the leading position. When applied to Texas, it probably refers to Texas's political influence due to the many people who live there.

- **The Blizzard State**—Not your normal snow blizzard, but a reference to the frequent dust and wind storms that sweep the state.

- **The Jumbo State**—P. T. Barnum brought Jumbo, the largest elephant in captivity, to the United States in 1882. Jumbo was used to describe anything huge or gigantic, including Texas.

- **The Super-American State**—*The New Yorker* magazine gave Texas this name in 1961. Looks like New Yorkers have some sense after all.

Texas by the Numbers

- Number of incorporated cities: 1,210

- Number of cities with 100,000 population or more: 25

- Number of cities with 50,000 population or more: 58

- Number of cities with 10,000 population or more: 221

- Area (total): 268,581 square miles

- Land area: 261,797 square miles

- Water area: 6,784 square miles

- Geographic center: About 15 miles northeast of Brady in northern McCulloch County

- Highest point: Guadalupe Peak (8,749 ft.) in Culberson County in far West Texas

- Lowest point: Gulf of Mexico (sea level)

- 28th State to enter the Union on Dec. 29, 1845

- Present constitution adopted: 1876

DALLAS COWBOY CHEERLEADERS

The Darlings of the NFL

In Texas, where football is the state religion, being a cheerleader is akin to being a traveling evangelist.

Among these icons, the Dallas Cowboys Cheerleaders are arguably the most famous. With their white and blue star spangled uniforms, dazzling smiles and stunning athleticism, these women have stood out since their first Championship days in the 1970s.

It was all the idea of Tex Schramm, the Cowboys' general manager. He talked the idea over with Dee Brock, the cheerleaders' manager, and the decision was made to expand the group into a sideline of glamorous, choreographed dancers. Brock recruited Texie Waterman, one of the top dancers in America, to judge the auditions and help create the group.

Sixty women attended the first audition. Seven were chosen. When the 1972–73 season kicked off that fall, the Cowboys introduced their cheerleaders and the crowd loved them. Nevertheless, it was not until 1976 that the nation fell under their spell. During Superbowl X, a television camera operator shot a close-up of one of the girls, and she winked. The nation was hooked. Seventy-five million viewers, one third of the nation, saw that wink and wanted more.

The phenomenon of the squad goes well beyond the football field. The cheerleaders have appeared in network television specials, several commercials, and have shared the stage with Clint Black, Shania Twain, Randy Travis, Reba McEntire, Jessica Simpson, and Billy Gilman. The Dallas Cowboys Cheerleaders made a two-hour, made-for-television movie, which aired January 14, 1979, that remains one of the highest rated in history.

The group travels internationally, entertaining crowds worldwide. In 1979, the U.S. Department of Defense requested a USO Christmas tour of installations in Korea. The cheerleaders were enthusiastically received, and since then the group has made a tradition of visiting military troops. At last count, the Dallas Cowboys Cheerleaders have performed 49 times to boost the military morale around the world. Most of the cheerleaders' non-game appearances are for charity.

3 CHEERS FOR "HERKIE"

Inventor of the POM PON

Lawrence "Herkie" Herkimer began his career as a cheerleader at North Dallas High School in Texas as a way to face his stuttering problem. He continued as a cheerleader at Southern Methodist University and as a graduate student at the University of Illinois. In 1948, he started the fledgling National Cheerleading Association in his hometown of Dallas.

Soon after, he held the first cheerleader camp at Sam Houston State University. Fifty-two girls attended the first camp, which included classes on public speaking and sessions with an English teacher to help with cheer rhymes. The girls weren't thrilled with speech and English, but they loved Herkimer's use of motions and gymnastics to motivate the crowd.

Shortly after the clinic, Herkimer was at the New York World's Fair, where he saw color television for the first time. He realized that cheerleaders needed something more colorful than their chrome batons. Herkimer had the idea of tying crepe paper ribbons to sticks and waving them at the crowd. The Wichita Falls, Texas, High School cheerleaders first used the pom pons at a halftime show, and the most popular tool in cheerleading was born.

Herkimer and his wife started the Cheerleader Supply Company in their garage, packing pom pon kits and sending them to schools. The company grew to supply skirts, sweaters, dancewear, and booster items to schools worldwide, and the spirit industry Herkimer started in 1948 is now a multimillion dollar business. ☉

★ Did You Know?

It's no typo! In cheerleading language, the proper spelling of the hand-held strips of plastic used to add flourish to cheers is Pom Pon. The commonly used spelling of Pom Pom refers to the smaller but similar decorative balls such as those used on clothing or curtains.

Famous Cheerleaders

George W. Bush	Meryl Streep
Halle Berry	Steve Martin
Paula Abdul	Teri Hatcher
Sandra Bullock	Samuel L. Jackson
Madonna	Katie Couric
Dwight D. Eisenhower	Kirk Douglas
Deana Carter	Michael Douglas
Jamie Lee Curtis	Sally Field
Cameron Diaz	Calista Flockhart
Ann-Margret	Ruth Bader Ginsburg
Franklin D. Roosevelt	Reba McEntire
Jimmy Stewart	Mandy Moore
Vanna White	Alicia Silverstone
Cybill Shepherd	Raquel Welch

MUSIC
of the
Lone Star State

Trying to list all the types of music—and musicians—in Texas is like trying to count the stars in the sky!

Country music would not have been the same without Ernest Tubb, Lefty Frizzell, Johnny Horton, and George Jones. Don't forget Alvin Crow, Bob Wills, Willie Nelson, Waylon Jennings, the Dixie Chicks, Ponty Bone, Joe Ely, Lloyd Maines, Butch Hancock, Terry Allen, Jimmie Dale Gilmore, Buck Owens, and Tommy Hancock. The list continues with the unforgettable Tex Ritter and Jim Reeves. Crooners George Strait, Pat Green, Cory Morrow, and Brian Burns all enriched the country music tradition, while folk artists like Guy Clark, Townes Van Zandt, Nanci Griffith, Lyle Lovett, and Steve Earle helped build a unique sound too.

Texas blues owes homage to Blind Lemon Jefferson, Blind Willie Johnson, Big Mama Thornton, the Fabulous Thunderbirds, and Stevie Ray Vaughan. Blues may have started in the Delta, but Texans painted them a true deep blue.

Rock in all its forms has roots in Texas. Where would it be without Buddy Holly, Roy Orbison, or ZZ Top? Then there was Doug Sahm's Sir Douglas Quintet and Roky Erickson's legendary 13th Floor Elevators. Garage Rock can be traced to the bands like Lift to Experience. Ragtime's Scott Joplin was born in Texarkana. Tejano, a mix of musical influences, is unique to Texas, and boasts the likes of the late Selena Quintanilla, as well as Flaco Jimenez and Narciso Martinez, as influential figures.

The wide variety of people immigrating to Texas brought their music too. African Americans brought gospel, rhythm and blues, and jazz. Polka arrived with the Germans, Czechs, and Poles. Mariachi came from Mexico . . . Phew! Does something listed here sound "foreign" to you? Then . . . put down this book, put on your boots, and go out and listen to some music! ☻

35 TUNES with "TEXAS" in the Title

All My Ex's Live in Texas | George Strait

Bluest Eyes in Texas | Restless Heart

Blue Texas Waltz | Billy Joe Shaver

Deep in the Heart of Texas | Gene Autry

The Eyes of Texas | Milton Brown

God Blessed Texas | Little Texas

Good Texan | The Vaughn Brothers

Hello, Texas | Jimmy Buffett

Hustled Down in Texas | Johnny Winter

If You're Gonna Play in Texas (You Gotta Have a Fiddle in the Band) | Alabama

I'll Take Texas | Clint Black

Luckenbach, Texas (Back to the Basics of Love) | Waylon Jennings with Willie Nelson

Memories of East Texas
Michelle Shocked

Miles and Miles of Texas
Asleep at the Wheel

Rolling Stone from Texas | Don Walser

T for Texas (Blue Yodel No. 1)
Jimmie Rodgers

Texas | Waylon Jennings/Willie Nelson/Johnny Cash/Kris Kristofferson

Texas Flood | Stevie Ray Vaughn & Double Trouble

Texas in 1880 | Foster & Lloyd

Texas in My Rear View Mirror
Mac Davis

Texas Is Bigger Than It Used to Be Mark Chestnutt

Texas Lullabye | David Allan Coe

Texas Me | Sir Douglas Quintet

Texas on a Saturday Night
Mel Tillis, Willie Nelson

Texas Size Heartache | Joe Diffie

Texas Tornado | Sir Douglas Quintet

Texas (When I Die) | Tanya Tucker

That's Right (You're Not from Texas) Lyle Lovett

Waltz across Texas | Ernest Tubb

The WASP (Texas Radio and the Big Beat) | The Doors

Way Down Texas Way | Asleep at the Wheel

West Texas Waltz | Butch Hancock

Yellow Rose of Texas | Gene Autry

Governors of Texas

Early Statehood

J. Pinckney Henderson (1846–1847)
George T. Wood (1847–1849)
Peter Hansbrough Bell (1849–1853)
J. W. Henderson (Nov.–Dec. 1853)
Elisha M. Pease (1853–1857)
Hardin R. Runnels (1857–1859)
Sam Houston (1859–1861)

War, Ruin, and Reconstruction

Edward Clark (March–Nov. 1861)
Francis R. Lubbock (1861–1863)
Pendleton Murrah (1863–1865)
Andrew J. Hamilton (1865–1866)
James W. Throckmorton (1866–1867)
Elisha M. Pease (1867–1869)
Edmund J. Davis (1870–1874)

The Wild West

Richard Coke (1874–1876)
Richard B. Hubbard (1876–1879)
Oran M. Roberts (1879–1883)
John Ireland (1883–1887)
Lawrence Sullivan Ross (1887–1891)

Gov. Francis R. Lubbock

Texas Rising

James Stephen Hogg (1891–1895)
Charles A. Culberson (1895–1899)
Joseph D. Sayers (1899–1903)
S. W. T. Lanham (1903–1907)
Thomas Mitchell Campbell (1907–1911)
Oscar Branch Colquitt (1911–1915)

The Politics of Personality

James E. Ferguson (1915–1917)
William Pettus Hobby (1917–1921)
Pat Morris Neff (1921–1925)
Miriam A. Ferguson (1925–1927)
Dan Moody (1927–1931)
Ross S. Sterling (1931–1933)
Miriam A. Ferguson (1933–1935)
James V. Allred (1935–1939)
W. Lee O'Daniel (1939–1941)
Coke R. Stevenson (1941–1947)
Beauford H. Jester (1947–1949)

Modern Texas

Allan Shivers (1949–1957)
Price Daniel (1957–1963)
John Connally (1963–1969)
Preston Smith (1969–1973)
Dolph Briscoe (1973–1979)
William P. Clements (1979–1983)
Mark White (1983–1987)
William P. Clements (1987–1991)
Ann Richards (1991–1995)
George W. Bush (1995–2000)
J. Richard Perry (2000–Present)

★ Famous Texas Governors' Quotes:

"I thought I knew Texas pretty well, but I had no notion of its size until I campaigned it."
Ann Richards

"Texas has yet to learn submission to any oppresson, come from what source it may."
Sam Houston

Great Women Behind the Great State

Susan Combs—Prior to her election as Texas's first female agriculture commissioner in 1998, Combs served two terms in the Texas House of Representatives. She was inducted into the Texas Women's Hall of Fame in 2004. Combs manages a cow-calf operation on the Brewster County ranch established by her great-grandfather over 100 years ago.

Barbara Jordan—A lawyer, college professor, and politician, Jordan broke both racial and gender barriers in her long career. The first Texas woman elected to Congress, she had previously been the first African American Texas state senator since 1883. Her keynote address at the 1976 Democratic National Convention is considered the best in modern history; she was again the keynote speaker in 1992. Jordan was awarded the Presidential Medal of Freedom in 1994, and was elected to both the Texas and National Women's Hall of Fame.

Laura Miller—Elected Dallas mayor in 2002 after serving on the city council, Miller was an award-winning journalist at major newspapers in Dallas, New York, and Miami before entering Dallas politics.

Ann Richards—Forty-fifth governor of Texas, 1988 Democratic National Convention keynote speaker, state treasurer, Travis County commissioner, teacher, and activist are just some of this remarkable woman's credentials. Richards continues her tradition of public service, serving on the boards of numerous philanthropic and educational organizations. She was inducted into the Texas Women's Hall of Fame in 1985.

Carole Keeton Strayhorn—The first woman in history elected the Texas Comptroller of Public Accounts, Strayhorn was also the first woman mayor of Austin and the only mayor elected for three successive terms. Her slogan: "One Tough Grandma—Watching Out for Texas."

Please Pass the Biscuits, Pappy!

"Please pass the biscuits, Pappy!" was a familiar call heard on Texas Depression-era radio. Led by Burrus flour mill sales manager Wilbert Lee (Pappy) O'Daniel, the Hillbilly Boys' daily 15 minutes of music, laughter, and entertainment convinced the Texas public to elect the colorful Pappy to a term as governor.

Pappy O'Daniel ran for governor on a platform of the Golden Rule and following the Ten Commandments, and won the election by a landslide. Everywhere Pappy went he attracted huge crowds, thus ushering in a unique era in Texas politics.

In 1941, he successfully beat out Lyndon Johnson for a seat in the Senate. He won the election by only a handful of votes. In Washington, veteran senators shunned Pappy, and he did not seek reelection. Later, he tried again but never returned to elected office.

Rangers
AND
OUTLAWS

The Texas Rangers have their roots in the militia Stephen Austin formed in 1823 to protect his colony from raids by the Comanche—and although the name wasn't actually used officially for another fifty years, this group of ranging lawmen was the only thing that stood between civilized folk and the wild lawlessness that plagued the West.

Captain Jack Hays

One of Austin's original—and most famous—Rangers was Captain Jack Hays. Hays earned a reputation as a fearless fighter, particularly against the Comanche; in fact, an Apache chieftan once said that Hays was "not afraid to go to Hell by himself." Although he and his men were often involved in battles where they were outnumbered, Hays's knowledge of Comanche warfare and the Rangers' superior firepower (the Rangers under Jack Hays were the first to use the Colt five-shot revolver) won the day. Smaller than average, exceptionally wiry, and tough enough to endure the Texas terrain, Hays continued as a Ranger until he caught gold fever in 1849. In California, he amassed a sizable fortune and became politically prominent. He died in Piedmont, California, on April 25, 1883.

John Wesley Hardin & John Barclay Armstrong

John Wesley Hardin, who claimed he "never killed a man who didn't need killing," lived a life of violence. It began in 1867, when he killed a fellow student in the schoolyard. In 1874 he killed Charles Webb, deputy sheriff of Brown County—and he was a wanted man, chased throughout Texas from that day on. Hardin's most persistent pursuer was John Barclay Armstrong, the Texas Ranger known as "McNelly's Bulldog." Armstrong tailed Hardin through Alabama and then to Florida, where he killed one of Hardin's men and knocked Hardin unconscious to take him into custody in 1877. Hardin was tried and sentenced to twenty-five years in prison. During that time,

Hardin made repeated attempts to escape, read theological books, was superintendent of the prison Sunday school, and studied law. Pardoned on March 16, 1894, and admitted to the bar, he was soon in trouble: he was shot to death in a saloon in 1895.

Sam Bass & Junius Peak

During the spring of 1878, Sam Bass and his gang held up four trains within 25 miles of Dallas. Governor Richard Coke commissioned Junius Peak and a Ranger detachment from Company B to track Sam Bass and his gang.

For several months Peak and his men harassed Bass, driving him from North Texas. Then one of Bass's men betrayed him, and the Rangers engaged Bass in a gunfight in Round Rock on July 19, 1879. The Rangers found Bass the next morning, lying wounded north of town. He died on July 21, 1878, on his 27th birthday.

The legend of Sam Bass has grown over the years. Referred to as "Texas's Beloved Bandit" or "Robin Hood on a Fast Horse," history has treated Bass kindly. A ballad written by John Denton and sung by cowhands on stormy nights helped Bass's legacy live on in infamy. ⊕

 ★ Did You Know?

The Rangers under Jack Hays were the first to use the Colt five-shot revolver.

From "The Ballad of Sam Bass"

by John Denton

Sam met his fate at Round Rock, July the twenty-first;

They pierced poor Sam with rifle balls
and emptied out his purse.

Poor Sam, he is a corpse and six foot under clay,

And Jackson's in the bushes trying to get away.

Jim had borrowed Sam's good gold and didn't want to pay.

The only shot he saw was to give poor Sam away.

He sold out Sam and Barnes and left their friends to mourn.

Oh, what a scorching Jim will get
when Gabriel blows his horn!

The 52-foot TEXAN

He towers a massive 52 feet high. He wears a size 100 180/181 shirt and size 284W/185L XXXXXL jeans. Needless to say, his clothes are tailor-made. The jeans alone require 72 yards of denim and weigh 65 pounds. His size 70 boots are 7 feet, 7 inches tall. His belt is 23 feet long with a 50 pound belt buckle. Perched atop his head is a five-foot tall, 75-gallon cowboy hat. Who is this Texas-sized man? Big Tex, of course!

Big Tex, the World's Largest Cowboy, greets visitors to the Texas State Fair every year with a "Howdy, folks" and updated fair information. It all began in 1949 when a 52-foot Santa was created to bolster sales in Kerens, Texas. After the 1950 Christmas season, the novelty wore off, and the 52-foot giant was transported 60 miles to Dallas and sold to the State Fair of Texas for $750.

What's a Ten-Gallon Hat?

"Ten-gallon hat" is the result of a linguistic mix-up. *Galón* is the Spanish word for "braid." Some Mexican vaqueros wore as many as ten braided hatbands on their sombreros, which were called "ten galón hats." English speakers heard *gallon*. Just so you know, a ten-gallon hat only holds three quarts of water.

In 1952, the statue was changed and dressed as a cowboy, and Big Tex was born. Big Tex talked for the first time in 1953. He says "Howdy" 60 times every day of the state fair. Seven different men have been the voice of Big Tex, but the most recognizable was Jim Lowe, the Dallas morning show broadcaster who was the voice of Big Tex for 30 years.

Big Tex waved for the first time at the 2000 Texas State Fair and turned 50 in 2002. He needs a little help getting up in the morning. Eight men use a giant crane to get Big Tex to stand up straight. ⊕

Cowboy Boots

SIGNS AND SUPERSTITIONS

A boot set on top of a fence post is a sign that someone is at home.

Boots hung with their toes pointed toward the wall are a sign that their owner is dead.

It is bad luck to step into your left boot first.

If you wear your boots out on the toe, you will spend money as you go.

Tripping over a boot is a bad omen.

To walk along wearing only one boot will bring you as many bad days as steps taken.

If a father wears his boots while his baby is born, it will be a boy.

If your new boots creak as you walk, it means that you still owe the bootmaker his/her bill.

Justin Boots

There are many types of cowboy boots today, but Justin Boots set the standard in early Texas. Herman Justin started the company in 1879 in Spanish Fort, where the Chisholm Trail crossed the Red River. Cowboys with their herds stopped to get measured for the hand-fitted boots.

The Justin family prospered and in 1925 moved to Fort Worth. The company has expanded over time and Justin boots are now known worldwide. The Justin Boot Company hasn't lost sight of its values, staying true to the words of founder H. J. Justin: "No boot shall ever bear the Justin brand unless it is the very best that can be produced from the standpoint of material, style, and workmanship. It is my wish that I might leave behind me an institution which will uphold the standards and spirit of the true West."

Want to DANCE?
Get in Line!

Dancing in Texas is special. It remains a family activity in many rural communities, the centerpiece of a social gathering to celebrate family, community, or holiday events. While all types of dance are performed and enjoyed in Texas, three that most have absorbed the Texan flare are line dancing, square-dancing, and the Texas two-step.

Line Dancing

Believe it or not, one of line dancing's most famous choreographers is from Canada! Check out some of Bill Bader's best:

Boot Scootin' Boogie—The original dance of this name! It was used to set the Guinness World Record for the World's Largest Line Dance in 1996, 1997, 1998, 1999, 2000, 2001, and 2003.

Chill—A little tricky, and not for everyone.

Cowgirls Twist—This is one of the world's most popular dances. It can be taught to total beginners to show how much fun they can have with line dancing from the get-go. "What the Cowgirls Do" by Vince Gill gave this dance its "Cowgirls" name.

Evil Weevil—Evil swivels in this dance explain the name. Very tricky.

Hot Pepper—A rousing dance with quick footwork. Danced to fast songs like Jimmy Buffett's "Pascagoula Run."

Long Live Love—The choreography is done entirely with "L" shapes inspired by the song title and carried through to the dance name.

No Trippin—Designed to introduce Applejacks, plus some other unusual and interesting moves.

Slap City—Old-style fun dance.

WOW—Loaded with interesting combinations. Inspired by the George Strait song "You Can't Buy Your Way Out of the Blues."

Square-Dancing Jargon

Arky—Dancing as a gent if you're a female or a lady if you're male.

Beau—Left-side dancer of a couple.

Belle—Right-side dancer of a couple.

Call—A set of moves that you do when the caller calls its name.

Frill—A fancy move that is added to or substituted for the standard way of doing it.

Hoedown—A large gathering held to square-dance.

Patter call—A call that is chanted.

Phantom—An imaginary dancer.

Sequence—A series of calls.

Sound effect—Something the dancers yell back.

Tip—Time spent dancing in one square without a break.

Zero—A call that leaves you in the same place at the end of the call as where you started.

HOW TO DO THE TEXAS TWO-STEP

Every respectable Texan has a two-step in his dancing repertoire. The Texas two-step is danced with two quick steps and two slow steps. In case you need to learn this dance, here is a quick how-to.

Leader

1. Stand with your feet together, facing your partner.
2. Put your right hand on your partner's waist.
3. Put your left hand out to your side with your arm slightly bent and gently grasp your partner's hand.
4. Wait for the music to start.
5. On the first beat, step forward quickly with your left foot.
6. On the second beat, step forward quickly with your right foot.
7. On the third beat, step forward slowly with your left foot.
8. Pause through the fourth beat.
9. On the fifth beat, step forward slowly with your right foot.
10. Pause through the sixth beat, and then pull your left foot even with your right.
11. Repeat.

Follower

1. Place your left hand on the leader's right shoulder.
2. Bend your right elbow and place the palm of your tight hand lightly on his outstretched palm.
3. Do the opposite of what your partner does. Move your right foot back when the leader moves his left foot forward on the first beat.
4. Continue following the directions for the leader, but in reverse, stepping back with your left foot when he steps forward with his right.

TEXAS SCRAMBLE

See if you can unscramble these famous Texans.

1. ISPSSYASCEK

2. ROLBUACTENTR

3. SHBUWORGEGE

4. CHAUBATSERORG

5. JSCTOLINTPO

6. ISYORROBNO

7. YAILALVNIE

8. OBWSLILB

9. ZTMIWLCHTRESELIANIIM

10. TARNREDAH

ANSWERS:

1. SISSY SPACEK; 2. CAROL BURNETT; 3. GEORGE W. BUSH;
4. ROGER STAUBACH; 5. SCOTT JOPLIN; 6. ROY ORBISON; 7. ALVIN AILEY;
8. BOB WILLS; 9. CHESTER WILLIAM NIMITZ; 10. DAN RATHER

Southern ZODIAC SIGNS

Okra
(December 22–January 20)

Okras appear tough and a little prickly but are really tender characters at heart. Okras have great influence on others, often spreading the seeds of their influence everywhere. And we mean everywhere. Beware Moon Pies!

Chitlin
(January 21–February 19)

Chitlins are not very self-aware because what they find is a little disturbing. Chitlins often alienate companions, but go well with Catfish and Okras.

Boll Weevil
(February 20–March 20)

Boll Weevils are extremely curious, often feeling the need to bore deep into the interior of things. You are very intense, as if driven by some inner hunger.

Moon Pie
(March 21–April 20)

Moon Pies are easy to recognize by their physical appearance—big and round. This might be the year you diet, but it's doubtful. You'll have to sell yourself on your sweet nature.

Possum
(April 21–May 21)

Possums have a natural tendency to withdraw into a don't-bother-me attitude. Sometimes you become so withdrawn you even appear dead. Possums like everyone, but the feeling is not often reciprocated. Check out Armadillos.

Crawfish
(May 22–June 21)

Crawfish are one of the water signs. You often prefer to hang out in the bathroom. When frightened, your instinct is to run backwards as fast as possible, and you turn bright red when overheated. Still, try meeting a Catfish.

Collards
(June 22–July 23)

Collards love to join the melting pot of life and mingle your essence with those around you. Collards make good social workers, psychologists, and professional baseball managers. Stay away from Moon Pies; it won't work. It's just not a good combination.

Catfish
(July 24–August 23)

Catfish are not easy to understand; even your name is confusing. You prefer the murky bottoms to the clear surface of life. You might get along well with Okras and Collards.

Grits
(August 24–September 23)

Grits enjoy being a small part of the larger whole. You especially like to huddle with a big crowd of other Grits. You enjoy all meals but breakfast is your specialty.

Boiled Peanut
(September 24–October 23)

Despite Boiled Peanuts' passionate desire to help mankind, your personality is often too salty, but you're actually soft underneath your hard shell. Boiled Peanuts go with anyone drinking a cola drink.

Butter Bean
(October 24–November 22)

Butter Beans have no enemies, which makes them great party guests. On the vine of life, you are at home no matter the setting. You can try a relationship with a Chitlin, but we can't guarantee anything.

Armadillo
(November 23–December 21)

Despite your hard exterior, Armadillos are actually quite soft inside. You're old-fashioned, a throwback to a previous era. Like, virtually prehistoric. You will probably marry another Armadillo but you might want to check out Possums, also.

WHAT WAS THE 7TH FLAG OVER TEXAS?

Six Flags over Texas refers to the slogan used to describe the six nations that had sovereignty over the land of Texas. The six nations were:

Spain (1519–1685; 1690–1821)

France (1685–1690)

Mexico (1821–1836)

Republic of Texas (1836–1845)

Confederate States of America
(1861–1865)

United States of America
(1845–1861; 1865–present).

The little-known 7th flag was the **Republic of the Rio Grande**. The independent state was only in existence for a short while and didn't encompass the whole state. It only covered a small region near Laredo.

Texas Fun Facts

RODEO is the official state sport of Texas!

- Seventy-five percent of the world's Snickers bars are made in Waco at the M&M/Mars plant.

- Fort Sam Houston has more historic buildings than Colonial Williamsburg.

- In Texas, it is illegal to put graffiti on someone else's cow.

- For $150, you can become a licensed dead animal hauler in Texas.

- The King Ranch in Texas is larger than the state of Rhode Island.

- The world's largest collection of beer bottles is in Wurstfest in New Braunfels.

- There is a forest of mature Harvard oak trees no taller than three feet high at Monahans Sandhills State Park.

- The lightning whelk is the official state shell.

- More wool comes from the state of Texas than any other state in the United States.

- The world's largest parking lot is located at Dallas-Fort Worth International Airport.

- Caddo Lake is the only natural lake in the state.

- Texas boasts the nation's largest herd of whitetail deer.

- In Houston, it is illegal to sell Limburger cheese on Sunday.

- Early Spanish missionaries in Texas hoped to encourage the spread of European values by offering flannel underwear to Native Americans.

- Texas is the only state to enter the United States by treaty instead of territorial annexation.

- Texas boasts the largest of all the state capitol buildings, constructed of 15,000 carloads of pink granite.

- Texas is home to Dell and Compaq computers, and central Texas is often referred to as the Silicon Valley of the South.

- There is a Texas law that forbids people from carrying around a fence cutter or a pair of pliers that could cut a fence.

- Texans consume forty percent of the farm-grown catfish in the United States.

33

Traveling

 They say everything is bigger in *Texas*—and with 268,581 square miles in the Lone Star State, they weren't kiddin'! We could spend a lifetime exploring every nook and cranny, but for now let's just get familiar with the regions . . . and a few interesting destinations.

Panhandle Plains

ABILENE—*The Friendly Frontier*

Home to 117,500 friendly people waiting to share their traditional frontier heritage, Abilene is located 150 miles west of Dallas, in the center of Texas. Three universities and Dyess Air Force Base are found here. Visitors should not miss the Grace Museum, Abilene Zoo, Center for Contemporary Arts, the 12th Armored Division Memorial Museum, or the National Center for Children's Illustrated Literature. Fort Phantom Hill offers ghostly ruins for the history-loving tourist too. Abilene's recent downtown renovation is a model for other towns that want to preserve their heritage. Unique architecture and cultural landscapes make this town a great stop on a Texas tour. For more information contact:

Abilene Convention and Visitors Bureau
1101 North First, Abilene, TX 79601, (325) 676-2556 or (800) 727-7704

AMARILLO—*Step into the Real Texas*

Amarillo is in the center of the Texas panhandle, where the desert meets the southern plains. Everything Texas can be found in Amarillo, from outdoor activities to art to history. Some must-see attractions include *Texas*, one of the nation's best outdoor theater performances, as well as Panhandle Plains Historical Museum, Don Harrington Discovery Center, Cadillac Ranch, Big Texas Steak Ranch, Route 66, Kwahadi-Kiva Indian Museum, and the Globe-News Center for the Performing Arts, home to ballet, opera, and symphony. See for yourself by contacting:

Amarillo Convention and Visitor Council (The second floor of the Bivins Mansion)
1000 S. Polk St., Amarillo, TX 79101, (800) 692-1338 or (325) 379-5361

LUBBOCK—*The Texas You've Always Dreamed Of!*

Small-town hospitality and West Texas charm ooze like oil in Lubbock. The town is famous as the home of Texas Tech University and the birthplace of Buddy Holly, as well as Prairie Dog Town. Texas Tech's museum has over two million items on display and is definitely worth a visit. Next, take a trip to the Buddy Holly Center to experience interactive music and dynamic displays. It might be the best way ever to discover art through music. Finally, a stopover in Lubbock would not be complete without a trip to Mackenzie Park to view the critters at Prairie Dog Town. Plan it all by contacting:

Lubbock Convention and Visitors Bureau
1301 Broadway Suite 200, Lubbock, TX 79401, (800) 692-4035 or (806) 747-5232

POSSUM KINGDOM—Restoration, Not Just Vacation

Prairie Dog

If you ever wanted to know what it is like to step off the edge of the civilized universe, Possum Kingdom just might be the location for you! Situated about eighty miles northeast of Abilene, both primitive and developed camping sites are available around this state park and lake. You'll find plenty of rainbow trout, as well as the state longhorn herd in quiet getaway. For directions and information about this oasis call:

Possum Kingdom Chamber of Commerce
362 N. FM 2353, Graford, TX 76449, (888) 779-8330

WICHITA FALLS—Absolutely

Located in north central Texas, Wichita Falls was founded in 1882, and is the home of Midwestern University. Nearby Sheppard Air Force Base is a technical training center, one of the largest of five in the United States, and hosts the only NATO pilot training program in the world. The city has attractions as the Hotter 'N Hell Hundred (the world's largest bicycle race) and a state-of-the-art multipurpose events and convention facility that includes the J. S. Bridwell Ag Center, the Event Center, and the Coliseum. Downtown offers dining, music, theater, and antique shopping. To visit, contact:

Wichita Falls Convention & Visitors Bureau
P.O. Box 630, Wichita Falls, TX 76301, (940) 716-5500

Big Bend Country

EL PASO—Do Texas Different

El Paso is short for El Paso del Rio del Norte, the name given to this pristine river valley by conquistador Don Juan de Oñate more than four centuries ago. The city encompasses countless museums, as well as a historical corridor that includes the Mission Trail, a twenty-nine-foot statue of Christ, Magoffin Homestead, the Fray Garcia Monument, and the Camino Real. El Paso's Amigo Airshow is recognized as one of the nation's best, while the Fort Bliss Army post and museums offer several days' entertainment and education. To enjoy El Paso, contact:

El Paso Convention & Visitors Bureau
One Civic Center Plaza, El Paso, TX 79901, (800) 351-6024

MIDLAND—Always in the Middle of Somewhere

Home to forty-third president George W. Bush and wife Laura Bush, Midland residents welcome the world with a friendly enthusiasm and down-home hospitality, combining a cosmopolitan atmosphere with the Texas ambiance of small-town America. The annual Haley Library Art Show is an excellent exhibit, and in June, the Mex-Tex Menudo, Chili, and Fajita Cook-Off will have you running for a glass of ice water. And don't forget to look up in the ClayDesta Atrium at the 40,000 square foot skylight master-piece. It's easy to feel at home in Midland by contacting:

Midland Convention & Visitors Bureau
109 N. Main, Midland, TX 79701, (800) 624-6435

PECOS—Home of the World's First Rodeo

Roughly 200 miles east of El Paso and 400 miles west of Fort Worth, Pecos prides itself on its rich western heritage (it was the location of the world's first rodeo, held here in 1883), and the West of the Pecos Museum allows you to step back into the town's colorful history. Across from the museum is the old T & P train depot, remind-ing visitors of earlier times. Pecos is nationally renowned for its cantaloupes—every year over 2,000 acres are planted in melons. To see this and Pecos, contact:

Pecos Area Chamber of Commerce
111 South Cedar / P.O. Box 27, Pecos, TX 79772, (432) 445-2406

ODESSA—The Right Place in Texas

Odessa, land of both cowboys and oil barons, is the gateway to three national parks, including Big Bend, Carlsbad Caverns, and Guadalupe Mountains. Odessa's annual Southwest Shakespeare Festival takes place in an authentic replica of Shakespeare's Globe Theatre, or you can drive out and see the second largest meteor crater in the United States. Check out the Presidential Museum, the only such museum dedicated to the office of the presidency, and drop by to see the "World's Largest Jack Rabbit," a fiberglass statue too! Visit him and the other sites by contacting:

Odessa, Texas Convention & Visitors Bureau
700 North Grant, Ste. 200, Odessa, TX 79761, (800) 780-4678

Hill Country

AUSTIN—Live Music Capital of the World

Texas state capital Austin is always hopping with activities. Be sure to visit the Lyndon Baines Johnson Library and Museum at the University of Texas, check out the exhibits at the Bob Bullock Texas State History Museum, and take a stroll through the Lady Bird Johnson

The State Capitol Building

Wildflower Center. Cap it off by going to one of the many live music venues in the Sixth Street entertainment district. For more information:

Austin Convention & Visitors Bureau
301 Congress Ave., Suite 300, Austin, TX 78701, (800) 926-2282

BANDERA — Cowboy Capital of the World

Bandera was the staging area for the great cattle drives of yesteryear, and calls itself the Cowboy Capital of the World. Today it has a bronze sculpture honoring the many National Rodeo Champions who call Bandera home, and plenty of Western atmosphere, including rodeos twice weekly. Surrounded by both working and guest ranches in the beautiful rolling hills, you'll find plenty of horseback riding and other outdoor activities. Contact the folks in Bandera at:

Bandera Texas Convention & Visitors Bureau
P.O. Box 171, Bandera, TX 78003, (800) 364-3833

BLANCO — Gateway to the Central Texas Hill Country

Pioneer stockmen, former Texas Rangers, and immigrants settled Blanco in 1853. Located just 45 miles north of San Antonio, Blanco boasts having the warmest welcome in the Hill Country. It may have something to do with the beautiful lavender fields and the festival held at seven local lavender farms. Maybe it is the Blanco State Park, one of the smallest—but loveliest—state parks in Texas. Finally, there is Old Blanco Community Court House, a fine example of late nineteenth century architecture. You can learn more about any of these by contacting:

Blanco Chamber of Commerce
312 Pecan / P.O. Box 626, Blanco, TX 78606, (830) 833-5101

GRUENE — Gently Resisting Change Since 1872

Gruene (pronounced "Green") is truly the picture of laid-back Texas. Visit Gruene Hall, the virtually unchanged center of social activity since 1878, which still hosts national musical acts like George Strait and Lyle Lovett. Designated a Historic Town, Gruene is filled with Victorian homes that are on the National Historic Register. Gruene is conveniently located between Austin and San Antonio and is, by the residents' own admission, a little behind the times. To find out more, contact:

601 Hunter Rd., New Braunfels, TX 78130, (830) 629-5077

KERRVILLE — Hill Country Paradise

The scenery is gorgeous in Kerrville, which is located along the Guadalupe River near Fredericksburg, Boerne, and Bandera. Kick back and do some horseback riding in the rolling hills, go rafting on the river, or visit a dude ranch. And don't forget the many excellent golf courses in the area! Contact the visitors bureau for more ideas at:

Kerrville Convention & Visitors Bureau
2108 Sidney Baker, Kerrville, TX 78028, (800) 221-7958 or (830) 792-3535

TRAVEL

MASON—*The Gem of Hill Country*

Established under the protection of the frontier Fort Mason, many local homes and businesses in Mason have been built with the sandstone blocks from the old fort. A beautiful historic town square, and a real bat cave—where four to six million bats can be found—are sights you'll enjoy in Mason. For more information about visiting Mason:

Mason County Chamber of Commerce
P.O. Box 187, Mason, TX 76856, (325) 347-5758

ROUND ROCK—*Purpose, Passion, Prosperity*

Rich in Old West history, the city's name derives from a round rock formation in the middle of Brushy Creek that was a natural marker during cattle drives on the Chisholm Trail. And downtown Round Rock is the site of the gunfight and subsequent capture of nineteenth-century train robber Sam Bass by Texas Rangers. Festivals held in Round Rock include the Daffodil Days Festival in March, Fiesta Amistad in May, Frontier Days in July, and Texas Outlaw 100 Cycling Tour in October. For more information:

City of Round Rock
221 E. Main St., Round Rock, TX 78664, (512) 218-5400

WIMBERLEY—*A Little Piece of Heaven*

Located on the banks of the Cypress Creek and the Blanco River, Wimberley is a slice of small-town rural America. Don't miss the Corral Theatre, an outdoor movie theatre with first-run movies—they'll even let you bring your own chair. Camping, swimming, and hiking abound in this area. And Market Days, held the first Saturday of every month from April to December, is the place to congregate. There are over 450 booths covering over 16 acres—a treasure hunter's paradise! Find out more:

Wimberley Chamber of Commerce
P.O. Box 12, Wimberley, TX 78676, (512) 847-2201

Prairies and Lakes

ARLINGTON—*Fun Central*

In Arlington, they believe that fun is more than a state of mind; it is a place to be. As home to Six Flags Over Texas, the Texas Rangers at Ameriquest Field, and Hurricane Harbor Water Park, Arlington does have more than its share of fun—with an entertainment district of mammoth proportions. Bring the family, 'cause there's something to please everyone! Restaurants and hotels in the area are also top-notch with shopping for every budget. Contact them at:

Visitor Information Center
1905 E. Randol Mill Rd., Arlington, TX 76011-8214, (800) 342-4305

DALLAS-FORT WORTH—*It's Everything Texas and More*

This is Texas all grown up—a sophisticated metropolitan area with a western flair. The DFW area is home to too many attractions to list, but a sample itinerary includes: Billy Bob's Texas, Cattle Raisers Museum, Cavanaugh Fight Museum, Cowtown Coliseum, the Dallas Arboretum, the Dallas Museum of Art, Fort Worth Museum of Science and History, Gilley's Dallas, Mesquite Championship Rodeo, Nasher Sculpture Center, Stockyards Station, the Western Currency Facility of the Bureau of Engraving and Printing . . . and the list could go on! To thoroughly enjoy DFW, find out more at:

Dallas Tourism Information Center
100 Houston St., Dallas, TX 75201, (800) 232-5527; or

Fort Worth Visitors Center
415 Throckmorton, Fort Worth, TX 76102, (817) 336-8791

PARKER—*Home of the Southfork Ranch and Country Living*

Parker is an unassuming suburban community that is home to one of the most famous locations in television history: the Southfork Ranch of Dallas. Although the ranch is an event and conference center, guided tours are available for groups and individuals. At the "Dallas Legends" exhibit you can see the gun used to shoot J. R., Lucy's wedding dress, the Dallas family tree, and Jock's Lincoln Continental. There is even a herd of Texas longhorns!

Southfork Ranch
3700 Hogge Rd., Parker, TX 75002, (972) 442-5259

PLANO—*Plan to Have Fun*

See these sights in Plano and plan to have fun: the Interurban Railway Station Museum, JC Penney Museum, Heritage Farmstead, Heard Natural Science Museum & Wildlife Sanctuary, and the Community Credit Union Plano Balloon Festival. For information and directions:

Plano Convention & Visitors Bureau
2000 East Spring Creek Pkwy., Plano, TX 75086, (800) 81-PLANO

WACO—*Gateway to Texas History*

This town located between Austin and Dallas offers eighteen museums and countless attractions that offer a unique, relaxing getaway from big city hustle and bustle. Take a peek at the suspension bridge built in 1870 that served as a model for the Brooklyn Bridge. Stop at the Dr. Pepper Museum and slurp a Pepper. And the Texas Sports Hall of Fame is a quick stop on your way to Baylor University. End the day viewing the Lake Waco Wetlands. Directions to everything can be found through:

Waco Convention & Visitor Bureau
P.O. Box 2570, Waco, TX 76702, (800) 962-6386

South Texas Plains

GOLIAD—*Birthplace of Texas Ranching*

One of Texas's oldest municipalities, "Remember Goliad" became a Texas Revolution battle cry honoring the men who were massacred at Goliad. Remembrance services are held on the weekend closest to March 27. The General Zaragoza State Historic Site honors one of Mexico's most famous military figures and is both a state park and international historic site. To find out more, contact:

Goliad County Chamber of Commerce
231 S. Market Street / P.O. Box 606, Goliad, TX 77963-0606, (361) 645-3563

SAN ANTONIO—*Home of the Alamo*

The eighth largest city in the United States, San Antonio is an exciting destination. Stroll the beautiful River Walk in the heart of the city, now also the heart of the entertainment district, as well as the location of the La Villita settlement. Come for Fiesta in April, or visit the lively Market Square Mexican Market anytime. A stop at the historic old Alamo is a must, and visit missions, historic trails, and ranches too. Find all San Antonio can offer at:

San Antonio Visitor Information Center

The San Antonio River 317 Alamo Plaza, San Antonio, TX 78205, (800) 447-3372

Piney Woods

HUNTSVILLE—*Home of Sam Houston*

Huntsville offers guests history, nature, prominent state institutions, antiques, and hospitality. Everything Sam Houston can be found in this town—from the Sam Houston Memorial Museum to the huge statue downtown. Outdoor activities abound in the surrounding area, including camping, fishing, hiking, boating, and swimming. Call the people of Huntsville at:

Huntsville Visitors Bureau
P.O. Box 1230, Huntsville, TX 77342-1230, (936) 295-8113

TYLER—*The Real Rose of Texas*

Home of the nation's largest municipal rose garden, the Tyler Rose Garden features more than 38,000 rose bushes of over 500 varieties. The history of the rose and the Texas Rose Festival are highlighted at the spectacular Tyler Rose Museum. Other natural highlights include the wildlife at the 85-acre Caldwell Zoo and Brookshire's World of Wildlife Museum and Country Store. Find more Tyler activities by contacting:

Tyler Convention and Visitors Bureau
315 N. Broadway, Tyler, TX 75702, (800) 235-5712

Gulf Coast

BEAUMONT—Texas with a Little Something Extra

This is Texas embracing its bayou roots—enjoy Zydeco music while eating spicy crawfish and waiting for your swamp tour, or head out to Spindletop (check first: it was damaged by Hurricane Rita) to see where the first big oil gusher came in. Museums are plentiful in Beaumont, including the Edison Museum, Dutch Windmill Museum, and Fire Museum, home of the World's Largest Fire Hydrant. You can do it all in Beaumont by contacting:

Beaumont Convention & Visitors Bureau
801 Main St., Ste. 100 / P.O. Box 3827, Beaumont, TX 77704, (409) 880-3749

CLUTE—Home of the Great Texas Mosquito Festival

Swimming, fishing, water-skiing, diving, picnicking, sailing, sunbathing, or shelling, you can do it in Clute. If you like bird-watching, the Gulf Coast Bird Observatory is a must-see site. However, Clute is probably most famous for the Great Texas Mosquito Festival with Willie Manchew, the festival's 30-foot tall mascot, welcoming warm-blooded humans to the fun event. The festival is held the last Thursday, Friday, and Saturday in July. Contact:

Clute Visitors Bureau
1014-B Lazy Ln., Clute, TX 77531, (800) 983-4853

HOUSTON—Space City

You won't have a problem finding something to do in Houston! The largest city in Texas, Houston has a downtown entertainment district that boasts over seventy bars, clubs, lounges, and restaurants, as well as ballet, Broadway, opera, and symphony. And did we mention sixteen museums within walking distance? If you love sports, take in a pro baseball game at Minute Maid Park or a football game at Reliant Stadium, or take a hike on the over eighty miles of trails within the city. And don't forget the Houston Space Center! Check it all out at:

Greater Houston Convention and Visitors Bureau
901 Bagby, Ste. 100, Houston, TX 77002, (800) 446-8786 or (713) 437-5200

WHARTON—Unwind Where the River Bends

Wharton is a paradise for bird-watchers and sportsmen, while stately plantation homes throughout the area are splendid sightseeing pleasures. A visit to the Wharton County Historical Museum or Marshall and Lillie A. Johnson Wild Game Exhibit will not disappoint—or just stroll or bike through Riverfront Park. In the middle of the river you'll find a fascinating educational exhibit on a boat. Find out more:

Wharton Chamber of Commerce & Agriculture
225 N. Richmond Road / P.O. Box 868, Wharton, TX 77488, (979) 532-0102

TRAVEL

MILEAGE CHART TEXAS

DISTANCE BETWEEN SOME TEXAS CITIES (IN ROAD MILES)

	Abilene	Amarillo	Austin	Brownsville	Corpus Christi	Dallas	El Paso	Houston	Lubbock	San Antonio	Texarkana
Abilene		266	218	514	387	183	429	351	159	245	358
Amarillo	266		480	763	636	356	414	593	121	494	488
Austin	218	480		324	192	194	569	161	371	77	338
Brownsville	514	763	324		157	516	796	347	652	269	633
Corpus Christi	387	636	192	157		377	684	203	525	142	488
Dallas	183	356	194	194	377		610	239	321	271	176
El Paso	429	414	569	796	684	610		726	338	544	785
Houston	351	593	161	347	203	239	726		510	194	285
Lubbock	159	121	371	652	525	321	338	510		383	470
San Antonio	245	494	77	269	142	271	544	194	383		414
Texarkana	358	488	338	633	488	176	785	285	470	414	

OUT-OF-STATE DESTINATIONS (IN ROAD MILES)

	Dallas	El Paso	Houston	San Antonio
Albuquerque, NM	634	267	827	700
Little Rock, AR	314	925	426	555
New Orleans, LA	487	1064	345	537
Oklahoma City, OK	202	667	442	458

TEXAS HIGHWAY FACTS

In 1917, the Texas legislature established the Texas Highway Department to administer federal funds for highway construction and maintenance. The first farm-to-market road was completed in 1937. The system now includes 40,900 miles of paved roadway.

In Texas, the maximum speed limit for cars and light trucks is 70 miles per hour (mph) daytime, 65 mph nighttime on all numbered highways in rural areas. Lower speed limits are posted on many Texas Highways. Speed limits on urban freeways typically range from 55 mph to 70 mph.

Texas state law requires that persons in the front seat must wear a seatbelt. Children under the age of four must be secured and children under the age of two must be in a federally approved car seat. The safest place for a child under the age of 12 is the backseat. Fines range from $25 to $200 for unrestrained drivers and passengers.

A motor vehicle may not be operated in Texas unless a policy of liability insurance is in effect. Evidence of insurance must be furnished when requested by a police officer.

Speeds, caution areas, stops, and directions are marked along the more than 79,000 miles of Texas highways by over half a million signs.

While traveling in Texas, call 1-800-452-9292 for emergency road condition information and travel assistance, or visit one of the sites listed below.

Amarillo	I-40 (from Oklahoma & New Mexico
Anthony	I-10 (from New Mexico)
Austin	Capitol Complex
Denison	U.S. 75/69 (from Oklahoma)
Gainesville	U.S. 77, I-35 (from Oklahoma)
Langtry	U.S. 90, Loop 25
Laredo	I-35 & U.S. 83
Orange	I-10 (from Louisiana)
Texarkana	I-30 (from Arkansas)
Valley	U.S. 77 & U.S. 83 in Harlingen
Waskom	I-20 (from Louisiana)
Wichita Falls	I-44, U.S. 277/281 (from Oklahoma)

The distance between Houston & El Paso **is greater** than the distance between Chicago & Washington, D.C.

The terrazzo star under the dome of the Texas State Capitol is the zero milestone for Austin.

Fredericksburg

The first letters of streets intersecting Main Street heading southeast from the center of town spell *ALL WELCOME* (Adams, Llano, Lincoln, Washington, Elk, Lee, Columbus, Olive, Mesquite, and Eagle).

The first letters of streets intersecting Main Street heading northwest from the center of town spell *COME BACK* (Crockett, Orange, Milam, Edison, Bowie, Acorn, Cherry, and Kay).

McAllen

A set of McAllen avenues are named alphabetically for trees: Ash, Beech, Cedar, Date Palm, Ebony, Fir, Gumwood, Hackberry, Ivy, Jasmine, Kendlewood, Laurel, Maple, Nyssa, Orange, Pecan, Quince, Redwood, Sycamore, Tamarack, Upas, Vine, and Walnut.

After skipping a few avenues, it starts again with flowers: Camellia, Daffodil, Esperanza, Fern, Gardenia, Hibiscus, Iris, Jonquil, Kerria, Larkspur, Mangold, Nolana, Orchid, Primrose, Quamasia, Redbud, Shasta, Tulip, Ulex, Violet, Wisteria, Xanthisma, Yucca, and Zinnia.

Finally, there is a set of birds (roughly in same area of town, not as neatly placed, but generally in order): Avocet, Bluebird, Cardinal, Dove, Eagle, Falcon, Flamingo, Goldcrest, Hawk, Heron, Jay, Kiwi, Lark, Martin, Mynah, Nightingale, Oriole, Pelican, Robin, Sandpiper, Swallow, Thunderbird, Toucan, Umar, Umbrellabird, Verdin, Warbler, Xenops, Yellowhammer, and Zenaida.

Whitewing Avenue is located between the trees and flowers.

Weslaco

A set of avenues in Weslaco were named for mostly northern states on the north or both sides of town, and a few southern states on the southern side. They run north to south, with a few Texas terms thrown in: Border, Colorado, Republic Street/Calle De La Republica, Oklahoma, Ohio, Georgia, Louisiana, Indiana, Nebraska, Missouri, Texas Boulevard, Kansas, Illinois, Iowa, Tennessee, Florida (next to Orange Avenue), Michigan, Oregon, Utah, and Nevada.

Did You Know?

Downtown Austin streets running north and south (skipping Congress Avenue) are named for Texas rivers: Sabine, Red River, Neches, Trinity, San Jacinto, Brazos, Colorado, Lavaca, Guadalupe, San Antonio, Nueces, and Rio Grande.

See Your Name in Lights!

Texas Towns Named after Male First Names (242):

Abner, Ace, Adrian, Albert, Alexander, Alfred, Allen, Alton, Alvin, Ambrose, Andres, Andy, Angus, Anson, Anthony, Antonio, Arney, Art, Arthur, Asa, Augustus, Austin, Bailey, Barry, Bedford, Benjamin, Bernard, Betram, Bob, Boyd, Brad, Brady, Brice, Brooks, Bruce, Bryan, Bryce, Buck, Buford, Burgess, Burke, Burton, Calvin, Cameron, Carey, Carl, Carlos, Carson, Carter, Carey, Charles, Charlie, Chester, Clark, Claude, Clay, Clayton, Cleo, Clint, Clyde, Coy, Craig, Curtis, Dale, Dallas, Dalton, Damon, Dan, Daniel, Davy, Dean, Dell, Dennis, Denny, Dewey, Dexter, Diego, Donie, Douglas, Doyle, Dudley, Dwight, Earle, Eddy, Edgar, Elbert, Elgin, Elliot, Elmo, Elton, Ely, Enoch, Ephriam, Erwin, Esteban, Everett, Ewell, Felipe, Fernando, Floyd, Forrest, Fostoria, Frank, Franklin, Fred, Frederick, Gabriel, Gary, George, Glen, Glenn, Graham, Grant, Gregg, Gus, Guy, Hamlin, Hampton, Harrold, Henry, Herbert, Herman, Hiram, Howard, Iago, Ike, Ira, Irby, Ivan, Jack, Jacob, Jake, James, Jasper, Jay, Jeff, Jim, Jimmy, Joaquin, Joel, John, Jose, Joshua, Juan, Jud, Justin, Keith, Kelly, Kent, Kermit, King, Knox, Kyle, Lamar, Laurel, Laurence, Lee, Leo, Leon, Leland, Leonard, Leroy, Lewis, Lloyd, Lorenzo, Luis, Luther, Marco, Marshall, Mart, Martin, Marvin, Matthew, Maurice, Melvin, Milburn, Miguel, Miles, Milton, Mitchell, Monroe, Morris, Morton, Neal, Newt, Newton, Nolan, Norman, Oliver, Ollie, Oscar, Otis, Patrick, Paul, Pedro, Perry, Preston, Quanah, Ralph, Randall, Ray, Raymond, Reagan, Rex, Ricardo, Riley, Rob, Roddy, Roland, Roscoe, Roy, Rudolph, Rush, Russell, Ryan, Scott, Sherman, Sidney, Silas, Solomon, Sterling, Sylvester, Taylor, Temple, Terrell, Thomas, Travis, Trent, Troy, Valentine, Van, Vernon, Vicente, Victor, Vincent, Warren, Washington, Wayne, Weldon, Wendell, Wesley, Whon, Willard, William, Wilson, Winfield, Wylie, and Ygnacio

Towns Named after Female First Names (175):

Ada, Adell, Ady, Agnes, Alice, Althea, Aldine, Allison, Alma, Amanda, Amelia, Amy, Angelina, Anna, Anneta, Ashley, Aubrey, Audrey, Augusta, Aurelia, Aurora, Bebe, Belle, Bess, Bessie, Bettie, Bettina, Beverly, Beulah, Bonnie, Bonita, Camilla, Caterina, Celeste, Charlotte, Chita, Clairette, Crystal, Daphne, Davilla, Dawn, Delia, Della, Desdemona, Diana, Dixie, Delores, Donna, Dora, Ebony, Edna, Elba, Elena, Elizabeth, Ella, Ellen, Elmina, Eloise, Elsa, Emma, Emory, Eola, Era, Erna, Estelle, Etta, Eula, Eunice, Fairlie, Fairy, Fate, Fay, Flo, Flora, Florence, Frances, Francitas, Gail, Gayle, Geneva, Gladys, Grace, Gustine, Helena, Hilda, Holly, Hope, Hub, Ida, Ilka, Inez, Iola, Irene, Isabel, Jane, Jean, Jewell, Jo, Josephine, Joy, Joyce, June, Karen, Kate, Katherine, Katy, LaRose, Lela, Leigh, Leila, Lena, Leona, Lesley, Lillian, Lillie, Linn, Lissie, Lois, Lolita, Lora, Lorena, Lorraine, Lotta, Lou, Louisa, Lydia, Lynn, Madison, Margaret, Margarita, Maria, Marion, Martha, Mary, Maud, May, Melissa, Mercedes, Merle, Merrill, Mildred, Minerva, Mona, Monica, Mozelle, Myra, Myrtle, Nancy, Natalia, Nell, Ola, Olga, Olive, Orla, Pansy, Patricia, Paulina, Pearl, Peggy, Penelope, Perlita, Polly, Ramona, Rebecca, Rhoda, Rosely, Rosita, Rowena, Roxana, Sarita, Thalia, Thelma, Velma, Vera, Victoria, Viola, Violet, Vivian, Winnie, and Zella

☆ Off the Beaten Path
Seven unusual and wacky wonders
of the lone star state

Looking for something unusual on your next road trip?
Here's a few odd—or just plain strange—places you might want to see!

Cadillac Ranch

Ten decorated classic Cadillacs, dating from 1949–1963, are artistically perched vertically along the horizon. They'd be considered collectors' items if they were not buried nose-down in the dirt. No, they're not the cast-offs of an eccentric Texas driver—millionaire ranch owner Stanley Marsh III actually intended to make a unique roadside art installation in 1973. Visitors are encouraged to add their own grafitti. Look for it just outside Amarillo, along eastbound I-40 between exits 60 and 62.

Marfa Mystery Lights

The Marfa Lights are are visible off and on from a viewing area about ten miles east of the town of Marfa on Highway 90. Are they ghosts, swamp gas, radioactive bursts, ball lightning, or navigational lights for space aliens? Skeptics say they are no more than the headlights of passing cars. The Texas Department of Transportation put up a Marfa Mystery Lights road marker—maybe they know something the rest of us don't know!

Forbidden Gardens

In 1997, millionaire real estate developer Ira P. H. Poon turned eighty acres of former rice land in Katy (outside Houston) into an outdoor museum that depicts, in miniature, several of China's most fascinating historical scenes—including a replica of the 6,000-piece terra-cotta army of the Chinese emperor Qin.

The Beer Can House

John Milkovisch thought his Houston home needed a little sparkle, so over a period of eighteen years, he flattened 39,000 beer cans into aluminum siding (he was also a prodigious beer-drinker)! Yep—the entire house is covered in beer can aluminum. Sadly, Milkovisch and his wife, Mary, have died, but there are plans to open the house as an exhibition. In the meantime, take Memorial Drive west from downtown past Shepherd; turn right on Malone, and go two blocks. The house is on your right.

Paisano Pete

Fort Stockton has its very own 11-feet tall and 22-feet long fiberglass bird, once billed as the world's largest roadrunner, but possibly dethroned by an even larger roadrunner in Las Cruces, New Mexico (who knew?). Doesn't matter—Paisano Pete still poses for dozens of photos every day—and from some angles it actually looks like he likes it! Look for him on U.S. 290 at Main Street in downtown Fort Stockton.

The Blarney Stone

Not content with just the name, Shamrock, Texas, imported a genuine chunk of the real Blarney Castle in 1959, and enshrined it in Elmore Park, three blocks east of U.S. 83, between Railroad Avenue and 1st Street. The town has an Irish festival every year too.

Eiffel Tower

There are plenty (fifteen, to be exact) of towns in the United States called Paris, and a few of them have replica Eiffel Towers. Although Paris, Texas's Eiffel Tower—on the east edge of town on U.S. 82, at the corner of Jefferson Road and South Collegiate Drive—only measures 65 feet tall, it boasts a huge red cowboy hat with a brim that's ten feet wide. Ooh la la, y'all!

Texas Tourist Information Hotlines

Austin: (866) GO-AUSTIN
Amarillo: (800) 692-1338
Athens: (888) 294-2847
Beaumont: (800) 392-4401
Corpus Christi: (800) 766-2322
Dallas: (800) C-DALLAS (232-5527)
El Paso: (800) 351-6024
Fort Worth: (800) 433-5747
Graham: (866) 549-0401
Huntsville: (800) 289-0389
Irving: (800) 2-IRVING (247-8464)

Laredo: (800) 361-3360
Lubbock: (800) 692-4035
Midland: (800) 624-6435
Odessa: (800) 780-HOST (4678)
Plano: (800) 81-PLANO (817-5266)
Rockport-Fulton: (800) 826-6441
San Antonio: (800) 447-3372
San Marcos: (888) 200-5620
Tyler: (800) 235-5712
Uvalde: (800) 588-2533
Waco: (800) 321-9226

TURKEY, TEXAS

UNUSUAL NAMES OF TEXAS TOWNS

When you go, don't forget to pick up a T-shirt!

1. ***Bee Cave:*** Founded around 1870 and named for a large cave of wild bees found nearby. Population 656.

2. ***Bigfoot:*** Settled about 1865 and orignally known as Connally's Store; later Mr. Connally named it Bigfoot, for William A. A. (Bigfoot) Wallace, a local resident. Population 304.

3. ***Cut-n-Shoot:*** Named after a 1912 confrontation over a church that almost led to violence! Population 1,158.

4. ***Dime Box:*** Until a post office opened in 1877, settlers deposited outgoing mail and a dime in a small box. Population 313.

5. ***Ding Dong:*** Apparently named for the only public building: a church. Population 22.

6. ***Dripping Springs:*** Started around 1849 by a man named Fawcett! Population 1,548.

7. ***Gun Barrel City:*** Developed around a reservoir in the mid-1960s and derived its name from its motto, "We shoot straight with you." Population 5,145.

8. ***Jot 'em Down:*** Known by various names until the Jot 'Em Down Gin Corporation, named for Lum and Abner's fictional store on the popular early '30s radio show, gave the town its name. Population 10.

9. ***Leakey:*** Named for John Leakey, who arrived with his wife Nancy and five other settlers in 1856. Population 399.

10. ***Loco:*** Early settlers arrived in the 1880s and named the town for the locoweed that grew in the area. Only farms and a cemetery remain.

11. ***Looneyville:*** First settled around the time of the Civil War, and named for John Looney, who opened a store there in the early 1870s. Now considered a "dispersed rural community."

12. ***Muleshoe:*** Founded when the Pecos and Northern Texas Railway laid tracks here in 1913 and named for the nearby Muleshoe Ranch. Population 4,571.

13. ***Notrees:*** Had one native tree before construction of a large Shell gas plant forced its removal in 1946, during the oil boom. With a post office in the grocery store, owner Charlie Brown provided the name. Population 338.

14. ***Poetry:*** Formerly Turner's Point, the postal service requested the community change its name to avoid confusion with a similarly named post office in 1876. A local merchant suggested the name Poetry because the area in springtime reminded him of a poem. Population 600.

15. ***Possum Kingdom:*** Named for Possum Kingdom bend in the Brazos River, an unincorporated community. No population figures available, although there are four businesses and two hotels.

16. ***Tarzan:*** In 1925 a two-room school was built to accommodate the local community, and postal officials chose the name from a list of possibilities submitted by the general store owner. Population 498.

17. ***Trophy Club:*** An upscale community planned in 1973 around a country club with a course designed by Ben Hogan; the name originated in the idea that the club would exhibit Hogan's golf trophy collection. Population 6,350.

18. ***Turkey:*** First settled in the early 1890s and originally called Turkey Roost, for the wild turkey roosts once found nearby; changed to Turkey in 1893, when a post office was established there. Population 507.

19. ***Twitty:*** Named for Asa Twitty, an early settler and store owner, around 1912. Population 60.

20. ***Uncertain:*** Local tradition says the town is named due to the uncertainty that residents had about their citizenship before the boundary between the United States and the Republic of Texas had been established. Population 194.

WINNERS
TOP10
Wines
Texas Best

TEXAS IS THE FIFTH LARGEST *wine-producing state in the nation, with more than one hundred wineries operational in the Lone Star State today. Although most of the state's vineyards are in the Lubbock and West Texas areas, the majority of Texas wineries are located in the Hill Country and Grapevine/North Texas areas, and many have developed award-winning vintages.*

Here are the top ten award-winning wines and their vineyards from the Texas's Best Wines competition. The Wine Society of Texas hosts the competition using scoring based on a 20-point evaluation method. Medals are awarded based on a competitive evaluation of the highest-scoring wines based on color, clarity, aroma, taste, and overall impression.

1. Fall Creek Vineyards: Granite Reserve, 2003

Fall Creek Vineyards was established in 1975 by a Texas businessman/rancher and his wife, who, when visiting France, noticed the similarities in the climate and soil to their Texas home. The vineyard is located about eighty miles northwest of Austin, where there is a spectacular 90-foot waterfall on the property.
1820 County Rd. 222, Tow, TX 78672 | (325) 379-5361

2. Spicewood Vineyards: Rosé of Merlot, 2004

Spicewood Vineyards has been commercially producing wine since 1995 in a handcrafted winery building designed to resemble a nineteenth-century Texas Hill Country home. All of the Spicewood Vineyards wines are estate bottled.
1419 Burnet County Rd. 409 | Spicewood, TX 78669, (830) 693-5328

3. Texas Hills Vineyard: Orange Moscato, Newsom Vineyard, 2003

Texas Hills Vineyards champions the environment, using environmentally friendly fertilizers and harvesting methods. Even the winery and tasting room, built from rammed earth, are environmentally sound. Located one mile east of Johnson City on Ranch Road 2766, the road to Pedernales Falls State Park.
P.O. Box 1480, Johnson City, TX 78636 | (830) 868-2321

4. Becker Vineyards: Claret, 2003

Located in the Texas Hill Country between Fredericksburg and Stonewall, Becker Vineyards was established in 1992 and housed in a reproduction nineteenth-century German stone barn. The wine is stored in the largest underground wine cellar in Texas. Visit this homestead by traveling eleven miles east of Fredericksburg or four miles west of Stonewall off U.S. Hwy 290 on Jenschke Lane.

P.O. Box 393, Stonewall, TX 78671 | (830) 644-2681

5-6. Llano Estacado: Chenin Blanc, 2004; Cabernet Sauvignon Cellar Reserve, Newsom Vineyard, 2002

Llano Estacado is the largest premium winery in Texas, established in 1976. They've planted an experimental vineyard, resulting in "Viviano," Texas's first ultra-premium wine. You can find them just over three miles east of U.S. 87 South on FM 1585 in Lubbock.

P.O. Box 3487, Lubbock, TX 79452 | (800) 634-3854 or (806) 745-2258

7. La Bodega Winery: Private Reserve Merlot, 2002

This is the world's only fully-licensed/bonded winery in an airport. Yes, you read that correctly—this winery offers Texas hospitality to guests in two distinctive locations inside Dallas-Fort Worth International Airport: American Airlines Terminal A, Gate A15, and Terminal D, Gate D14, pouring over thirty private reserve and exclusive, limited-production Texas wines from privately owned boutique wineries.

P.O. Box 613136, Dallas-Ft. Worth Airport, TX 75261 | (972) 574-1440

8-9. Flat Creek Estate: Travis Peak Select, Reserve Cabernet Sauvignon, 2002; Muscato Blanco, 2004

Established in 1998, Flat Creek Estates Winery is nestled in the hills just west of Austin and prides itself on its quiet, retreat-like surroundings. In fact, you can book rooms here for a wedding or corporate event. The estate currently has twenty acres of grapes and mimics Tuscany in its surroundings, while making award-winning wines.

24912 Singleton Bend East Rd., Marble Falls, TX 78654 | (512) 267-6310

10. Delaney Vineyards: Sauvignon Blanc, 2002

Delaney Vineyards is an Old World chateau in the middle of Texas—and during the grape harvest, you can attend the Annual Grape Stomp! You'll enjoy a visit here any time of the year, though, visiting the state-of-the-art facilities or relaxing in the tasting rooms.

2000 Champagne Blvd., Grapevine, TX 76051 | (817) 481-5668

JANUARY

El Paso—Southwestern International Livestock Show and Rodeo

Ft. Worth—Stock Show and Rodeo

Mission—Texas Citrus Festival, parades, bands, floats, food, and fun

Port Arthur—Janis Joplin Birthday Bash, a one-night party honoring Janis Joplin and the music she made famous

FEBRUARY

Brownsville—Charro Days, billed as the best homegrown international celebration

El Paso—Southwestern International Livestock Show and Rodeo

Fort Worth—Stock Show and Rodeo (cont.)

Galveston—Mardi Gras

Houston—Livestock Show and Rodeo

Laredo—Washington's Birthday Celebration

MARCH

Dallas—Dallas Blooms

Dublin—St. Patrick's Day Festival

Fulton—Oysterfest, a celebration of all foods having anything to do with oysters

Goliad—Goliad County Fair Festival

Halletsville—South Texas Sausage and Polka Festival

Houston—Should Have Been a Cowboy Association BBQ Cook Off

Spring—Springfest, a Texas-style celebration of wine, food, and art; celebrates Texas wine and wineries

Washington—Texas Independence Day

APRIL

Austin—Old Settler's Music Festival, central Texas's premier music festival

Corpus Christi—Buccaneer Days

Dallas—Dallas Blooms (cont.)

Dayton—Ole Tyme Days Festival

Halletsville—Texas State Championship Fiddlers' Frolics

Port Aransas—Texas Sand Sculpture Festival

Poteet—Strawberry Festival

San Antonio—Fiesta San Antonio, one of the biggest festivals in the United States

Turkey—Bob Wills Day

MAY

Abilene—Western Heritage Classic

Athens—Athens Old Fiddlers' Contest and Reunion

Columbus—Live Oak Art and Music Festival

Corpus Christi—Buccaneer Days (cont.)

Crystal Beach—Texas Crab Festival

Kerrville—Texas State Arts and Crafts Fair

Marshall—Stagecoach Days

Port Neches—Riverfest, boating activities, car show, fishing tournament, and festival

Temple—Central Texas Air Show

JUNE

Albany—Fort Griffin Fandangle

Canyon—Musical drama *Texas*, performances through August

Longview—AlleyFest, a three-day art, music, and food festival with a Kids Fest and sporting events

Luling—Watermelon Thump

San Antonio—Texas Folklife Festival

Seadrift—Shrimpfest

JULY

Lampasas—Spring Ho Festival

Longview—Great Texas Balloon Race

Port Aransas—Deep Sea Roundup, the oldest fishing tournament on the Gulf Coast

Stamford—Texas Cowboy Reunion

Weatherford—Parker County Peach Festival

AUGUST

Amarillo—Cal Farley's Boys Ranch Rodeo

Dalhart—XIT Rodeo and Reunion

Fredericksburg—Gillespie County Fair

Wichita Falls—Hotter 'N Hell Hundred Bike Ride and Festival

SEPTEMBER

Abilene—West Texas Fair and Rodeo

Amarillo—Tri-State Fair

Anahuac—Texas Gatorfest

Aransas Pass—Shrimporee

Boerne—Kendall County Fair

Brenham—Washington County Fair

Caldwell—Kolache Festival

Corpus Christi—Bayfest

Dallas—State Fair of Texas. If you only choose one annual affair to go to, make it this one. It is HUGE!

Del Rio—Diez y Seis de Septiembre Celebration

Hallettsville—Hallettsville Kolache Fest

Lakehills—Medina Lake Cajun Festival

Lubbock—Panhandle South Plains Fair

Lufkin – Texas State Forest Festival

Odessa – Permian Basin Fair and Exposition

Plano—Balloon Festival

Rockport/Fulton—Hummer/Bird Celebration

OCTOBER

Austin—Legends of Rasta Reggae Festival

Flatonia—Czhilispiel

Fort Worth—Red Steagall Cowboy Gathering and Western Swing Festival, one of the top cowboy events in the country featuring cowboy poetry and music, trail rides, chuck wagons, and rodeos

Galveston—ARToberFEST

Gilmer—East Texas Yamboree

Gonzales—"Come and Take It" Days

Helotes—Texas Shrimp Fest

Tyler—Texas Rose Festival

NOVEMBER

Crystal City—Spinach Festival

Marshall—Wonderland of Lights, displays through New Year's Eve

New Braunfels—Wurstfest

Port Isabel—World's Championship Shrimp Cookoff. Chefs from around the country compete in this one-day event that is a must for all shrimp lovers.

San Antonio—Holiday River Parade and Lighting Ceremony

Seguin—Pecan Fest

DECEMBER

Buda—Budafest Festival and Extravaganza

Galveston—Dickens on the Strand. Galveston is transformed into Victorian England.

Granbury—Candlelight Tour of Homes

Palestine—Victorian Christmas Train Ride

Port Isabel—Christmas Lighted Boat Parade

San Angelo—Christmas at Old Fort Concho

San Antonio—Fiesta de las Luminarias

Uncertain—The Annual Uncertain Floating Christmas Parade

Photo Spots in Texas

Popular Tourist Towns and Top Texas Attractions

The Riverwalk, San Antonio

Paseo del Rio is the Spanish translation for *river walk*, or literally *walk of the river*. San Antonio's Riverwalk is one of the most visited places in Texas. In January, parts of the river are drained for cleaning. Seizing any excuse to party, the city holds the San Antonio Riverwalk Mud Festival and Mud Parade. Whether you choose the dry walk along the river or the tour boat version, this is a great adventure in shopping and fine dining.

> **Q:** What is the longest river located wholly within the border of Texas?
>
> **A:** The Brazos. The Rio Grande is not within the border but on the border. It begins in Colorado and flows through New Mexico before it reaches Texas.

Granbury

Granbury is a popular tourist town about 35 miles southwest of Fort Worth. Granbury is a historic town rich in legends. History involving the famous and infamous, including Davy Crockett and John Wilkes Booth, can be found here. In Granbury Cemetery you'll find the resting places of General Hiram B. Granbury, Jesse James, and Ashley Crockett, grandson of Davy Crockett. After touring the town, relax at Lake Granbury by going fishing or kayaking. This friendly town awaits your arrival!

Schlitterbahn Waterpark Resort, New Braunfels

This is a destination with over 3 miles of tubing adventures, 7 children's water playgrounds, 17 water slides, the world's first surfing machine, and 3 uphill water coasters. Schlitterbahn Waterpark Resort, on the banks of the spring-fed Comal River in historic New Braunfels, opened in 1979 and today includes a huge water park and two resorts spread across sixty-five acres. **Hot tip from Schlitterbahn's:** To avoid crowds on weekends, come early or late in the season. Weekends in April, May, early June, late August, and September are less crowded than weekends in late June, July, and early August.

The Sixth Floor Museum, Dallas

The Sixth Floor Museum at Dealey Plaza contains a permanent exhibition that examines John F. Kennedy's life and presidency, his assassination, and the historical legacy of that tragic event. Each year, over two million visitors come to this location in downtown Dallas.

Corpus Christi

Voted an all-American city in 2003, Corpus Christi is one of Texas's most popular tourist cities. Located on the Gulf Coast, Corpus Christi offers beach activity, boating, fishing on the gulf, and more in approximately 255 days of vacation sunshine a year. The Museum of Science and History gives a unique look South Texas and its place in the world. Visit the USS *Lexington*. See a play at Harbor Playhouse. Stroll through the peaceful oasis of the Corpus Christi Botanical Garden. Corpus Christi truly has something for everyone.

Jefferson

The historic steamboat port of Jefferson has steamboat tours, a steam train, and riverboat bayou tours. There is plenty of shopping with dozens of antique and gift shops. Situated on the Big Cypress Bayou, Jefferson became a bustling riverport town early on and is described as the "Riverport to the Southwest."

Museum of Fine Arts, Houston

The Museum of Fine Arts, Houston, is the largest art museum in America south of Chicago, west of Washington, D.C., and east of Los Angeles. More than two million people visit the MFAH each year. The museum contains a collection of over 51,000 pieces that cover many periods and geographic regions.

Dallas World Aquarium

The aquarium features more than 85,000 gallons of saltwater with marine life from around the world. Take a stroll through the 22,000-gallon tunnel to see marine life surround you without getting wet. This site remains one of the best-kept secrets in Dallas.

Leakey

Leakey is sometimes referred to as "The Swiss Alps of Texas." Elevations in the area range from 1,500 to 2,400 feet with deep canyons cut by the Frio and Nueces Rivers. The Frio River offers anything from whitewater rapids to flats to swimming holes and great fishing. Camping and hunting are very popular, as is tubing in the crystal clear water of the Frio River.

SeaWorld, San Antonio

Amazing shows, animal entertainment, and a theme park combine to make SeaWorld a must-see Texas attraction. It is actually four parks in one on 250 acres: a show park, rides, a water park, and an amazing animal park. Visiting this park is a true adventure.

Canyon Lake

The city of Canyon Lake is on Canyon Lake, which has 80 miles of scenic shoreline. Canyon Lake is located approximately halfway between San Antonio and Austin. The Army Corps of Engineers built Canyon Dam and Canyon Lake for the primary purpose of flood control and water conservation. Today, Canyon Lake is a prime spot for recreational activities.

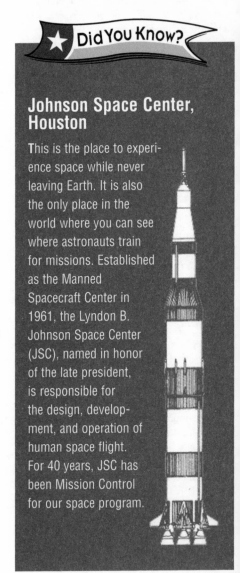

★ Did You Know?

Johnson Space Center, Houston

This is the place to experience space while never leaving Earth. It is also the only place in the world where you can see where astronauts train for missions. Established as the Manned Spacecraft Center in 1961, the Lyndon B. Johnson Space Center (JSC), named in honor of the late president, is responsible for the design, development, and operation of human space flight. For 40 years, JSC has been Mission Control for our space program.

Fredericksburg

This town is the shoppers paradise of Texas, with well over 150 shops featuring antiques, hand-constructed merchandise, clothing, gifts, jewelry, western items, and furniture. There are also several local wineries to help you stock your wine cellar with Texas wines. Fredericksburg is located 70 miles west of Austin and 68 miles northwest of San Antonio.

Texas State Railroad State Park, Rusk

The historic state railroad is still maintained as a fully self-contained railroad system that operates between Rusk and Palestine, Texas. Its train crews maintain and operate four steam engines, four antique diesel locomotives, and a complete steam-engine restoration shop, while its track crew maintains over 25 miles of track and 24 bridges. This is a fantastic 1-1/2 hour trip to the opposite station. Once visitors arrive, they have 1-1/2 hours to eat lunch, shop, and then return home.

Galveston Island

This is one of Texas's most popular tourist destinations for people who love beaches. Thirty-two miles of beach, historic homes, museums, shopping, and seafood restaurants are what Galveston is known for. The island has over 1,500 designated historical landmarks on the National Register of Historic Places. Recently, Galveston seaport also became a

cruise ship port for major cruise lines. The island is a quick 50 miles southeast of Houston.

Q: Who operates the world's most complete collection of working WWII combat aircraft?

A: The Commemorative Air Force in Midland, Texas.

Fort Griffin State Park and Historic Site, Albany

Located 15 miles north of Albany, Fort Griffin offers plenty of frontier history in the Texas Panhandle. Fort Griffin was established in 1867 and was a strategic unit in the string of border and frontier outposts defending Texas settlers against hostile Indians and outlaws. Today, visitors can see the partially restored ruins of the fort. The park has camping, hiking, fishing, picnicking, historical reenactments, and much more. The park is also home to a portion of the state's longhorn herd.

Wouldn't You Like to Be a PEPPER?

Dr Pepper Bottling Plant, Dublin

Dublin, Texas is officially known as Dr Pepper Texas for one week each summer in June. Dr Pepper was invented in nearby Waco. The Dublin location is the oldest Dr Pepper bottler in the world. It is also the only plant where the original Dr Pepper formula is still in use. They opt for pure cane sugar over the cheaper, more common corn sweeteners used in most soft drinks today. Some Dr Pepper addicts swear they can tell the difference between the original formula and others. Additionally, they preach of the original formula's healing properties. The annual birthday celebration sponsored by the plant is a fantastic weekend getaway for Peppers everywhere.

Kingsland

Located 66 miles northwest of Austin on Lake LBJ, where the Llano and Colorado rivers join the lake, Kingsland is a great place to rent a lake cabin or park your RV for the weekend. It is popular for boating, fishing, swimming, and the town of Kingsland has antique shops, arts and crafts venues, and restaurants serving a variety of menus. Both a recreation and a retirement town, many snowbirds from the north spend the winter here.

Uncertain

Located in eastern Texas on Caddo Lake, the town of Uncertain offers a unique opportunity to enjoy nature. Fishing, canoeing, hunting, and birding are popular. And there are steamboat tours of Caddo Lake. The meandering channels, bayous, and sloughs of Caddo Lake cover 32,700 acres. In 1971, Caddo was designated a "Wetlands of International Importance." Its natural beauty has made it one of the best—if not *the* best—photos spots in Texas.

Salado

This quaint and historic village is located 45 miles north of Austin and 45 miles south of Waco. Over 100 stores tempt the tourist to browse and stay in one of the many bed-and-breakfast hotels. The town of Salado was originally a stop for the stagecoach lines and home to the first coeducational college in the state of Texas. *Salado* is an Indian word describing the spring-fed creek. During Salado's frontier days, the village was a home-away-from-home for such historical figures as Sam Houston, General George Custer, and outlaw Sam Bass. Now Salado is an artists' colony, with more than 100 working artists in residence.

Billy Bob's Texas, Fort Worth

The building that is now known as Billy Bob's Texas was built in 1910 and was once a large open-air barn for housing prize cattle during the Fort Worth Stock Show. In 1936, as a Texas Centennial Project, the building was enclosed by the City of Fort Worth at a cost of $183,500 and the tower added. The "new" structure contained 1,257 animal stalls, and a 1,200-seat auction ring that is now the bull riding arena. Throughout its history, it has been many things, but since 1981, it has been the premier place for musical entertainment and live Pro Bull Riding. More than fifteen million visitors have come through Billy Bob's doors since 1981. Repeatedly named Country Music Club of the Year, Billy Bob's has the true Texas honky-tonk attitude.

You oughta go on stage. ...there's one leaving in five minutes.

★ **Billy Bob's Trivia:**

The most bottled beer sold in one night was at a Hank Williams, Jr., concert. 16,000 bottles were sold. Merle Haggard once bought a round of drinks for the whole club and set a world record.

The Alamo

The Alamo
Cradle of Texas Liberty

Any state, anytime, anywhere, everyone does "Remember the Alamo." During the Texas Revolution, San Antonio and the Alamo played a vital role. Mexican general Santa Anna and his men stormed the Alamo. After a bloody and ferocious fight, only a few defenders were left alive. Santa Anna had them executed. The Alamo stirred the rest of Texas, culminating in the battle of San Jacinto and Texas independence. The place where men fought against overwhelming odds and gave their lives has become the shrine of Texas liberty.

The Texas State Capitol

Widely recognized as one of the most spectacular state capitols, the Texas State Capitol building is an extraordinary historical building. The Texas State Capitol is the largest in gross square footage of all the state capitols, second only in size to the National Capitol in Washington, D.C. The capitol's exterior walls are "Sunset Red" granite, which gives the building its pink color. It took seven years and over three million dollars to complete the construction.

Washington-on-the-Brazos

Washington, called Washington-on-the-Brazos, was the site where Texans finally declared their independence from Mexico in 1836. A state historic site and a marriage of history and nature, Washington-on-the-Brazos is a visit to the history of Texas. The picturesque park grounds along the Brazos River and the Star of the Republic Museum, Independence Hall, and the Barrington Living History Farm allow the visitor to pretend to be back in the lives and times of the fight for Texas independence. Contact: Box 305 Washington, Texas 77880-0305. Phone (936) 878-2214

Texas State Cemetery

This is the Lone Star State's version of Arlington National Cemetery. The site honors the lives of some of the most famous and notable Texans, such as Stephen F. Austin, General Albert Sidney Johnston, Governor Allan Shivers, Governor John Connally, and Lieutenant Governor Bob Bullock. The cemetery has a Confederate section, an Honored Texans section, and a September 11th Memorial. Visitors may make a reservation for a guided tour. The cemetery is located at 909 Navasota Street, Austin, Texas 78702. Phone (512) 463-0605.

Spelling Bee "Capital" refers to the city. Austin is the capital of Texas. "Capitol" refers to the building. The Texas Capitol was completed in 1888.

> *"History like that of Texas is rare. In its color, its dramatic movement, and its instructiveness when viewed from the standpoint of political and social science, it has few parallels. These characteristics make it well worth preservation and study. To the genuine Texan . . . one of the strongest motives to the cultivation of the subject will be found in his patriotism."*
>
> *George P. Garrison*

Point Isabel Lighthouse

Constructed in 1852, the Point Isabel Lighthouse was built to protect and guide ships through Brazos Santiago and the barrier islands. In 1952, the lighthouse was opened as a state park and remains the only lighthouse on the Texas coast open to the public. It is also the second smallest state park in the state of Texas. Point Isabel Lighthouse has been activated and deactivated many times over the years and today provides a glimpse into Texas maritime history. Point Isabel Lighthouse is located at 421 East Queen Isabella Blvd., on the Lower Laguna Madre in the City of Port Isabel, approximately 26 miles east of U.S. Hwy. 77/83 on State Hwy. 100.

Battleship *Texas*

Permanently anchored on the Buffalo Bayou and the busy Houston Ship Channel, Battleship *Texas* became the first battleship museum in the United States in 1948. The *Texas* is the last of the battleships to have participated in World Wars I and II, and is credited with the introduction and innovation of advances in gunnery, aviation, and radar. A tour of this naval vessel will allow you a look into the life of the men aboard the *Texas* during World War II. The *Texas* is part of the San Jacinto Battleground State Historic Site. Visit it at: 3523 Highway 134, Laporte, TX 77571. Phone (281) 479-2431.

San Jacinto Monument

The world's tallest memorial column, 15 feet taller than the Washington monument, the San Jacinto Monument is a sight to see. The monument and museum honor all who fought for Texas independence. At 570 feet, this giant is one of the finest examples of Moderne (Art Deco) architecture in the United States. The octagonal shaft is 48 feet at its base, 30 feet at the observation level, and 19 square feet at the base of the 220-ton star made of stone, steel, and concrete. The American Society of Civil Engineers has recognized the monument as a National Historic Civil Engineering Landmark. At the base of the monument is the museum and gateway to Texas cultural history. The museum is located just 20 minutes from Houston at One Monument Circle, La Porte (Houston), Texas 77571-9585. Phone (281)479-2421.

Moody Mansion

This four-story, 28,000 square-foot structure was completed in 1895 and became home to the Moody family soon after the great hurricane of 1900. The Moody family fortune was based on cotton, banking, ranching, insurance, and hotels. Moody family members remained in the home until 1986. Two Moody charitable foundations support worthy causes.

The mansion has been restored to its turn-of-the century splendor and now houses the furnishings and personal effects of the Moody family. The mansion is located at 2618 Broadway, Galveston, Texas 77550. Phone (409) 762-7668.

Texans Love the
Sun of a Beach

With over 600 miles of coastline, sandy beaches, and a beautiful temperate climate, Texas beaches are a hidden American treasure. The best beaches in Texas are centered around three locations: Galveston, Corpus Christi and Port Aransas, and South Padre Island.

The warm waters of the Gulf of Mexico meet 80-degree average temperatures up and down the coastlines.

Start the sandcastle building at any of these beaches.

Corpus Christi Beaches

Corpus Christi Beach This urban beach includes rinse-off showers, restrooms, picnic tables, and cabana. This beach is a popular kiteboarding spot because of the excellent wind and wave conditions. Locals call it "North Beach." It is also home to the Texas State Aquarium and the USS *Lexington* Museum.

McGee Beach This beach has recently had a facelift that extended the shore, so there is more room to play. This is a child-friendly beach with little seaweed and no undertow. You can watch sailboats, windsurfers, and the shrimpers hauling in their catch, or turn toward the street to watch pedal carts, in-line skaters, and passersby.

Padre Balli County Park This is a fishing beach about 15 minutes south of Corpus Christi. It is also home to the well-known local landmark Bob Hall Pier.

J. P. Luby Surf Park The pier was built specifically to generate waves. You won't find monster waves here—waves along the Texas Gulf Coast are generally two to three feet high, at most. This is the beach where young singles go to ogle and be ogled.

Galveston Island Beaches

East Beach Located just 45 minutes south of Houston, East Beach is known as "Houston's Playground." East Beach is the largest beach in Texas, and it is a lively place, with beach parties, outdoor concerts, special events, and bikini contests. Facilities include showers, game room, and volleyball courts. The beach also has the Big Reef Nature Park. East Beach is also called R. A. Apffel Park.

Seawall Beaches There are a number of beaches along the seawall. Beach bums can rent boogie boards and umbrellas and grab a bite to eat anywhere along this strip. Fishing is permitted from atop the concrete jetties.

Stewart Beach Families flock to this beach with its lifeguards, miniature golf course, waterslide, and easy access to food. Located between the East End and Seawall Beach, there is parking (for a fee) and peace of mind from April to October.

Galveston Island State Park Found on the west end of Galveston Island, travelers can enjoy camping, bird-watching, beachcombing, and stargazing on over 2,000 acres.

Padre Island National Seashore

Padre Island National Seashore stretches 130,454 miles and is the longest remaining stretch of undeveloped barrier island in the United States. In 1998, it was designated a Globally Important Bird Area.

The National Seashore is subdivided into several beaches, of which five are named. From north to south, they are North Beach, Closed Beach (which includes the Malaquite Beach area), South Beach, Little Shell Beach, and Big Shell Beach.

Major attractions at this national park are fishing, camping, and windsurfing. The Bird Island Basin area of Laguna Madre is one of the top spots in the nation for windsurfing.

Port Aransas Beaches and Mustang Island

Port Aransas This intimate coastal community is the best jumping-off point for a deep-sea fishing trip. Port Aransas is on Mustang Island, a barrier island north of North Padre Island. It is accessible by road from Corpus Christi or by ferry from Aransas Pass. Great seafood restaurants are an added incentive at this beach.

Mustang Island State Park This park is a great place for hiking and fishing. At just under 4,000 acres, the park features five miles of beach and beautiful dunes. The dunes were recently damaged by hurricanes but are recovering.

South Padre Island Beaches

Not to be confused with Padre Island, South Padre Island is a barrier island at the southernmost tip of Texas. South Padre Island is a resort beach, and there are hotels, condominiums, restaurants, gift shops, bars, and all the other luxuries associated with a resort beach. These beaches attract many visitors from across the United States and Mexico. At spring break time, there is a deluge of visitors that only the hardiest beach lover could handle.

THE STATE FAIR OF TEXAS
Livestock Competition

More than a Pretty Face

Since 1886, Fair Park in Dallas has been the location of the State Fair of Texas—an event that hundreds of thousands of people attend every year. Livestock has always been a major draw, as the fair is host to over 8,000 head of cattle, sheep, swine, goats, poultry, and llamas.

The livestock competitions offer more than bragging rights. High school seniors who have participated in the State Fair Youth Livestock Show are eligible for a State Fair Scholarship. In 2006, forty-four students across Texas received scholarships of $1,000. Renewal grants in this amount were given to an additional sixty undergraduates at Texas colleges and universities who maintained a minimum 3.0 GPA. Since this program began in 1992, more than $1.8 million in new and renewed scholarships have been awarded. Congratulations to the latest winners, and the critters who did them proud!

Animals Exhibited

- Beef and Dairy Cattle
- Youth Beef Heifers, Dairy Cattle, Market Steers, and Prospect Steers
- Donkeys and Mules
- Miniature Donkeys
- Angora and Dairy Goats
- Boer and Meat Goats
- Cashmere Goats
- Youth Dairy and Market Goats
- Poultry
- Fine and Medium Wool Sheep

- Natural Colored Sheep
- Youth Breeding Sheep
- Youth Market Lambs (wethers)
- Pan-American and Junior Breeding Swine
- Youth Market Barrows
- Llamas
- Miniature Zebu Cattle
- Nigerian Dwarf Goats
- Pygmy Goats
- Pigeons

And the Winner is . . .
Some of Our Previous Celebrities:

Headline, Red, Buckwheat, Aggie, GoTo, Hurricane,

Mini Me, Atlas, Tuition, Weebull, Tex, and Giant

NO BULL!

Look what these prize winners sold for at the auction . . .

Grand champion steer sold for a record-breaking $88,000.

The top market swine sold for $12,700.

The grand champion market lamb sold for $9,000.

Grand champion market goat sold for $9,000.
Prize winning pen of three market broilers sold for $9000.

Grand Champion Youth Market Barrow sold for $12,700.

Reserve Grand Champion Youth Market Steer sold for $25,000.

Reserve Grand Champion Market Barrow sold for $8,000.

State Fair Facts:

- Fair's economic impact on Dallas: approximately $350 million annually

- Exhibit space: approximately 370,000 sq. ft. in six buildings

- Amusement rides: 70–75

- The 212-ft. Texas Star is the tallest Ferris wheel in North America.

- Livestock entries: approximately 8,000

- Creative Arts entries: approximately 7,000

- Food service locations: approximately 200

- Ride and food revenues: $23 million (2004)

- The Texas-OU football game has been played during the fair every year since 1929.

- Big Tex made his first state fair appearance in 1952.

- Corn dogs were invented in 1942 by state fair concessionaires Carl and Neil Fletcher.

- Since 1992, the State Fair of Texas Scholarship program has awarded more than $1.5 million in new and renewed college grants to eligible students.

Join the Corn Club

Texas 4-H started with the first county Extension agent in Texas in 1906. Two years later, T. M. (Tom) Marks, county agricultural agent, organized the first "corn club" for boys in Jack County. Marks found that he had more success teaching new farming and production technology to youngsters rather than to adults. Within a matter of years, "pig clubs," "beef calf clubs" (Coleman County, 1910), and girls' "tomato clubs" (Milam County, 1912) were born.

From those first 25 corn club members to the more than 750,000 4-H club members in Texas today, 4-H has grown and thrived. Boys and girls, ages 5 to 19, contact their local county extension agent to find the nearest club and join. The Texas 4-H Museum is located in Jacksboro (Jack County), the birthplace of 4-H in Texas.

What's the "4-H" for?

The foundation of all 4-H programs is: "Head, Heart, Hands, Health."

Find out more about 4-H and how to join at 4husa.org.

★ 4-H Projects

Aquatic Science, Automotive, Beef, Bicycle, Biological Sciences, Citizenship, Clothing and Textiles, Companion Animals, Computer Science, Consumer Education, County Government, Dairy Cattle, Dog Care, Electric, Energy, Entomology, Entrepreneurship, Exotic Animals, Family Life, Field and Stream, Food and Nutrition, Forestry, Goats, Health, Horse, Horticulture, Housing and Home Environment, Investigating Water, Leadership, Meat Science, Photography, Public Speaking, Poultry, Rabbits, Range Science, Recreation, Safety, Sea Science, Sheep, Shooting Sports, Small Engines, Sport Fishing, Swine, Veterinary Science, Wildlife and Fisheries, and Wood Science

THE TEXAS FFA

Q: What is the FFA?

A: FFA stands for the Future Farmers of America. FFA uses the initials instead of the full name because agriculture is more than farming and ranching. It is a student-led leadership group dedicated to agricultural education.

Q: Is everyone in FFA going to be a farmer?

A: No. Agriculture is an ever-expanding subject that includes landscaping, computer applications, accounting, environmental science, mechanics, and engineering.

Q: How do kids become involved in FFA?

A: Unlike 4-H, which is run by the county extension office, FFA is part of the teaching of agricultural science in school. The programs are funded through grants, private donations, and sponsorships at the local and national level.

Texas Pride

Texas FFA is proud to have one of the largest state memberships within the National FFA Organization. Texas FFA membership has steadily grown toward a new membership record with over 61,000 members in 2005.

YOU JUST WON'T BELIEVE WHAT THEY CAUGHT!

Texas fishing, like everything else in Texas, is huge. Finding a place to fish isn't difficult. There are more than a hundred lakes in Texas for freshwater fishing, and the Gulf of Mexico offers saltwater marine fishing opportunities.

The Fishing Tackle Loaner Program

If you want to try fishing and don't own your own equipment, Texas has a program where you can borrow what you need. The Fishing Tackle Loaner program loans fishing equipment just like a library book. Future or "wanna be" fishermen can borrow rods, reels, and tackle boxes with hooks, sinkers, and bobbers for up to seven days of fishing. Loaner sites in Texas are in Arlington, Austin, Channelview, College Station, Conroe, El Campo, Freeport, Hamilton, Houston, Laredo, Quintana, San Angelo, San Antonio, Sherman, Southlake, Valley View, and Watauga.

Remember: If you are over 17 years old, you will need a fishing license. If you are under 18 years old, an adult must be with you when you check out equipment.

Once you have your equipment, where are the best spots to fish? Fishing is best in a spot that provides fish with the right amount of food, oxygen, water, shelter, and space. Next, try to find a spot down current from structures such as jetties, piers, stumps, trees, and rocks.

When do the fish bite?

It isn't an exact science, but here is a chart of the approximate dates.

- **CATFISH: Mid-April to mid-October**
- **CRAPPIE: March to May**
- **LARGEMOUTH BASS: March to June**
- **STRIPED BASS: All year, especially November to February and June to September**
- **SUNFISH: May to June**
- **TROUT: November to December and mid-February to mid-April**
- **WALLEYE: Mid-February to mid-April**
- **WHITE BASS: Mid-March to May**

★ Texas Fishing License

Required of any resident who fishes in the public waters of Texas (Note: All members of the U.S. Armed Forces on active duty and their dependents are considered residents).
For more information about licenses, you can phone (800) 792-1112 or (512) 389-4800 (9 a.m.– 6 p.m., Monday through Friday, closed Saturday, Sunday, and most holidays).

How to Measure a Fish

1. Lay the fish on its side.
2. Close its mouth and then squeeze the tail fins together.
3. Measure from the tip of its snout to the farthest tip of its tail.

Common freshwater fish caught in Texas include the black crappie, bluegill, largemouth bass, freshwater drum, rainbow trout, white bass, and the channel catfish. Saltwater fish common on the Texas shorelines are the southern flounder, the red drum, sheepshead, Atlantic croaker, sand trout, spotted seatrout, and the black drum.

Hints for Catching Fish

Channel Catfish They are most active in the evening or early night. You can catch one easily during the day by baiting holes with soured grain, dog food, cottonseed cake, or alfalfa cubes. Use shrimp, worms, cutbait, blood, and stink bait for the most luck.

Bluegill They are easiest to catch with worms, crickets, mealworms, small jigs, spinners, and crankbaits.

Largemouth Bass They will bite artificial bait and love live bait, such as minnows, worms, crawfish, leeches, frogs, lizards, and insects.

Black Crappie These fish love minnows, small flies, or plastic jigs and worms.

Southern Flounder Fish for these with live mullet, minnows, live shrimp, or artificial lures close to the bottom.

Red Drum Catch these by baiting with live mullet and croaker, live or dead shrimp, and lures sunk close to the bottom.

Spotted Seatrout Use live shrimp, mullet, or croakers for the best luck catching these fish.

Atlantic Croaker Offer these fish peeled shrimp, fishing close to the bottom. You can also catch these in the fall during the migration to the Gulf.

The ShareLunker program

The ShareLunker program is designed to encourage anglers who have caught 13-pound-plus largemouth bass to lend or donate the fish to the Texas Parks and Wildlife Department for spawning purposes. In a production hatchery, these large fish are paired and mated with other fish. The goal is to improve the quality of largemouth bass in Texas in hopes of creating the next world-record largemouth bass.

Until then, the offspring are used to improve the quality of fish in Texas lakes and rivers. Participating anglers who donate their fish to the program receive a fiberglass replica of their catch, ShareLunker clothing, and recognition at an annual awards banquet at Texas Freshwater Fisheries Center.

Did You Know?

The Texas resident catching the largest fish of the season is awarded a lifetime fishing license for the state of Texas.

Catch and Release

The old saying "limit your catch, don't catch your limit" defines this fishing philosophy. Catch and release is a form of recreational fishing where releasing the fish is used as a technique of conservation. After capture, fish are returned to the water before they are completely exhausted or otherwise injured.

Texas Fishing Records

Freshwater - Rod and Reel

Largemouth Bass
18.18 pounds, 25.5 inches
01/24/91 in Fork

Bighead Carp
90 pounds, 55.5 inches
07/22/00 in Kirby

Blue Catfish
121.5 pounds, 58 inches
01/16/04 in Texoma

Black Crappie
3.92 pounds, 18.5 inches
04/27/03 in Fork

Southern Flounder
11.35 pounds, 26 inches
10/16/87 in Brazoria Reservoir

Alligator Gar
279 pounds
01/01/51 in Rio Grande River

Walleye
11.88 pounds, 31.75 inches
02/26/90 in Meredith

Freshwater - Fly Fishing

Bowfin
7.26 pounds, 26.5 inches
08/17/04 in Tyler

Grass Carp
13.13 pounds, 31 inches
03/17/03 in Brays Bayou

Freshwater Drum
8.14 pounds, 24 inches
07/22/99 in Lewisville Lake

Spotted Sucker
1.14 pounds, 14.5 inches
07/02/02 in Catfish Creek, Engeling

Blue Tilapia
4.5 pounds, 18.5 inches
01/30/01 in Gibbons Creek Reservoir

Catch and Release

Largemouth Bass
25 inches
02/14/06 in Alvarado Park

Smallmouth Bass
22.75 inches
01/29/06 in Lake Texoma

White Bass
17.5 inches
02/09/06 in Stillhouse Hollow

Flathead Catfish
49 inches
02/14/06 in Sam Rayburn

"A bad day of fishing is better than a good day of work."
Author Unknown

World's Largest Fly Fishing Rod

The world's largest fly fishing rod measures 71 feet, $4^1/_2$ inches in length. The functional reel is 4 feet in diameter and 10 inches wide. It would require the combined strength of two dozen strong men to operate the fly rod. Later, a giant tarpon was built to accompany the fly rod. Both can be seen at Pirate's Landing Restaurant in Port Isabel.

Are We Batty?

Largest Bat Colony at Bracken Cave

Bracken Cave in central Texas is about 20 minutes from San Antonio. Every spring, for almost 10,000 years, 20 million Mexican free-tailed bats return here to make their summer home.

Each year, these bats form the largest bat colony in the world and the largest concentration of mammals. The majority of this colony is female. Bracken Cave is actually the largest maternity ward for bats. In March and April, the pregnant females return to Bracken after spending the winter in Mexico and give birth in late June. By late July, the young bats are ready to join their mothers on flights outside the cave.

The bats' nightly feeding excursions are a sight to see. At first, only a few bats circle outside the cave entrance. Soon, more and more bats join them until the bats fill the air, their millions of pair of wings creating a soft breeze. As they rise above the mouth of the cave, they create swirling columns that can be seen for miles. Flocks can climb to nearly 10,000 feet. The bats cover thousands of square miles and consume about 20 tons of insects.

Bat Conservation International (BCI) was able to purchase the Bracken Cave site to preserve it from urbanization and is in the process of creating a nature preserve and visitors' center. Until these plans are completed, the Bracken Cave site is open only on select nights and almost exclusively for BCI members.

Largest Urban Bat Colony

Congress Avenue Bridge in downtown Austin is the spring and summer home to Mexican free-tailed bats, with up to 1.5 million bats at the peak of the bat-watching season. It is the largest urban bat colony in North America. But why did the bats choose the Congress Avenue Bridge? It was not until the Congress Avenue Bridge over Town Lake was renovated in 1980 that the bats found their favorite hangout. Narrow but deep openings created in the bridge construction became perfect housing for the bats.

Austin loves these bats that return each spring. There is even a Batfest combining Austin's love of music and the bats. During Batfest, the observer can hang around listening to music and waiting for the bats to take flight.

During the season, fans can call the Bat Hotline at (512) 416-5700, Category 3636 for estimated times of bat flights. The best place to view the bats is the Statesman Bat Observation Center adjacent to the the bridge. You can also take a bat-watching cruise on Town Lake.

For information on the Bracken Cave bats or the Congress Avenue Bridge bats, contact:
Bat Conservation International
P.O. Box 162603   Austin, TX 78716
(512) 327-9721
http://www.batcon.org

The Allure of the Horny Toad

If you grew up in Texas, you know what a horny toad is. Correctly identified it is a horned lizard.

There are three species of horned toads. The round-tailed variety lives in the Texas Panhandle and the Trans-Pecos. The mountain short-horned is only found in the Guadalupe and Davis mountains. Texas horned lizards are found all over the state.

Texas horned lizards are typically 3 to 5 inches long with yellow, brown, and tan markings. Rings of tan or yellow are found behind the head. They also have spines to aid in defending themselves.

Horny toads can puff up to twice their original size and can squirt blood from their eyes.

Horny toads don't adjust well to captivity. Still, it is difficult to find an adult Texan who hasn't had one at some time in their life. In 1967, the state of Texas began protecting the horny toads, and it is no longer legal to keep one as a pet.

THE LEGEND OF OLD RIP

In July 1897, the town of Eastland began construction to replace their fire-damaged courthouse. A ceremony was held when the cornerstone of the new courthouse was put in place. Inside the hollow block of marble, officials placed a Bible and other mementos. As a joke, County Clerk Ernest Wood added a horned lizard his son had brought along.

Thirty-one years later, it was decided that the courthouse needed to be replaced. People remembered the entombed lizard and on February 18, 1928, 3,000 people gathered to see the cornerstone opened. The horny toad was removed, apparently lifeless. He twitched and the town cheered. He was named Rip, as in Rip Van Winkle.

Rip the horny toad went on tour. He went to Washington, D.C., to meet President Calvin Coolidge. He sadly did not enjoy his celebrity for long. He died on January 19 of pneumonia, less than a year after his release. Rip was embalmed and displayed in the new courthouse, where he remains today.

Did You Know?

If the story of Old Rip sounds familiar, it is because cartoonist Chuck Jones created the 1955 epic, "One Froggy Evening," based on the tale. In the cartoon, a demolition worker opens a cornerstone and discovers a frog who sings ragtime, but only for the worker. The frog, later named Michigan J. Frog, became host of the WB television network.

More Than Road Kill

Rattlesnakes

Texas has ten species of rattlesnakes, more than any other state except Arizona. Only three of these species interact with humans: the western diamondback, the prairie, and the eastern timber or canebrake.

Did You Know?

The western diamondback accounts for almost all the serious cases of venomous poisonings in the state.

Snakebite Statistics

- About 7,000 people are bitten by venomous snakes in the U.S. annually.

- Only 0.2% (1 out of 500) venomous snakebites result in death.

- On average, 1 to 2 people die each year from venomous snakebites in Texas.

- Roughly half of all venomous snakebites are "dry." That is, the snake does not inject venom into the victim.

Armadillo Fact File

The often misunderstood, fascinating world of the armadillo proves they are more than just Texas road kill.

- Armadillos are the state mammal of Texas.

- Armadillos always give birth to four identical young—the only mammal known to do so.

- Contrary to popular belief, the nine-banded armadillo CANNOT roll itself into a ball to escape predators! Only one of the 20-odd varieties of armadillos—the three-banded armadillo (*Tolypeutes tricinctus*)—is able to roll up. The other types are covered with too many bony plates to allow them to curl up.

- Baby armadillos have soft shells, like human fingernails. They get harder as the animal grows, depositing bone under the skin to make a solid shell. The process of laying down bone is known as "ossification."

- A single armadillo may have up to 15 burrows (each 8 inches in diameter and 2–25 feet long) in its 10-acre range.

- Outside of the breeding season, adult armadillos generally live alone.

- Armadillos make grunting sounds as they forage for food. They also may squeak or squeal when they feel threatened.

★ Armadillo Joke

Q: Why did the chicken cross the road?

A: To show the armadillo that it could be done.

EMPIRE of CATTLE

Texas is the nation's leading cattle producer with 14.8 million head. Texas cowboys, with their attitude toward their life and their job on the great trail drives, are the ones who made the wilderness of Texas into an empire of cattle.

Cattle have been raised in Texas as early as the 1690s. Many of the early cattle were longhorns, descendants of Spanish ranch and mission herds, with Texas-sized horn spreads from four to eight feet. These longhorns formed the first cattle population in North America.

The longhorn is a survivor. Hardy, aggressive, and adaptable, Texas Longhorns are well suited to the rigors of life in Texas.

The first Anglo-American settlers of Texas came to raise cotton. They brought cows with them, mostly of northern European breeds. The Spanish breeds already in Texas mixed with these cows and soon considerable herds grew. Most of the cattle used to stock the central and northern plains came from these herds.

When the cowboys left to fight in the Civil War, the cattle were left to survive in the wild. The cattle were mostly left to roam, graze, grow fat, and multiply. The longhorns flourished. It is estimated that there were five million longhorns in Texas by the end of the Civil War.

Early 20th-century economics nearly drove the longhorn to extinction. Tallow from rendered animal fat was in high demand for candles, soaps, and lubricants. Beef was merely a by-product of the rendering plants. Cattle ranchers were raising animals with high tallow content. The longhorn, being naturally lean with 80 percent less renderable tallow, was not wanted. However, some ranchers recognized the longhorn's qualities, and six genetically unique strains were preserved. A seventh "family" was created when the U.S. government established a herd in 1927 at the Wichita Mountains Wildlife Refuge in Oklahoma. Today, there are seven breeds of longhorn cattle: Milby Butler, M. P. Wright, Emil Marks, Cap Yates, Wichita Refuge, Jack Phillips, and the Graves Peeler.

★ **The Silver Spurs**

The Silver Spurs is the honorary service and spirit organization responsible for the caretaking and transportation of the University of Texas Longhorn mascot, BEVO.

More Cow Sense

Santa Gertrudis was the first new breed produced in the Western hemisphere in 1910 on the King Ranch. It is a cross between Shorthorn and Brahman cattle. The name Santa Gertrudis comes from the name of the original Spanish land grant given to Captain Richard King. This land grant is where the King Ranch was first established.

In 1940, the United States Department of Agriculture recognized the **Santa Gertrudis** as a purebred. Santa Gertrudis cattle are called "America's First Beef Breed."

The **Salorn** is a cross between Texas longhorns and Salers, a French breed known for its tremendous growth ability and high-quality beef. By combining these two hardy breeds, a tropically adapted animal that also works well in the cooler climates of western America has been produced.

Texas State Longhorn Herds

In 1936, Texas businessman Sid Richardson believed that the longhorn was closer to extinction than the buffalo. He talked about gathering a state longhorn herd with his friend, historian J. Frank Dobie. Dobie recruited rancher Graves Peeler, and together they selected twenty head of cattle for the herd. By 1941 they had a herd of cattle but needed a place to put them.

The Texas Parks and Recreation Department saved the day and placed the cattle at the Lake Corpus Christi State Park. Richardson asked Dobie and Peeler to find more cattle for more herds. By the end of 1942 they had found the cattle and they were placed at Lake Brownwood State Park.

In 1948, all the longhorns were rounded up. Twenty-one were sent to Fort Griffith State Park, and the remaining cattle were sold. Since that time, the Longhorns have been one of the greatest assets at Fort Griffin, drawing visitors from all over the world. This herd has been the official state longhorn herd since 1948. Fort Griffin places longhorns in other state parks for exhibition, range management, and breeding.

Fort Worth Herd Cattle Drives

The Old West comes to life before your eyes as a team of cowhands drives a herd of longhorns along Exchange Avenue through the Stockyards on the world's only twice-daily cattle drive.

The cattle drive begins at the far east end of Exchange Avenue. Traveling west past the Stockyards Visitor's Center and Livestock Exchange Building, the cattle drive ends at Cowtown Coliseum.

You can see the herd from the observation deck in the visitors center.

★ IRON SIGNATURES

In the American West, cattle rustling was a killing offense and the cattle brand a rancher's mark of ownership. Branding iron art, historically and across many cultures, has featured common symbols such as moon and star, pitchfork or heart, letters or digits, with bars or slashes to render them lazy, flying, or rocking.

State Parks with Texas Longhorns

- **Abilene State Park**

- **Big Bend Ranch State Park. The Longhorns here are a part of the Big Bend Ranch heritage, not a part of the official Texas longhorn herd.**

- **Copper Breaks State Park**

- **Fort Griffin State Park and Historic Site**

- **Lyndon B. Johnson State Park and Historic Site. The longhorns are not part of the official Texas longhorn herd.**

- **Palo Duro Canyon State Park**

- **San Angelo State Park**

Dreaming of Cattle

To dream of seeing beautiful, fat cattle grazing in green pastures denotes prosperity and happiness.

* * *

To see cattle lean and poorly fed, you will work hard all your life because of wasted energy and lack of attention to details.

* * *

To see cattle stampeding means that you will have to do everything you can to keep your career on track.

* * *

To see a herd of cows at milking time means you will be wealthy.

* * *

To dream of milking cows with udders well filled means great fortune is in store for you.

* * *

To see young calves in your dream means you will be popular among friends.

* * *

Long-horned and dark, vicious cattle denote enemies.

ENDANGERED AND THREATENED SPECIES IN TEXAS

Have you seen one of these endangered animals in Texas?

Amphibians

Barton Springs Salamander, Houston Toad, San Marcos Salamander, Texas Blind Salamander

Arachnids

Bee Creek Cave Harvestman, Bone Cave Harvestman, Tooth Cave Pseudoscorpion, Tooth Cave Spider

Birds

Attwater's Prairie Chicken, Bald Eagle, Eskimo Curlew, Golden-cheeked Warbler, Interior Least Tern, Mexican Spotted Owl, Northern Aplomado Falcon, Piping Plover, Red-cockaded Woodpecker, Whooping Crane

Fish

Big Bend Gambusia, Clear Creek Gambusia, Comanche Springs Pupfish, Leon Springs Pupfish, Pecos Gambusia, San Marcos Gambusia

Insects

Coffin Cave Mold Beetle, Kretschmarr Cave Mold Beetle, Tooth Cave Ground Beetle

Mammals

Black Bear, Black-footed Ferret, Jaguarundi, Mexican Long-nosed Bat, Ocelot

Reptiles

Atlantic Hawksbill Sea Turtle, Concho Water Snake, Green Sea Turtle, Kemp's Ridley Sea Turtle, Leatherback Sea Turtle, Loggerhead Sea Turtle, Louisiana Pine Snake, Northern Cat-eyed Snake

List is from the U.S. Fish & Wildlife Service

Black-footed Ferret

Black-footed ferrets have not been seen in Texas since 1963. Ferrets hunt mostly at night, so they are rarely seen. The black-footed ferret has a long, slim body with short legs. It has raccoon-like markings on its face and light-brown fur. Its feet and tail are black. The black-footed ferret lives in burrows made by prairie dogs. It takes about 100 acres of prairie dog colony to support one ferret family. Short grass prairies are their ideal habitat.

Owls, eagles, hawks, coyotes, badgers, foxes, and bobcats are the ferrets' main predators.

Houston Toad

The Houston toad lives primarily on land. The toads burrow into the sand for protection from the cold during winter hibernation and from hot, dry conditions in the summer.

The Houston toad is easily detected during mating season, when males may be heard calling. Their call is a high clear trill that lasts about 14 seconds.

The Houston toad lives from two to three years. The largest population of Houston toads exists in Bastrop County.

Golden-cheeked Warbler

Golden-cheeked warblers nest only in central Texas, preferring a habitat of mixed Ashe juniper and oak woodlands in ravines and canyons.

Adult golden-cheeked warblers reach a length of 4 1/2 inches. They use long strips of cedar bark and spider webs to build their nests. They come to Texas in March to nest and raise their young, and leave in July to spend the winter in Mexico and Central America. Of the nearly 360 bird species that breed in Texas, the golden-cheeked warbler is the only one that nests exclusively in Texas.

Attwater's Prairie-chicken

The Attwater's prairie-chicken is found only on the tall grass coastal prairies of Texas. It's a small, brown bird about 17 inches long, with a short, rounded, dark tail. Males have large, yellow air sacs on the sides of their necks, which they use to attract a mate.

Ocelot

Ocelots are members of the cat family. Ocelots have beautiful cream-colored fur covered with reddish-brown spots outlined in black. They have two stripes extending from the inside corner of their eyes and over the back of their heads. Ocelots are about 30 to 41 inches long and weigh 15 to 30 pounds.

Historical records indicate that ocelots once ranged throughout south Texas, the southern Edwards Plateau, and along the Coastal Plain. Today, they range the south Texas brush country and lower Rio Grande valley.

Whooping Crane

Whooping cranes are one of the rarest bird species in North America. They are white with rust-colored patches on the top and back of the head, yellow eyes, and long, black legs and bills. They lack feathers on both sides of the head. Their main wing feathers are black but can only be seen when they are flying. Whooping cranes are the tallest birds in North America at nearly five feet.

Whooping cranes migrate more than 2,400 miles a year. They begin their fall migration south to Texas in mid-September and begin the spring migration north to Canada in late March or early April.

4-LEGGED TEXANS

The horse is as important to Texas's heritage as the cowboys who rode them and the cattle they helped herd. While still used for ranch work, these horses are in demand for racing, rodeo, show jumping, and recreational riding.

American Quarter Horse

The American Quarter Horse is known as America's Horse. Quarter Horses are famous for their quarter-mile sprints. The fastest can cover the distance in 21 seconds or less!

American Paint Horse

This horse looks like someone took a solid-colored horse and painted white splotches on it. Paint Horses are descendants of two-toned horses brought to the Americas by the Spanish Conquistadors. Native Americans and cowboys came to appreciate the hardiness and athleticism of these colorful horses.

Appaloosa

Like the Paint Horse, Appaloosas are descended from Spanish explorers' horses. Later, Appaloosas were bred and refined by the Nez Perce Indians of the Northwest. Appaloosas are noted for their distinctive spotted markings.

Texas Race Horses

Assault

Asault had what horsemen call "heart," overcoming health problems and a severely injured hoof to win the Triple Crown—the Kentucky Derby, the Preakness, and the Belmont—in 1946. Assault is the only Texas-bred horse to date to have won the Triple Crown.

Pan Zareta

Pan Zareta was known as the Queen of the Turf. In her lifetime she won 76 races—more than any other mare. She also regularly carried more weight than the other mares. In seven of her races, she carried 140 or more pounds. Pan Zareta also set or equalled 11 track records during her remarkable career.

★ Invention

MAXIMILIAN JUSTICE HIRSCH

Hirsch trained race horses for many years at the King Ranch, which produced Bold Venture, Assault, and Middleground. Assault suffered from a serious foot injury and would never have been able to race but for a special steel spring, devised by Hirsch and inserted into the hoof, which enabled the animal to run without stumbling.

Texas Horseshoes
A Favorite Texas Pastime

No one is sure how washer pitching (sometimes called Texas horseshoes) came to be, but one thing is certain: it has become a favorite pastime in Texas.

The rules and playing field for washing pitching vary. Traditionally, the game is played outdoors by two to four players pitching washers at pits dug into the ground. Another version uses two boards or boxes with a hole in the middle. This version can be played indoors or out and is very popular.

Washer pitching may have begun in the oil fields of Texas. Oil field workers in need of entertainment might have simply created their own version of horsehoes with the materials they had on hand: pipe and big machine washers.

Did You Know?

In Tennessee, there is a rumor that Davy Crockett had to move to Texas because of a game of washer pitching. According to the story, Crockett bet his farm on the outcome of a game and lost. To escape the humiliation, Crockett moved to Texas.

Terms You'll Need to Know

Cap—When a washer lands inside the cup after the previous player has thrown a washer inside the cup.

Diddle—One toss per player that determines the starting order of each new game.

Hanger—A washer that hangs over the edge of the cup but is not in the cup.

On the Fly—Washers that land directly in the cup without first hitting the pit are said to have landed on the fly.

Skunk—Reaching a score of 11 points before the opposing player has scored at all.

Whitewash—Reaching a score of 17 points when your opponent has only scored one point.

A LITTLE-KNOWN EXPERIMENT IN
TEXAS HISTORY

Texas: home of cowboys, cattle, and . . . camels? That's right, camels. In an almost-forgotten chapter in Texas history, the U.S. Army Camel Corps called Texas home. Horse and mules, the army's traditional mounts, weren't suited to the Texas desert's harsh climate and rugged terrain. It was suggested that camels, the traditional "ships of the desert," might be a better animal to use in the desert. Many ridiculed the idea, but others listened and the experiment began.

The story begins with George H. Crosman, a second lieutenant in the U.S. Army. He proposed the camel idea to the government. Few people in Washington took Crosman seriously except for Major Henry C. Wayne. Wayne was able to convince Mississippi senator Jefferson Davis that the army should give camels a trial.

Davis was chairman of the Senate Committee on Military Affairs. Davis used his position to argue for importing camels on an experimental basis, but it was no use. Davis was able to make an official recommendation after being appointed secretary of war in 1852; even then, it was another three years before any action was taken. On March 3, 1855, Congress appropriated $30,000 for the project.

Wayne was given the responsibility of purchasing camels for the U.S. Army. He boarded the USS *Supply*, commanded by Lieutenant David Dixon Porter, on July 3, 1855, and sailed for Tunisia. Upon arrival, Wayne and Porter were so excited about

buying the camels that they bought the first one offered to them. It was sickly and promptly died.

Healthy camels were difficult to find. The Crimean War was in progress, and most of the camels were being used to carry troops and supplies. Wayne and Porter traveled to Malta, Greece, and Turkey, but did not have any luck in finding healthy animals. They learned a lot about the camel trade, though.

They learned that the one-humped Arabian camel was best for riding, while the two-humped Bactrian camel was best for carrying loads. They also learned how to spot sick animals, and they learned that camel dealers sometimes faked good health in a sick camel by artificially inflating its hump.

Finally, Wayne and Porter found healthy camels in Egypt. They headed back to America with 33 camels and five camel drivers, hired to look after the camels during the journey home and to educate the American soldiers how to care for and handle the camels when they arrived in the United States.

Back on dry land after a two month voyage, the camels were given several weeks of rest. During this time the camels were occasionally used to bring supplies from town. The reports were very positive. The camels could carry four bales of hay (1,200 pounds), much more than a mule could carry. The camels were taken to Camp Verde and Wayne sent favorable reports about them to Secretary of War Davis. Unfortunately, Davis and Wayne had a falling out about breeding the camels (Davis was against it), and Wayne requested a transfer.

A series of leadership changes followed, and the camels were put to little use. However, in June of 1857, the Camel Corps was assigned to survey the unexplored territory between El Paso and the Colorado River. The first few days the camels did not keep up with the rest of the party. As they got used to the task, the camels outpaced the party and led the way over terrain, which caused the horses and mules to balk. The camels even saved the expedition when it became lost and water supplies ran low. Only the camels were fit to travel; they found a river 20 miles from camp and led the expedition to it. The camels won over the skeptics in the expedition but not in Washington.

When James Buchanan took office as President in 1857, he appointed a new secretary of war, John B. Floyd. Secretary Floyd supported the Camel Corps, but the commander of the army in Texas did not. The new commander hated the camels intensely and so did some of the soldiers in his command. Many found the camels to be bad tempered and difficult to work with. The camels' smell was also a source of disagreement. It was unpleasant to men. Horse and mules panicked and stampeded when they smelled the strong, unfamiliar scent. The camels also held grudges, something the mules did not do.

By 1860, the looming Civil War occupied the nation and the camels were all but forgotten. The Texas camels were auctioned off in 1865, though some of the camels sold were later reclaimed as stolen property by the government, which promptly released them into the desert.

The short career of the U.S. Camel Corps had ended.

For years after the dispersal of the camels, the animals wandered at will across the American desert. Many roamed through Texas, California, and Arizona. Although no sightings of camels in the wild have been authenticated since the early years of this century, there are locals who claim that the camels thrive in remote areas to this day. So if you see a camel wandering in Texas, there's no need to get your eyes checked; it just might be a living legacy of a unique chapter in Texas history.

"And that's the way it is . . ."

If you are talking about reporters anywhere, let alone Texas, you must begin with **Walter Cronkite**. Cronkite got his start in journalism as a high-school student and college freshman, covering campus events for the *Houston Post*. In Oklahoma City, Cronkite worked as a sports announcer for a local radio station, and in 1937 he joined United Press. Cronkite covered World War II for United Press, taking part in the Normandy invasion in 1944.

Cronkite joined CBS News in 1950. He worked on a variety of programs and covered national political conventions and elections from 1952 to 1980. He became anchorman of the *CBS Evening News* in 1962, and anchored the broadcast until his retirement in 1981. The public's perception of him as honest, objective, and levelheaded led to his popular title as "the most trusted man in America." His nightly sign-off, "and that's the way it is," was his trademark.

Wharton, Texas, native **Dan Rather** succeeded Cronkite as *CBS Evening News* anchor.

Rather began his career in 1950 as an Associated Press reporter in Huntsville, Texas. In 1953, he received a bachelor's degree in journalism from Sam Houston State Teachers College, where he was editor of the school newspaper, the *Houstonian*. Following graduation, he spent a year as a journalism instructor. Later, he was a reporter for United Press International, several Texas radio stations, and the *Houston Chronicle*. In 1959, he entered television as a reporter.

In 1962, Rather joined CBS News as chief of its Southwest bureau in Dallas. In 1963, he was named chief of the Southern bureau in New Orleans. During this time he covered the assassination of President Kennedy and the civil rights movement. Rather worked his way up the ranks in CBS News. His first broadcast as Cronkite's replacement took place on March 9, 1981. On March 9, 2004, Rather retired as anchor and managing editor of the *CBS Evening News*, but did not retire completely. Often referred to as "the hardest working man in broadcast journalism," Rather lives up to the description. Rather is passionate about writing and recently published his seventh book. He also works as a correspondent for *60 Minutes*.

Another news legend in Texas is **Walter Furley**, Guinness World Record holder for Most Durable Newsreader. He was at station KZTV (famous for giving many successful journalists their start) in Corpus Christi for 45 years before retiring on May 31, 2002. He presented the news every weekday from 1957 to 2002 without any significant breaks. Furley still lives in Corpus Christi.

Not really a newsman, but colorful and famous all the same, is writer **Richard "Kinky" Friedman**. He is an American singer, songwriter, novelist, columnist, and an independent candidate for governor of Texas.

Friedman was born in Chicago in 1944, and the family moved to Texas in 1945. Friedman graduated from the University of Texas at Austin in 1966. He then served with the Peace Corps in Borneo. After leaving the Peace Corps in 1968, he lived in Nashville, trying to make a living as a songwriter. He put a band together, and in 1973 the Texas Jewboys released their first album. The band drifted apart, and Friedman's career faltered. He began writing mysteries as a way to earn money. In 1985 he came home to Texas and continued to write novels and record.

Friedman has also written a regular column for *Texas Monthly* since April 2001, although it has been suspended during his run for governor. His last essay appeared in the March 2005 issue. Friedman's serious, though colorful, campaign to be elected governor of Texas began in 2004. One of his stated goals is the "dewussification" of Texas. Among his campaign slogans are "How Hard Could It Be?" and "Why the Hell Not?"

College Newspapers

Walter Cronkite and Dan Rather started their journalism careers in college. Here is a list of a few college newspapers in Texas. Maybe the next famous Texas journalist will get his or her start at one of them!

Abilene Christian – *The Optimist*

Baylor – *The Baylor Lariat*

Del Mar College – *The Foghorn*

Midwestern State – *The Wichitan*

Rice – *The Rice Thresher*

Sam Houston State – *The Houstonian*

SMU – *The Daily Campus*

Stephen F. Austin State – *The Pine Log*

Texas A&M-College Station – *The Battalion*

Texas Christian University – *Daily Skiff*

Texas State – *The Daily University Star*

Texas Tech – *The University Daily*

University of Houston – *The Daily Cougar*

University of Mary Hardin-Baylor – *The Bells*

University of North Texas – *North Texas Daily*

University of Texas-Austin – *The Daily Texan*

25 RICHEST TEXANS

Name	Net Worth (Millions)	Source of Wealth
1. Michael Dell	$18,000*	Dell computers
2. Alice L. Walton	$15,500	Wal-Mart
3. Dan L. Duncan	$6,000	Energy
4. Robert Rowling	$4,800	Oil, gas, hotels, investments
5. H. Ross Perot	$4,200	Computer services, real estate
6. Robert Muse Bass	$3,000	Oil, investments
7. Ray Lee Hunt	$2,500	Inheritance, oil, real estate
8. Richard Kinder	$2,500	Pipelines
9. George Phydias Mitchell	$2,500	Mitchell Energy
10. Harold Clark Simmons	$2,500	Investments
11. Richard Edward Rainwater	$2,300	Real estate, energy, insurance
12. Charles C. Butt	$2,200	Supermarkets
13. Lee Marshall Bass	$2,000	Oil, investments
14. Sid Richardson Bass	$2,000	Oil, investments
15. Mark Cuban	$1,800	Broadcast.com
16. Fayez Shalaby Sarofim	$1,800	Money management
17. E. Pierce Marshall	$1,700	Investments
18. T. Boone Pickens	$1,500	Oil, gas, investments
19. Gerald J. Ford	$1,400	Banking
20. Donald R. Horton	$1,400	D. R. Horton
21. Joseph Dahr Jamail, Jr.	$1,400	Lawsuits
22. Robert C. McNair	$1,400	Energy, sports
23. Christopher Goldsbury	$1,300	Salsa
24. Billy Joe "Red" McCombs	$1,300	Radio, oil, real estate
25. Edward Perry Bass	$1,200	Oil, investments

* Note: $18,000 million = 18,000,000,000 or $18 billion

THE 50 BEST COMPANIES TO WORK FOR IN TEXAS

Best Companies Group, the Texas Association of Business, and the Society for Human Resource Management Texas State Council named these companies the "Best Companies to Work for in Texas 2006."

1. Kaye Bassman International Corp.
2. Catapult Systems, Inc.
3. Coors Brewing Company Sales, Southern Region
4. Edward Jones
5. Patrick Henry Creative Promotions, Inc.
6. Highland Homes
7. DPR Construction, Inc.
8. SICOLAMARTIN
9. Flintco, Inc.
10. Higginbotham & Associates, Inc.
11. Camden
12. TRANS-TRADE, INC.
13. Navigator Systems, Inc.
14. DATCU
15. Medical City Dallas
16. Rackspace Managed Hosting
17. Valero Energy Corporation
18. The Beryl Companies
19. MATRIX Resources, Inc.
20. The Richards Group
21. The Staubach Company
22. Keller Williams Realty, Inc.
23. Insurance & Bonds of Texas
24. HCSS
25. B. Lowry Management, Inc.
26. Walter P. Moore
27. McQueary Henry Bowles Troy, LLP
28. A&E-The Graphics Complex
29. K2Share, LLC
30. Vinson & Elkins, LLP
31. SpawGlass
32. CHRISTUS St. Michael Health System
33. Ebby Halliday Real Estate
34. Central Texas Workforce
35. Merrick Systems, Inc.
36. Hermes Sargent Bates, LLP
37. American Campus Communities, Inc.
38. Handango
39. Hines
40. United Supermarkets, Ltd.
41. AMERIGROUP Texas, Inc.
42. Brookshire Grocery Company
43. Magnum Staffing Services, Inc.
44. HKS, Inc.
45. Administaff, Inc.
46. Wells Fargo and Company
47. Texas Children's Hospital Integrated Delivery System
48. Four Hands
49. Hill Partners
50. Whole Foods Market, Inc.

TEXANS TAKE FLIGHT

First Flight in Texas

As early as the 1860s, balloonists took to the air over Texas in gravity-defying experiments. Within a few years, these efforts were redirected toward winged aircraft. Claims persist that Texas inventor Jacob F. Brodbeck became the world's first aviator. According to one account, he flew his "air-ship" on September 20, 1865, almost 40 years before the Wright brothers' famous flight at Kitty Hawk, North Carolina. Brodbeck's flight allegedly took place about three miles east of Luckenbach. Another account says the flight took place at San Antonio's San Pedro Park. A third account claims the flight took place in 1868, not 1865. All agree the flight ended in an unfortunate landing, which destroyed the craft but left Brodbeck without serious injury.

The first confirmed winged flight in Texas took place in South Houston several years after the Wright brothers' flight. Louis Paulhan, a Frenchman, made the historic flight on February 18, 1910. Flights in other Texas cities soon followed. Within two weeks of Paulhan's flight, army Lt. Benjamin Foulois successfully completed a similar feat in San Antonio. Foulois used a Wright biplane, which had been purchased by the U. S. Army. Three years later, the army's First Aero Squadron was assigned to Texas City with a fleet of nine aircraft.

Bessie Coleman

Bessie Coleman, the first African American pilot, was born in Atlanta, Texas, in 1892. At the age of 23 she moved to Chicago to live with her brothers, hoping to find more opportunities there. It was hearing the wild stories of aviation exploits during World War I that ignited Coleman's desire to fly. Her brother fanned the flame by claiming French women were superior because many of them could fly airplanes. In 1918, the few American women who had pilot's licenses were white and wealthy.

Because of her race, Coleman had to go to Paris, France, to learn how to fly. It took her seven months to learn.

Coleman returned to the United States in September 1921, and was met by a crowd of reporters eager to write about her acheivement.

Coleman spent the next five years performing at air shows. Over 3,000 people attended her first air show performance on September 3, 1922, in Garden City, Long Island. Coleman used her fame to encourage other African Americans, particularly those who wanted to fly. She also refused to perform at places that wouldn't admit African Americans.

Coleman took her last flight on April 30, 1926, in Jacksonville, Florida. Coleman and William Wills, a mechanic from Texas, were preparing for an air show, when at 3,500 feet a wrench got caught in the control gears and the plane plummeted to earth. Coleman was not wearing a seatbelt and fell to her death.

Coleman's legacy is still honored. In 1992 the Chicago City Council passed a resolution asking the U.S. Postal Service to issue a Bessie Coleman stamp. The resolution stated, "Bessie Coleman

continues to inspire untold thousands, even millions, of young persons with her sense of adventure, her positive attitude, and her determination to succeed."

Howard Hughes

Howard Hughes was an aviation innovator. He formed Hughes Aircraft Company as a division of Hughes Tool Company to defray the costs of converting a military plane for racing. Hughes entered the converted plane in the 1934 All-America Air Meet in Miami and won.

Hughes then began work on the H-1, designed to be the fastest landplane in the world. On September 13, 1935, Hughes flew the H-1 to a new world speed record of 352.322 mph. After fitting the plane with a different set of wings designed for the purpose, Hughes and the H-1 broke the transcontinental speed record on January 19, 1937. In 1938, Hughes completed an around-the-world flight in 3 days, 19 hours, and 17 minutes.

Hughes tried to get into military aircraft but had difficulty selling his planes and ideas to the government. The only plane to be completed was a massive flying boat. Hughes couldn't meet the original contract for three of these planes, but was awarded a contract for one. The HK-1, called the "Spruce Goose" by the public, was completed and Hughes flew it on November 2, 1947. Hughes's involvement with aviation was dramatized in the 2004 film *The Aviator*.

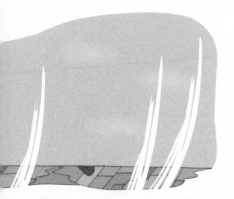

THE EAGLE HAS LANDED

JOHNSON SPACE CENTER

Houston, Texas, holds another flight of fancy for Texans: the Johnson Space Center. Established as the Manned Spacecraft Center in 1961 and later renamed the Lyndon B. Johnson Space Center, the Johnson Space Center (JSC) is responsible for the design, development, and operation of human space flight.

The Mission Control Center at JSC has been the heart of all American human space missions since *Gemini IV* in 1965. JSC is also the home of the NASA astronaut corps and is responsible for training astronauts from the United States and space station partner nations.

After the *Columbia* disaster, the people of East Texas became the first response team. The communities of Nemphill, Nacogdoches, Lufkin, Palestine, and Corsicana, all helped with the recovery efforts after the February 1, 2003, tragedy.

Texans are proud of the space program and JSC's place in American, and world, history.

Did You Know?

- **NASA** was established in October 1958.

- **Unity (Node 1)** is the name of the first U.S.-built element of the International Space Station (ISS).

- **Ms. Barbara Morgan** was selected for training in the Teacher in Space program and is the first Educator Astronaut.

- A dog named **Laika** was the first animal to orbit the earth.

- The **Ninety-Nines** was the first organization for licensed female pilots and was named for the 99 charter members in 1929. **Amelia Earhart** served as its first president.

- **The Spruce Goose** holds the record for the largest wingspan of any aircraft ever made, at 319 feet, 11 inches. It was flown only once, for about one mile at a top speed of 70 mph, in 1947.

- The first word spoken in space was "Houston." Neil Armstrong said: "Houston, Tranquility Base here; The Eagle has landed."

Kissed
by SUCCESS

Mary Kay Ash

One month in 1963, while preparing to write a book to help women succeed in business, Mary Kay Ash created one list of good business practices she had observed and another list of things she would improve. She then realized that she had created a marketing plan for a successful business. Ash used her life savings of $5,000 to launch Mary Kay Cosmetics on Friday, September 13, 1963. From those small beginnings, Mary Kay Cosmetics Corporation has grown into one of the leading direct-sales companies in the world.

Conrad Hilton

Conrad Hilton got his first taste of the hotel trade in 1907, when part of his family's general store was converted into a hotel. In 1919, Hilton purchased the Mobley Hotel in the small Texas town of Cisco. Between 1925 and 1930 he opened a new hotel in Texas every year. Nearly bankrupted by the Great Depression, Hilton rebounded to become chairman of the Hilton Hotels Corporation. In 1948, Hilton International Company

was organized, building hotels in exotic locations: Madrid, Istanbul, Havana, Berlin, and Cairo. Eventually, Hilton owned 188 hotels in 38 U.S. cities and 54 hotels abroad.

Michael Dell

At age 19, Dell began selling custom-built personal computers out of his dorm room at the University of Texas in Austin. The company, called PCs Limited, was successful enough that he dropped out of college to run the business full-time. He sold six million dollars worth of computers in his first year. Nine years later, Dell Computer was one of the Fortune 500, had sales of over two billion dollars, and was the world's fourth-largest computer maker.

George Foreman

In addition to being a World Heavyweight Champion, George Foreman has been a rancher, a preacher, and an entrepreneur. Foreman's most successful venture, far surpassing the financial success of his boxing career, is the George Foreman Grill. Known as a "lean, mean, fat reducing grilling machine," the hugely successful product resulted from collaboration with small appliance manufacturer Salton, Inc. Although grill sales have contributed the most to Foreman's wealth, he admits it may not have been achieved without his boxing career.

TEXAS SUCCESS

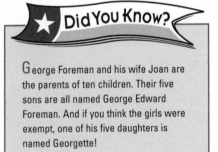

Did You Know?

George Foreman and his wife Joan are the parents of ten children. Their five sons are all named George Edward Foreman. And if you think the girls were exempt, one of his five daughters is named Georgette!

Unexpected Weather

Cycles of Drought and Heat

Approximately every 20 years, a new drought cycle begins in Texas. Most of Texas experiences warmth year-round; however, the Panhandle can experience cool weather on a regular basis. The eastern half of Texas typically receives the most rain, while the western half is quite dry. Dry weather and hot weather are often paired together. Dry soil heats up faster than moist soil, so the air becomes hotter as well. The worst drought in Texas

history occurred between 1950 and 1957. October 1952 had the lowest statewide average of precipitation ever recorded in Texas: only 0.02 inches of rain fell on the entire state.

Hail and High Winds

Texas hosts some of the most devastating tornadoes on record, including the most devastating tornado to hit the area, on April 9, 1947. This massive tornado first touched down in the Panhandle near Amarillo, causing damage in White Deer, in Carson County. After proceeding into Oklahoma and Kansas before dissipating, the final tally was 68 dead and 201 injured, making it the fourth most deadly tornado ever to strike Texas.

Tornadoes terrify almost everyone, but for ranchers and farmers in Texas, the most dreaded weather event is hail. For them, the damage from hail has a much bigger economic impact.

The Perfect Storm

The worst hailstorm on record was a thunderstorm that struck Dallas—Fort Worth on May 5, 1995. This was the "perfect storm" of hailstorms: a supercell, a squall line, an outdoor festival, and sunset all came together to maximize the impact. The storm started with a supercell forming near Mineral Wells in late afternoon. It moved east and intensified, dropping baseball-sized hail in downtown Fort Worth during their May festival. Many people who were caught out in the open were injured. As the storm moved toward Dallas, the hail combined with rain, causing a flash flood just after dark that killed 19 people.

Floods

Floods can occur at any time, but they are more prevalent in hotter weather. Flash floods are the most dangerous type of flood because they develop quickly and usually without warning. Luckily, they typically affect only very small areas.

Ben Ficklin, the county seat of Tom Green County, experienced a flash flood on August 23–24, 1882. Heavy thunderstorms upstream of Ben Ficklin sent a rapidly rising mass of water into the unsuspecting town during the night. The rush of water destroyed the town. Ben Ficklin was not rebuilt, and the county seat was moved to San Angelo.

Snow

Snow often falls in Texas, especially in the Panhandle. However, when snow falls in other parts of the state, it becomes a national news event. The greatest amount of snow that has ever fallen in Texas occurred in February 1956 when Hale received 33 inches of snow. However, the snowstorm of February 1971 became the most significant storm for Texas due to the accompanying wind, which buried and killed thousands of cattle.

It's not the heat, it's the humidity!

Port Arthur is the third most humid city with an average relative humidity of 77.5%.

Corpus Christi is the seventh most humid city with an average relative humidity of 76.0%.

Houston is the tenth most humid city with an average relative humidity of 75.0%.

El Paso is the fifth least humid city with an average relative humidity of 42.5%.

Brownsville is the sixth hottest city with an average annual temperature of 73.6°F.

Corpus Christi is the ninth hottest city with an average annual temperature of 72.1°F.

• • •

Extreme Weather Events

Heaviest Rain

Alvin, Texas, holds the U.S. record for the most rainfall in a 24-hour period. Measured in 1979 at an official measuring site of the National Weather Service, the total rainfall on that memorable day was 40 inches. At a nearby unofficial measuring site, 43 inches of rain fell in 24 hours.

Worst Hurricane

The 1900 Galveston hurricane killed nearly 10,000 people and destroyed the city of Galveston. This hurricane was the greatest natural disaster in the history of the United States. Only Hurricane Katrina of 2005, primarily affecting the New Orleans and Mississippi area, can be considered a comparable storm.

Dust Storms

April 14, 1935, is the only named day in Texas weather history. Black Sunday, when it seemed that day became night with a snap of one's fingers, marked a dramatic end to an already devastating drought and dust storm season. This day of worship and rest was instantaneously blackened by a blizzard of fine dirt driven by fifty-mile-per-hour winds.

Coldest Day

The most memorable cold snap on record in Texas occurred on February 12, 1899. Half of Texas had temperatures below 0°F on that day. The state record for coldest temperature was set that day at Tulia, Texas, which registered a temperature of -23°F.

★ **On the Sunny Side**

El Paso is the fifth sunniest city, receiving an average of 83 percent of the annual possible sunshine. (Statistics on sunscreen sales were not available.)

FUN FACTS
ABOUT WEATHER AND CLIMATE

The National Weather Service urges everyone to **"Turn Around, Don't Drown!"** when encountering a flooded road. Either find another route to get to your destination or wait for the floodwaters to recede. Getting to your destination quickly is not worth risking your life.

"A rainbow in the morning gives fair warning."

In the morning, when the sun is in the east, the rain shower and its rainbow are in the west. In the northern hemisphere, weather generally moves from west to east. A morning rainbow means that rain is moving in from the west toward the observer.

"Sea gull, sea gull, sit on the sand; it's a sign of rain when you are at hand."

Low pressure is a sign of impending rain. Generally, birds tend to roost more during low pressure than during high pressure. The lowering of air pressure makes flying more difficult.

"When the ditch offends the nose, look for rain and stormy blows."

High-pressure conditions trap a certain amount of odors in ditches and other low-lying areas. As pressure decreases, such as before a storm, odors from ditches, swamps, and cellars are able to escape.

"When smoke descends, good weather ends."

Air pressure instability before a storm keeps smoke from chimneys or bonfires from rising quickly. Smoke curls downward in the face of a storm wind.

"Red sky at night, sailor's delight; red sky in morning, sailors take warning."

When the western sky is clear, there is often a red sunset because the setting sun and its light passes through dust and pollution particles in the lower atmosphere, especially in high pressure regions. However, if the sky is red in the eastern morning sky, then the high-pressure region has already passed, and an area of low pressure may follow, possibly bringing clouds, rain, or storms.

"A clear moon means frost soon."

If the atmosphere is clear, the Earth's surface is able to cool quickly at night because there is no "blanket" of clouds to hold in the heat absorbed during the day. If the temperature is low enough on these clear nights and there is no wind, frost may form.

"A halo around the sun or moon will likely bring rain or snow soon."

A layer of cirrus clouds causes a halo around the sun or moon. These clouds are made of ice crystals that act as tiny prisms, forming a white or sometimes colorful halo around the sun or moon. Clouds often indicate an approaching warm front and an associated area of low pressure. Rain or snow will not always follow, but there is a higher probability of it after a halo is seen. The brighter the halo, the greater the probability.

HOT
WEATHER IN TEXAS

Month	Highest Temperature Recorded (°F)	Year	City	Lowest Temperature Recorded (°F)	Year	City
January	98	1997	Zapata	-22	1959	Spearman
February	104	1902	Fort Ringgold	-23	1933	Seminole
March	108	1954	Rio Grande	-12	1948	Spearman
April	113	1984	Catarina	5	1936	Romero
May	116	1989	Boquillas	15	1909	Tulia
June	120	1994	Monahans	32	1917	Tulia
July	119	1910	Tilden	40	1906	Claytonville
August	120	1936	Seymour	39	1910	Plemons
September	116	2000	Columbus	25	1983	Bravo
October	109	1926	Victoria	8	1993	Dalhart
November	102	1988	McAllen	-10	1976	Stratford
December	98	1951	Cotulla	-16	1983	Lipscomb

Summer Survival Tips

- Drink two to five times your usual amount of water and sugarless, nonalcoholic beverages to replace fluids lost in perspiration.
- Wear clothing that is loose-fitting, lightweight, and light-colored.
- Wear a wide-brimmed hat.
- Use sunscreen with SPF 30 or higher.
- Limit physical activity and take frequent breaks.
- Choose the cooler hours of the day for outside activities.
- Use a buddy system between coworkers in a high heat-stress job.
- Watch for symptoms of heat exhaustion when being active with friends or family.

Is Your Texan in Trouble?

Symptoms of Heat Exhaustion

A person who shows these symptoms should be moved to a cool location such as a shaded area or air-conditioned building. They should lie down with their feet slightly elevated. Loosen their clothing, and apply cool, wet cloths. Fanning will also help. They should drink water or electrolyte drinks. Be sure to have them checked by medical personnel.

Symptoms include: headache, dizziness, heavy sweating, extreme thirst, fatigue, loss of coordination, nausea, impaired judgment, loss of appetite, hyperventilation, anxiety, tingling in hands or feet, and cool, moist skin. Person may have a weak and rapid pulse (of 120–200), and low to normal blood pressure.

Let It Snow! Let It Snow! Let It Snow!

Snow in Texas? Of course it snows. It is just that snow is not a very commonplace occurrence in most areas of Texas. Snow is most common in January and early February.

The northern half of Texas usually gets at least one significant snow event per season. A heavy snowfall of five or more inches at once occurs once every two or three years.

Does snow fall in the southern portion of Texas? It is a rarity, but it does happen. Most often, any such snow melts on ground impact, just causing wet roads, although it might slightly accumulate on grassy surfaces.

The Panhandle is known to receive the most amount of snow, 15 to 18 inches on average.

Exceptional Snowstorms in Texas History

February 12–15, 1895: A rare Gulf storm brought upwards of 20 inches on a line from Houston to Orange.

February 2–5, 1956: Hale received the greatest amount of snow ever recorded in Texas—33 inches.

February 1–7, 1964: A Panhandle blizzard occurred in Berger, dumping 25 inches of snow. Winds of 30 miles per hour created drifts 10 feet deep.

January 12–13, 1985: San Antonio received 13.5 inches; the city shut down because snow removal equipment was inadequate to meet the demand.

December 25–27, 2000: Freezing rain affected most of the area north of Interstate 20. Up to 4 inches of ice was reported from Montague County east to Lamar County. Sleet and snow occurred over much of north Texas. A band of 4 to 8 inches fell over northern Hamilton, northwest Bosque, and western Palo Pinto counties. A foot of snow closed Ranger Hill for three days. Another band of 3 to 6 inches fell from the northern Hill County into southern Dallas County, with 7 inches in Itasca.

February 5–6, 2002: Snow fell over the northern sections of north Texas, accumulating between 4 and 5 inches on a line from Gainesville to Paris and from McKinney to Greenville to Cooper. Elsewhere, 1 to 3 inches fell.

The 10 Deadliest Tornadoes in Texas

Although not technically in tornado alley, tornadoes can wreak havoc throughout Texas.

All tornadoes are classified according to the Fujita scale.

10. The Lubbock Tornado *(May 11, 1970):* The Lubbock tornado formed over the southwest corner of the city and touched down just outside the city limits. It destroyed over 1000 homes and 100 aircraft, killing 28 and injuring 500.

9. The Saragosa Tornado *(May 22, 1987):* An F4 tornado touched down near Saragosa in Reeves County. It destroyed 80 percent of the town, killing 30 and injuring 121. Over 70 percent of the deaths occurred at the city hall where a group had gathered for a children's graduation ceremony. Most of these deaths were the parents and grandparents who shielded the children from the debris with their bodies.

8. The Zephyr Tornado *(May 30, 1909):* Having formed somewhere near Zephyr in Brown County, this tornado destroyed large parts of the town in the early morning. Rated an F4, 50 homes and businesses, 2 churches, and a high school were leveled. It killed 34 and injured 70.

7. The Karnes-Dewitt Tornado *(May 6, 1930):* Occurring on the same day as the Frost tornado, it touched down near Kenedy in Karnes County. Along its path, this F4 tornado caused 36 deaths and 60 injuries.

6. The Frost Tornado *(May 6, 1930):* It touched down in Bynum, in Hill County, crossing into Navarro County and Mertens, before striking the town of Frost with its F4 force. It killed 41 people in all and caused 200 injuries.

5. The Wichita Falls Tornado *(April 10, 1979):* This huge F4 tornado first touched down about 3 miles from Holliday, a town near Wichita Falls. The storm killed 42 people, injured 1700, and destroyed 3000 homes. More than 20,000 people were left homeless.

4. The Tri-State Tornado *(April 9, 1947):* Part of a family of deadly twisters, it killed 17 and injured 40 in Glazier, and injured 51 in Higgins.

3. The Rocksprings Tornado *(April 12, 1927):* This F5 tornado touched down 3 miles northwest of Rocksprings in Edwards County and moved southeast. It measured nearly 1 mile wide, killed 74 people, and destroyed 235 out of the 247 buildings in the town.

2. The Goliad Tornado

(May 18, 1902): This F4 tornado killed 114 people and injured 250. It touched down near Berclair and then moved 15 miles southwest to Goliad.

1. The Waco Tornado

(May 11, 1953): The deadliest tornado in Texas history struck the day after Mother's Day in 1953. It touched down north of Lorena and began moving north-northeast. It injured 597 people, killed 114, and destroyed around 600 homes. Some of the survivors waited 14 hours for rescue. It was a massive F5 tornado.

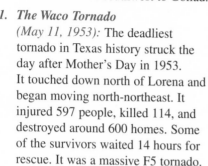

The Fujita Scale

F0—40–72 mph: *minimal damage,* with some damage to chimneys, TV antennas, roof shingles, trees, and windows.

F1—73–112 mph: *moderate damage,* with automobiles overturned, carports destroyed, and trees uprooted.

F2—113–157 mph: *major damage* occurs, with roofs blown off homes, sheds and outbuildings demolished, and mobile homes overturned.

F3—158–206 mph: *severe damage* is evident, with exterior walls and roofs blown off homes. Metal buildings collapse or are severely damaged. Forests and farmland are flattened.

F4—207–260 mph: the *damage* is *devastating.* Few walls, if any, are left standing, even in well-built homes. Large pieces of steel and concrete are thrown great distances.

F5—261–318 mph: widespread, *incredible damage,* as homes are leveled with all debris removed. Schools, motels, and other larger structures have considerable damage with exterior walls and roofs gone.

F6—319–379 mph: *inconceivable and incomprehensible damage,* as nothing recognizable would be left. Such winds most likely would be surrounded by F4 and F5 damage, so identifying the differences between wind speeds is not very likely.

 ## What Are Some Tornado Danger Signs?

Be aware of these tornado danger signs:

- Tornadoes are usually spawned from powerful thunderstorms, and many powerful thunderstorms produce large hail. Tornadoes frequently emerge from near the hail-producing portion of the storm.

- Before a tornado hits, the wind may die down and the air may become very still.

- An approaching cloud of debris can mark the location of a tornado even if a funnel is not visible.

- A visible rotating extension of the cloud base is a sign that a tornado may develop. A tornado is evident when one or more of the clouds turns greenish (a phenomenon caused by hail) and a dark funnel descends.

Hurricane Naming

Hurricanes are named from *A* to *Z*, with the exception of the letters *Q*, *U*, *X*, *Y*, and *Z*. There are 21 names available each year, alternating between male and female names. (At one time, all of the names for a year would be male, and then the next year would be female, and so on.) If there are more than 21 named storms in one year, Greek letters are used—Alpha, Beta, etc. The year 2005 was a record-breaking year, when 27 named storms formed during the season from June to November.

Different regions uses different names. The names given in this section refer to the North Atlantic region. Unique name groups exist for the north Pacific (three regions depending on longitude of origin), Philippines, Indian Ocean, Australia (three regions—western, northern, and eastern), Fiji, and Papua New Guinea.

Storms are named by the U.S. National Hurricane Center in Miami, Florida. The official name lists have been agreed upon by the World Meteorological Organization.

The Six-Year Name Cycling

2001: Andrea, Barry, Chantal, Dean, Erin, Felix, Gabrielle, Humberto, Ingrid, Jerry, Karen, Lorenzo, Melissa, Noel, Olga, Pablo, Rebekah, Sebastien, Tanya, Van, Wendy

2002: Arthur, Bertha, Cristobal, Dolly, Edouard, Fay, Gustav, Hanna, Isidore, Josephine, Kyle, Lili, Marco, Nana, Omar, Paloma, Rene, Sally, Teddy, Vicky, Wilfred

2003: Ana, Bill, Claudette, Danny, Erika, Fabian, Grace, Henri, Isabel, Juan, Kate, Larry, Mindy, Nicholas, Odette, Peter, Rose, Sam, Teresa, Victor, Wanda

2004: Alex, Bonnie, Charley, Danielle, Earl, Frances, Gaston, Hermine, Ivan, Jeanne, Karl, Lisa, Matthew, Nicole, Otto, Paula, Richard, Shary, Tomas, Virginie, Walter

2005: Arlene, Bret, Cindy, Dennis, Emily, Franklin, Gert, Harvey, Irene, Jose, Katrina, Lee, Maria, Nate, Ophelia, Philippe, Rita, Stan, Tammy, Vince, Wilma

2006: Alberto, Beryl, Chris, Debby, Ernesto, Florence, Gordon, Helene, Isaac, Kirk, Leslie, Michael, Nadine, Oscar, Patty, Rafael, Sandy, Tony, Valerie, William

The storm names being used in 2006 are the same as those used in 2000. The storm names to be used in 2007 are those that were used in 2001. The naming pattern continues in a six-year cycle.

WHAT NAMES HAVE BEEN RETIRED?

If a particular hurricane is deadly or very destructive, the name is officially retired and replaced with another name of the same gender and letter. After ten years, a retired name may be used again, but most of these hurricanes were so destructive that there has been no desire to potentially repeat history. The following Atlantic hurricane names have been retired:

Agnes, Alicia, Allen, Allison, Andrew, Anita, Audrey, Betsy, Beulah, Bob, Camille, Carla, Carmen, Carol, Cesar, Celia, Cleo, Connie, David, Diana, Diane, Donna, Dora, Edna, Elena, Eloise, Fifi, Flora, Floyd, Fran, Frederic, Georges, Gilbert, Gloria, Hattie, Hazel, Hilda, Hortense, Hugo, Inez, Ione, Iris, Janet, Joan, Keith, Klaus, Lenny, Luis, Marilyn, Michelle, Mitch, Opal, Roxanne

It is expected that the name Katrina will be retired. And it is possible that Rita and Wilma, which also did significant damage in 2005, may be retired.

On This Date in History is designed to spotlight a historical event, particularly if it's significant to Texas.

Day of Month	Sunrise (AM)	Sunset (PM)	Moon Phase	Normal High Temp. (°F)	On This Date in History
1	7:52	5:50	○	56	1863—The Emancipation Proclamation took effect.
2	7:52	5:51	○	56	1776—Congress published the Tory Act.
3	7:52	5:52	○	56	1823—Stephen F. Austin received a grant from the Mexican government and began colonization in the region of the Brazos River.
4	7:52	5:53	○ *Full*	56	1863—Confederate General Roger Hanson died. 1959—Spearman recorded the lowest high temperature ever recorded in Texas (below 0°F).
5	7:52	5:53	○	56	1959—Buddy Holly's last record was released.
6	7:53	5:54	○	56	The wedding anniversary for two presidents: George Washington and George H. W. Bush.
7	7:53	5:55	○	56	1940—The debut of Gene Autry's *Melody Ranch* radio show.
8	7:53	5:56	○	56	1977—Up to 3 inches of ice fell on a line north of Waco and Longview.
9	7:53	5:57	◑	56	1768—First modern circus.
10	7:53	5:58	◑	56	1901—Oil was discovered at Spindletop, near Beaumont.
11	7:52	5:59	◑ *Last Quarter*	56	1914—Pancho Villa drove 4,500 Mexican soldiers across the Rio Grande.
12	7:52	5:59	◐	56	1906—Tex Ritter was born.
13	7:52	6:00	◐	56	1910—First radio demonstration.
14	7:52	6:01	◐	56	1888—A rare South Texas ice storm coated the lower valley with 1 inch of ice.
15	7:52	6:02	●	56	1978—The Dallas Cowboys defeated the Denver Broncos 27-10 in Super Bowl XII.
16	7:52	6:03	●	56	1951—The world's largest gas pipeline opened, running from Brownsville, TX, to 134th Street in New York City.

JANUARY 2007

January is the first month of the year in the Gregorian Calendar and one of seven Gregorian months with the length of 31 days.

★ Did You Know?

January in the Northern Hemisphere is the seasonal equivalent to July in the Southern Hemisphere and vise versa.

Day of Month	Sunrise (AM)	Sunset (PM)	Moon Phase	Normal High Temp. (°F)	On This Date in History
17	7:51	6:04	●	56	1874—The inauguration of Democrat Richard Coke as governor marked the end of Reconstruction in Texas. 1949—The debut of the first TV sitcom.
18	7:51	6:05	● *New Moon*	58	1978—"Take This Job" became a #1 hit.
19	7:51	6:06	●	57	1846—Texas government is installed.
20	7:50	6:07	●	57	1891—James Hogg became the first Texas governor who was also a Texas native.
21	7:50	6:08	●	57	1855—Gun designer John Browning was born.
22	7:50	6:09	●	57	1779—Claudius Smith, "Cowboy of the Ramapos," was hung.
23	7:49	6:10	◐	57	1875—Molly Armstrong, the first woman optometrist in Texas, is born in Bell County.
24	7:49	6:11	◐	58	1952—Dallas Texans team established.
25	7:48	6:12	◐ *First Quarter*	56	1845—The House of Representatives voted to admit Texas to the Union. 1965—A dust storm in Lubbock produced 3 inches of dust in an official rain gauge.
26	7:48	6:13	◐	56	2001—The largest cooked breakfast ever to be served in Texas occurred in San Antonio with 18,941 people eating.
27	7:47	6:14	◐	56	1970—The age for admittance to an R-rated movie changed from 16 yrs to 17yrs.
28	7:47	6:15	◐	56	1986—The space shuttle *Challenger* exploded, trailing debris across North Texas.
29	7:46	6:16	○	56	1834—President Andrew Jackson sent troops to put down a labor riot.
30	7:45	6:17	○	56	1969—The Beatles' last public appearance.
31	7:45	6:18	○	56	1947—Nolan Ryan was born. 1993—The Dallas Cowboys won Super Bowl XXVII.

Day of Month	Sunrise (AM)	Sunset (PM)	Moon Phase	Normal High Temp. (°F)	On This Date in History
1	7:44	6:19	○	59	1861—Texas voted to secede from the Union.
2	7:43	6:20	○ Full	60	1848—The Treaty of Guadalupe Hidalgo was signed, ending the war with Mexico and specifying the location of the international boundary.
3	7:42	6:21	○	60	1956—The greatest snowfall ever recorded in Texas in a 24-hour period occurred in the town of Plainview (24.0 inches). 1959—Buddy Holly was killed in a plane crash.
4	7:42	6:21	◗	60	1789—The first U.S. president was elected. 1956—The greatest depth of snow after a snowfall lasting more than one day ever recorded in Texas occurred in the towns of Hale Center and Vega.
5	7:41	6:22	◗	60	1865—Battle of Dabney's Mill (Hatcher's Run) 1956—Hale, Texas, records 33 inches of snow.
6	7:40	6:23	◗	61	1854—The State of Texas allocated land for two Indian reservations in Young and Throckmorton counties.
7	7:39	6:24	◗	61	2002—President George W. Bush announced his plan for "faith-based initiatives."
8	7:38	6:25	◗	61	1915—The movie *Birth of a Nation* opened. 1933—The coldest temperature ever recorded in Texas occurred in the town of Seminole (-23°F).
9	7:38	6:26	◗	62	1864—Elizabeth Bacon married George Custer.
10	7:37	6:27	◑ Last Quarter	62	1899—Herbert Hoover married Lou Henry.
11	7:36	6:28	◑	62	1850—The first railroad to actually begin operation in Texas was chartered, and the first railroad began operation in 1853. 1937—The Battle of the Running Bulls.

FEBRUARY 2007

February is the second month of the year in the Gregorian Calendar. It is the shortest month and the only month with the length of 28 or 29 days. The month has 29 days in leap years, when the year number is divisible by four, but not years that are divisible by 100. In other years the month has 28 days.

Day of Month	Sunrise (AM)	Sunset (PM)	Moon Phase	Normal High Temp. (°F)	On This Date in History
12	7:35	6:29		62	1899—The coldest temperature ever recorded in Texas occurred in town of Tulia (-23°F). 1999—President Clinton was acquitted of perjury and obstruction of justice.
13	7:34	6:30		63	1905—Teddy Roosevelt discussed America's "race problem."
14	7:33	6:31		64	2004—Five inches of snow fell in the northern half of Texas.
15	7:32	6:32		64	1876—Texas citizens adopted their constitution.
16	7:31	6:33		64	1861—Sam Houston refused to support the Confederacy, and Edward Clark became governor.
17	7:30	6:34	New Moon	64	1889—H. L. Hunt was born. 1929—The League of United Latin American Citizens (LULAC) was founded in Corpus Christi.
18	7:29	6:35		65	1928—Horned toad Rip was taken out of the courthouse cornerstone.
19	7:28	6:35		65	1846—The Texas government was formally installed.
20	7:27	6:36		65	1972—Walter Winchell died.
21	7:25	6:37		66	1902—Dallart became the county seat of Dallart County.
22	7:24	6:38		66	1819—Treaty renounced of the U. S. claim to Texas.
23	7:23	6:39		66	1945—U.S. flag flown on Iwo Jima
24	7:22	6:40	First Quarter	66	1968—The TET offensive was halted.
25	7:21	6:41		67	1848—Railroad baron Edward Harriman was born.
26	7:20	6:42		64	2001—John Justin of Justin Boots dies.
27	7:19	6:42		64	1936—Shirley Temple received $50,000 for a film role.
28	7:17	6:43		64	1984—Dr Pepper became a privately owned company.

Day of Month	Sunrise (AM)	Sunset (PM)	Moon Phase	Normal High Temp. (°F)	On This Date in History
1	7:16	6:44		67	1845—The U.S. Congress passed a joint resolution for annexing Texas. 1861—Texas was accepted as a state by the provisional government of the Confederate States of America.
2	7:15	6:45		67	1910—Lt. Benjamin D. Foulois made the first military air flight in a Wright brothers plane at Fort Sam Houston in San Antonio, marking the beginnings of the U.S. Air Force.
3	7:14	6:46	Full	67	1873—Congress authorized a survey for a system of waterways.
4	7:12	6:46		68	1904—Batson-Old Oilfield reached peak production, producing 150,000 barrels.
5	7:11	6:47		68	1842—Rafael Vasquez invaded San Antonio.
6	7:10	6:48		68	1836—The Alamo fell to General Santa Ana.
7	7:09	6:49		69	1731—Fifty-five Canary Islanders arrive in San Antonio to establish a civilian settlement, San Fernando de Béxar.
8	7:07	6:50		69	1936—The first 58-mile electric line was energized to serve 120 farmers in Bartlett, Texas.
9	7:06	6:50		69	The founder of the Daughters of the Republic of Texas died.
10	7:05	6:51		69	1938—The Bette Davis movie *Jezebel* was released.
11	7:04	6:52		70	1890—Pappy O'Daniel was born
12	7:02	6:53	Last Quarter	70	1991—Howard E. Butt died at the age of 92.
13	7:01	6:54		70	The bill passed establishing the Texas State Penitentiary at Huntsville.
14	7:00	6:54		70	1888—A railroad connecting Denver, Colorado, and Fort Worth, Texas, was completed.
15	6:58	6:55		71	1967—Southwest Airlines was incorporated.
16	6:57	6:56		71	1861—Sam Houston resigned as governor in protest against secession.

MARCH 2007

March is the third month of the year in the Gregorian Calendar and one of seven Gregorian months with the length of 31 days.

Day of Month	Sunrise (AM)	Sunset (PM)	Moon Phase	Normal High Temp. (°F)	On This Date in History
17	6:56	6:57		71	1909—Lubbock was incorporated as a city.
18	6:54	6:57		71	1685—La Salle established Fort St. Louis at Matagorda Bay. 1937—A massive natural-gas explosion at the London Consolidated School in Rusk County resulted in the Texas legislature requiring that a malodorant be added to the gas so that leaks could be more easily detected.
19	6:53	6:58	New Moon	72	1899—Texas Rangers arrived in Laredo to help vaccinate against a smallpox epidemic.
20	6:52	6:59		72	1964—The daily newspaper, the *Houston Press*, ceased publication.
21	6:50	7:00		72	1858—Mollie Kirkland married Gus Bailey.
22	6:49	7:00		72	1920—The Great West Mill and Elevator Company opened for business.
23	6:48	7:01		72	1906—Joan Crawford was born.
24	6:46	7:02		73	1846—Texas's First Legislature was established in Burleson County.
25	6:45	7:03		73	1911—Jack Ruby was born.
26	6:43	7:03		74	1953—Jonas Salk announced the first polio vaccine.
27	6:42	7:04		74	1836—James Fannin and 400 Texans were executed in the Goliad Massacre, under the order of Santa Ana.
28	6:41	7:05	First Quarter	74	1862—"The Gettysburg of the West"
29	6:39	7:06		74	1973—The United States withdrew from Vietnam.
30	6:38	7:06		75	1981—President Reagan was shot.
31	6:37	7:07		75	1928—Musician William "Lefty" Frizzell was born.

Day of Month	Sunrise (AM)	Sunset (PM)	Moon Phase	Normal High Temp. (°F)	On This Date in History
1	6:35	7:08		75	1833—Convention of 1833 meets in San Felipe
2	6:34	7:09		75	1689—Spanish Gen. Alonso de León's expedition found the remains of Fort St. Louis. Fearing French intentions to lay claim to Spanish territory, the Spanish began establishing missions and settlements in East Texas. 1902—First movie theater opened.
3	6:33	7:09	Full	76	1817—"Bigfoot" Wallace was born.
4	6:31	7:10		76	1969—*The Smothers Brothers Show* was cancelled.
5	6:30	7:11		76	1976—Howard Hughes died. 2003—Sixteen north-central counties experienced a supercell thunderstorm that dropped 4.5-inch hailstones.
6	6:29	7:12		76	1896—The Olympics were reborn.
7	6:28	7:12		77	1891—P. T. Barnum died.
8	6:26	7:13		77	1968—The Padre Island National Seashore was dedicated by "Lady Bird" Johnson.
9	6:25	7:14		77	1947—The most devastating tornado in Texas history struck near Amarillo. 1959—The first astronauts were introduced.
10	6:24	7:14		77	1972—Charlie Chaplin received an Oscar. 1979—The most damage ever recorded in Texas for a tornado occurred in Wichita Falls ($442 million).
11	6:22	7:15	Last Quarter	78	1970—*Apollo 13* was launched to the moon.
12	6:21	7:16		78	1961—Soviet Cosmonaut Yuri Gagarin became the first man in space.
13	6:20	7:17		78	1997—Tiger Woods won his first major golf tournament.
14	6:19	7:17		78	1865—President Lincoln was shot.
15	6:17	7:18		79	1912—The *Titanic* sunk.

APRIL 2007

April is the fourth month of the year in the Gregorian Calendar and one of four with the length of 30 days.

Day of Month	Sunrise (AM)	Sunset (PM)	Moon Phase	Normal High Temp. (°F)	On This Date in History
16	6:16	7:19		79	1947—The French-owned SS *Grandcamp* exploded in the Texas City harbor. The concussion was felt 75 miles away in Port Arthur, and the force created a 15-foot tidal wave.
17	6:15	7:20		79	1790—Benjamin Franklin died.
18	6:14	7:20		79	1842—Juan Seguin resigned as mayor of San Antonio.
19	6:13	7:21	*New Moon*	79	1875—Kiowa Chief White Horse surrendered. 1993—Ending a siege that began on Feb. 28, federal agents stormed the compound called Mount Carmel near Waco, where cult leader David Koresh and his followers (Branch Davidians) had reportedly been storing a large cache of assault weapons.
20	6:11	7:22		80	1902—The Curies isolated radium.
21	6:10	7:23		80	1836—The Battle of San Jacinto.
22	6:09	7:24		80	1689—Mexican explorer Alonso de Leon reached Fort St. Louis.
23	6:08	7:24		81	1936—Roy Orbison was born.
24	6:07	7:25		81	1911—Magnolia Petroleum Company was founded.
25	6:06	7:26	*First Quarter*	81	1859—Ground was broken for the Suez Canal.
26	6:05	7:27		82	1854—Land surveys ordered for Indian reservations.
27	6:03	7:27		82	1907—Tornado in Hemming.
28	6:02	7:28		82	1789—Mutiny on the HMS *Bounty*.
29	6:01	7:29		82	1856—Fifty-three camels arrived at the port of Indianola for a 10-year U.S. Army experiment on using them as pack animals in the arid areas of the Southwest. They were quartered at Camp Verde, near present-day Kerrville.
30	6:00	7:30		83	1598—A ceremony of thanksgiving was held near present-day El Paso by Juan de Oñate, the members of his expedition, and natives of the region. The Spaniards provided game and the Indians supplied fish for the feast, the Franciscan missionaries celebrated mass, and Oñate claimed all land drained by the Rio Grande in the name of the King Philip II of Spain. 1933—Willie Nelson was born.

Day of Month	Sunrise (AM)	Sunset (PM)	Moon Phase	Normal High Temp. (°F)	On This Date in History
1	5:59	7:30	○	83	1718—The San Antonio de Valero mission was founded in San Antonio. The Alamo was the chapel. 1980—The Dallas Mavericks became part of NBA.
2	5:58	7:31	○ Full	83	1874—John Jones was appointed to lead Frontier Battalion of Texas.
3	5:57	7:32	○	84	1937—*Gone with the Wind* won a Pulitzer Prize.
4	5:56	7:33	○	84	1864—The Army of the Potomac crossed the Rapidan.
5	5:55	7:33	○	84	1995—The greatest damage ever caused by a hailstorm in Texas history occurred in Parker and Tarrant counties ($1.2 billion)—also a U.S. record.
6	5:55	7:34	○	84	1954—The first four-minute mile was run.
7	5:54	7:35	◐	85	1947—*Kraft Television Theater* made its debut.
8	5:53	7:36	◑	85	1846—The first major battle of the Mexican War was fought at Palo Alto.
9	5:52	7:36	◑	85	1541—De Soto reached the Mississippi.
10	5:51	7:37	◑ Last Quarter	85	1977—Joan Crawford died. 1996—Five-inch hailstones fell on Howard County.
11	5:50	7:38	◑	86	1953—Tornado in Waco.
12	5:49	7:39	◑	86	1903—"Eyes of Texas" sung for the first time at the University of Texas.
13	5:49	7:39	◑	86	1865—The last battle of the Civil War was fought at Palmito Ranch near Brownsville.
14	5:48	7:40	●	86	1888—The capitol building in Austin was dedicated.
15	5:47	7:41	●	87	1896—Tornados killed 78 people.
16	5:46	7:42	● New Moon	87	1888—The capitol building in Austin opened. 1898—Teddy Roosevelt arrived in San Antonio to recruit and train Rough Riders for the First Volunteer Cavalry to fight in the Spanish-American War in Cuba. 1917—Hail fell in Ballinger to a depth of three feet.

MAY 2007

May is the fifth month of the year in the Gregorian Calendar and one of seven Gregorian months with the length of 31 days.

Day of Month	Sunrise (AM)	Sunset (PM)	Moon Phase	Normal High Temp. (°F)	On This Date in History
17	5:46	7:42	◑	87	1992—Lawrence Welk died.
18	5:45	7:43	◑	87	1871—Chief Satanta massacred teamsters at Red River. 1923—A downpour in Beaumont dropped 12.8 inches of rain in 4.5 hours.
19	5:44	7:44	◑	88	1910—During the passing of Haley's comet, a 500-pound meteorite fell into Charleston, Texas.
20	5:44	7:45	◑	88	1920—Amarillo became the Porter county seat.
21	5:43	7:45	◑	88	1539—Black Spanish explorer Estevan was reportedly killed.
22	5:43	7:46	◑	88	1953—The Tidelands Bill was signed by Pres. Eisenhower, giving Texas the rights to its offshore oil. 1999—The largest pecan pie in history was made in El Paso.
23	5:42	7:47	◐ *First Quarter*	89	1934—Bonnie and Clyde were killed. 1859—Baylor and Charles Goodnight (and 250 other soldiers) attacked the Brazos Reservation.
24	5:42	7:47	◐	89	1869—24 defendants stood trial in the Stockade case.
25	5:41	7:48	◐	89	1896—The Daughters of the Confederacy met for the first time. 1981—Five and one-half inches of rain fell in one hour in Austin.
26	5:41	7:49	◐	89	1885—Al Jolson's birthday.
27	5:40	7:49	◐	89	1870—First printed reference to the Chisholm Trail.
28	5:40	7:50	○	90	1924—The U.S. Border Patrol was established.
29	5:39	7:51	○	90	1953—Men reach Everest summit.
30	5:39	7:51	○	90	1431—Joan of Arc was martyred.
31	5:39	7:51	○	90	1919—The first wedding in a flying aircraft occurred over Houston.

Day of Month	Sunrise (AM)	Sunset (PM)	Moon Phase	Normal High Temp. (°F)	On This Date in History
1	5:38	7:52	○ *Full*	91	1969—The Lyndon B. Johnson State Historical Park opened.
2	5:38	7:53	○	91	1911—Carrie Nation died.
3	5:38	7:54	○	91	1965—San Antonio native Ed White became the first American to walk in space. 1973—Bilingual education in schools in Texas was approved.
4	5:38	7:54	○	91	1967—Bill Cosby won an Emmy.
5	5:37	7:55	○	91	1956—Elvis created an uproar on the *Milton Berle Show*.
6	5:37	7:55	○	91	1936—The Texas Centennial Exposition opened in Dallas.
7	5:37	7:56	◑	92	1876—Construction began on Fort Sam Houston.
8	5:37	7:56	◑ *Last Quarter*	92	1925—Barbara Bush was born.
9	5:37	7:57	◑	92	1894—The Corsica oilfield was discovered.
10	5:37	7:57	◑	92	1821—Moses Austin died.
11	5:37	7:58	◑	92	1865—The infamous State Treasury robbery 1965—A flash flood in Sanderson caused $2.7 million in damage.
12	5:37	7:58	◐	92	1924—George Herbert Walker Bush was born.
13	5:37	7:58	◐	93	1875—Miriam Ferguson was born.
14	5:37	7:59	●	93	1920—Sul Ross State Normal College began operations, later becoming Sul Ross State University.
15	5:37	7:59	● *New Moon*	93	1921—Bessie Coleman became the world's first licensed African American pilot.
16	5:37	7:59	●	93	1943—A race riot in Beaumont occurred.

JUNE 2007

June is the sixth month of the year in the Gregorian calendar, with a length of 30 days. The month is named after the Roman goddess Juno, wife of Jupiter and equivalent to the Greek goddess Hera.

Day of Month	Sunrise (AM)	Sunset (PM)	Moon Phase	Normal High Temp. (°F)	On This Date in History
17	5:37	8:00		93	1899—Brazos River flood
18	5:37	8:00		93	1997—Enis became the home of the official state Bluebonnet Trail.
19	5:37	8:00		93	1846—Evan Jones, Populist spokesman and farmer, was born. 1865—Gen. Gordon Granger arrived at Galveston to announce that slavery had been abolished, an event commemorated by the festival known as Juneteenth.
20	5:38	8:01		93	1977—Oil began flowing in Alaska.
21	5:38	8:01		93	1864—Grant extended the Petersburg line.
22	5:38	8:01	First Quarter	94	1824—The Battle of Jones Creek
23	5:38	8:01		94	1845—Special session for Texas Annexation
24	5:39	8:01		94	1699—San Juan Bautisto Mission was founded.
25	5:39	8:01		94	1961—Miriam Ferguson died.
26	5:39	8:01		94	1832—The Battle of Velasco 1928—The opening of the Democratic National Convention in Houston, the first nominating convention held in a Southern city since 1860.
27	5:39	8:02		94	1957—Hurricane Audrey
28	5:40	8:02		94	1880—Texas Jack Omahundro died. 1994—The hottest temperature ever recorded in Texas occurred in the town of Monahans (120°F).
29	5:40	8:02		94	1899—Rain ended in the Brazos River flood.
30	5:41	8:02	Full	94	1882—Henry Flipper was dismissed from the army.

Day of Month	Sunrise (AM)	Sunset (PM)	Moon Phase	Normal High Temp. (°F)	On This Date in History
1	5:41	8:02	◯	94	1879—Jake Atz was born.
2	5:41	8:02	◯	94	1863—Hood's Texas Brigade joined the battle at Gettysburg.
3	5:42	8:01	◯	94	1884—Austin City Hospital opened
4	5:42	8:01	◑	94	1845—The Texas Constitutional Convention voted to accept the United States's annexation proposal; an Annexation Ordinance and State Constitution was drafted for the voters of Texas. 1883—The world's first rodeo was held in Pecos.
5	5:43	8:01	◑	94	1956—The first licensed pilot, Slats Rodgers, died.
6	5:43	8:01	◑	94	1946—George W. Bush was born.
7	5:44	8:01	◑	94	1891—The Port of Velasco opened on the Brazos River.
8	5:44	8:01	◑ *Last Quarter*	94	1911—Alfonso Steel died.
9	5:45	8:00	◖	94	1941—The Enigma key was broken, cracking the Nazi code.
10	5:45	8:00	◖	94	1842—Ben Stockton Terrell, soldier, lawyer, and Populist, was born.
11	5:46	8:00	◖	94	1919—The Longview race riot occurred.
12	5:46	7:59	◕	94	1861—Confederacy signed treaties with Choctaw and Chickasaw tribes.
13	5:47	7:59	◕	94	1985—Live Aid concert.
14	5:48	7:59	● *New Moon*	94	1938—Howard Hughes circled globe.
15	5:48	7:58	●	94	1882—The Texas Bar Association was organized.

JULY 2007

July is the seventh month of the year in the Gregorian Calendar and one of seven Gregorian months with the length of 31 days.

Day of Month	Sunrise (AM)	Sunset (PM)	Moon Phase	Normal High Temp. (°F)	On This Date in History
16	5:49	7:58		94	1839—Cherokee War began.
17	5:49	7:58		94	1945—Clara Driscoll died.
18	5:50	7:57		95	1936—The Spanish Civil War started.
19	5:50	7:57		95	1878—Sam Bass was wounded.
20	5:51	7:56		95	1876—Death of Santa Anna 1969—*Apollo 11* astronaut Neil Armstrong transmitted the first words from the surface of the moon: "Houston, The Eagle has landed."
21	5:51	7:56		95	1851—Sam Bass was born. 1878—Sam Bass died.
22	5:52	7:55	*First Quarter*	95	1864—The Battle of Atlanta
23	5:53	7:55		95	1937—Orson Welles's first radio drama aired.
24	5:53	7:54		95	1979—Tropical Storm Claudette brought 45 inches of rain to the area around Alvin.
25	5:54	7:54		95	1943—Mussolini toppled from power.
26	5:55	7:53		95	1845—The U.S. flag was flown for the first time.
27	5:55	7:52		94	1888—Randall County was organized.
28	5:56	7:51		94	1973—The March for Justice
29	5:57	7:51		94	1958—NASA was created.
30	5:58	7:50	*Full*	94	1936—Margaret Mitchell sold the film rights to *Gone with the Wind*.
31	5:58	7:49		94	1902—Charles Rath died.

Day of Month	Sunrise (AM)	Sunset (PM)	Moon Phase	Normal High Temp. (°F)	On This Date in History
1	6:00	7:48		94	1731—In the first election held in Texas, voters chose officials of the municipal government of San Fernando. 1966—In one of the worst massacres in Texas history, Charles Whitman killed 17 people, shooting them from the tower on the University of Texas campus in Austin. 1978—Remnants of Hurricane Amelia dropped 30 inches of rain in the Albany area.
2	6:00	7:47		94	1882—Roy Bean was appointed justice of the peace.
3	6:01	7:46		94	1861—The federal fleet bombed Galveston. 1970—The highest peak wind gust ever recorded in Texas occurred in Aransas Pass as a result of Hurricane Celia (180 miles per hour).
4	6:02	7:45		94	1941—Coke Stevenson became governor. 1978—The greatest amount of rain ever recorded in Texas in a 24-hour period fell in Albany (29.05 inches).
5	6:02	7:44		94	1838—Point Bolivar was settled.
6	6:03	7:43	Last Quarter	94	1726—Missionary Antonio Margil died.
7	6:04	7:42		94	1989—Mickey Leland died in a plane crash.
8	6:05	7:41		94	1812—Gutierrez-Magee Expedition crossed the Sabine.
9	6:05	7:40		94	1973—Billy Martin became manager of the Texas Rangers.
10	6:06	7:39		94	1935—The Texas Department of Public Safety was established.
11	6:07	7:38		94	1811—The Battle of Plum Creek
12	6:07	7:37	New Moon	94	1936—The hottest temperature ever recorded in Texas occurred in the town of Seymour (120°F).
13	6:08	7:36		94	1906—An all-black army unit was accused of a shooting rampage that left one civilian dead at Fort Brown in Brownsville, Texas.
14	6:09	7:35		93	1957—Jane McCallum died.
15	6:10	7:34		93	2000— Governor Bush appointed the Texas Quarter Dollar Design Advisory Committee.

August is the eighth month of the year in the Gregorian Calendar and one of seven Gregorian months with the length of 31 days.

Day of Month	Sunrise (AM)	Sunset (PM)	Moon Phase	Normal High Temp. (°F)	On This Date in History
16	6:10	7:33		93	1925—Fess Parker was born.
17	6:11	7:32		93	1786—Davy Crockett was born.
18	6:12	7:31		93	1983—The greatest damage ever caused by a hurricane in Texas occurred as a result of Hurricane Alicia ($3.0 billion).
19	6:12	7:29		93	1886—A hurricane destroyed every house in the port of Indianola, finishing a job started by another storm 11 years earlier. Indianola was never rebuilt. 1895—John Wesley Hardin died in gunfight.
20	6:13	7:28	First Quarter	93	1866—President Andrew Johnson issued a proclamation of peace between the United States and Texas. 1984—The opening of the National Republican Convention in Dallas
21	6:14	7:27		92	1928—Pauline Wells died.
22	6:14	7:26		92	1977—Texas A&M College of Medicine opened.
23	6:15	7:25		92	1917—Houston race riot
24	6:16	7:23		92	1882—The town of Ben Ficklin was washed away in flood. 1949—The University of Texas Medical Branch in Galveston admitted its first black student. 1979—A hailstorm destroyed 150,000 acres of crops and damaged another 550,000 acres.
25	6:17	7:22		92	1915—Galveston hurricane
26	6:17	7:21		91	1920—The 19th Amendment was adopted.
27	6:18	7:20		91	1990—Stevie Ray Vaughn died in a helicopter crash.
28	6:19	7:18		91	1963—Martin Luther King, Jr. presented his "I Have a Dream" speech.
29	6:19	7:17		91	1908—Alton Strickland was born.
30	6:20	7:16	Full	90	1956—Mansfield High School mob prevented black students from attending.
31	6:21	7:14		90	1871—James "Gentleman Jim" Ferguson was born.

Day of Month	Sunrise (AM)	Sunset (PM)	Moon Phase	Normal High Temp. (°F)	On This Date in History
1	6:21	7:13	◐	90	1807—Former U.S. Vice President Aaron Burr was found innocent of treason.
2	6:22	7:12	◐	90	1789—The U.S. Treasury Department was established.
3	6:23	7:11	◐	89	1891—Cotton pickers organized their own union.
4	6:23	7:09	◐ *Last Quarter*	89	1766—The first ever hurricane recorded in Texas struck near Galveston. 2001—Authorities confirmed a tabloid editor had contracted anthrax. He died the next day.
5	6:24	7:08	◐	89	1836—Sam Houston was elected president of the Republic. 1930—The Daisy Bradford #3 well, near Turnertown in Rusk County, blew in, heralding the discovery of the huge East Texas Oil Field. 2000—Most of the eastern and central parts of Texas experience temperatures in excess of 100°F.
6	6:25	7:07	◑	89	1876—The new constitution of Texas was established.
7	6:25	7:05	◑	88	1943—Fire in Gulf Hotel in Houston
8	6:26	7:04	◑	88	1900—The deadliest hurricane ever to strike Texas occurred in Galveston.
9	6:27	7:02	◑	88	1961—A meteor hit Grayson County.
10	6:27	7:01	◑	88	1993—Final episode of *Late Night with David Letterman* aired.
11	6:28	7:00	● *New Moon*	87	1961—The highest sustained wind speed ever recorded in Texas occurred in the towns of Matagorda and Port Lavaca as a result of Hurricane Carla (145 miles per hour). 2001—Terrorists flew planes into the World Trade Center and the Pentagon, with another plane crashing into a Pennsylvania field.
12	6:29	6:58	●	87	1909—Kenneth Threadgill was born. 1958—The integrated circuit, developed at Texas Instruments in Dallas, was successfully tested, ushering in the semiconductor and electronics age.
13	6:29	6:57	●	87	1925—Alexander Singer died.
14	6:30	6:56	●	86	1919—A hurricane destroyed Spohn Hospital in Corpus Christi.

September is the ninth month of the year in the Gregorian Calendar and one of four Gregorian months with 30 days.

Day of Month	Sunrise (AM)	Sunset (PM)	Moon Phase	Normal High Temp. (°F)	On This Date in History
15	6:31	6:54		86	1858–The southern route of the Butterfield Overland Mail crossed Texas on its way between St. Louis, Mo., and the West Coast. 1883–The University of Texas at Austin opened.
16	6:31	6:53		86	1832–Confederate General Custis Lee was born.
17	6:32	6:51		86	2002–The largest piece of toffee weighing 2,940 pounds was made in Midland.
18	6:33	6:50		85	1971–Lance Armstrong was born.
19	6:33	6:49	First Quarter	85	1863–Texas units fought at the Battle of Chickamauga.
20	6:34	6:47		85	1967–Hurricane Beulah hits.
21	6:35	6:46		85	1971–Texas Rangers in Arlington began.
22	6:35	6:45		84	1915–Southern Methodist University held its first class.
23	6:36	6:43		84	1863–Lincoln planned to send relief to the beleaguered Union force at Chattanooga.
24	6:37	6:42		84	1844–Mier Expedition returned to Texas.
25	6:37	6:40		84	1867–Oliver Loving died.
26	6:38	6:39	Full	83	1935–Andy Adams died.
27	6:39	6:38		83	1952–Big Tex, the 52-foot cowboy, joined the state fair.
28	6:40	6:36		83	1874–Col. Ranald Mackenzie led the 4th U.S. Cavalry in the Battle of Palo Duro Canyon, which ended with the confinement of southern Plains Indians in reservations in Indian Territory. This made possible the wholesale settlement of the western part of the state. 1948–Fort Worth WBAP-TV began broadcasting.
29	6:40	6:35		83	1923–"Bum" Phillips was born.
30	6:41	6:34		82	1925–Texas Tech University began classes in Lubbock as Texas Technological College. 1972–Guadalupe National Park was established.

Day of Month	Sunrise (AM)	Sunset (PM)	Moon Phase	Normal High Temp. (°F)	On This Date in History
1	6:42	6:32	◑	82	1937—The General Land Office opened in Houston.
2	6:42	6:31	◑	82	1835—A battle fought at Gonzales, was known as the opening battle of the Texas Revolution.
3	6:43	6:29	◑ *Last Quarter*	82	1954—Stevie Ray Vaughan was born.
4	6:44	6:28	◑	81	1876—Texas A&M opened.
5	6:45	6:27	◑	81	1863—Federal Fleet occupied Galveston.
6	6:45	6:25	◑	81	1989—Bette Davis died.
7	6:46	6:24	◐	80	1883—Susanna Wilkerson Dickinson, survivor of the Alamo, died.
8	6:47	6:23	◐	80	1926—The Witte Memorial Museum opened.
9	6:47	6:22	◐	80	1835—The first offensive action of the Texas Revolution occurred in Goliad.
10	6:48	6:20	◐	80	1835—The *Telegraph* and *Texas Register* began publishing.
11	6:49	6:19	● *New Moon*	79	1962—Pope opened Vatican II.
12	6:50	6:18	●	79	1886—Indianola hurricane hits.
13	6:50	6:17	●	79	1792—The White House cornerstone was laid.
14	6:51	6:15	●	78	1890—Dwight Eisenhower was born.
15	6:52	6:14	●	78	1853—New Braunfels held the First Saengerfest.

OCTOBER 2007

October is the tenth month of the year in the Gregorian Calendar and one of seven Gregorian months with the length of 31 days.

Day of Month	Sunrise (AM)	Sunset (PM)	Moon Phase	Normal High Temp. (°F)	On This Date in History
16	6:53	6:13		78	1925—The Texas School Board prohibited the teaching of evolution.
17	6:54	6:12		77	1839—Lamar arrived in new capital city of Austin.
18	6:54	6:10		77	1928—Charles Siringo died.
19	6:55	6:09	First Quarter	77	1919—The League of Women Voters was organized.
20	6:56	6:08		76	1807—Aaron Burr was found not guilty of treason.
21	6:57	6:07		76	1822—The Texas National Bank was established.
22	6:58	6:06		75	1836—Sam Houston was inaugurated.
23	6:58	6:05		75	1883—Abilene became the county seat of Taylor county.
24	6:59	6:04		75	1971—The first game in Texas Stadium was played.
25	7:00	6:03		74	1886—The first Texas State Fair opened.
26	7:01	6:02	Full	74	1930—The first Cotton Bowl was played.
27	7:02	6:00		73	1858—Theodore Roosevelt was born.
28	7:03	5:59		73	1835—The Battle of Conception
29	7:04	5:58		73	1946—Crane Webster Furr died.
30	7:04	5:57		72	1938—"War of the Worlds"—a realistic radio dramatization of a Martian invasion of Earth—aired.
31	7:05	5:57		72	1926—Houdini was found dead.

Day of Month	Sunrise (AM)	Sunset (PM)	Moon Phase	Normal High Temp. (°F)	On This Date in History
1	7:06	5:56	Last Quarter	71	1866—Belle Star married outlaw Jim Reed.
2	7:07	5:55		71	1828—Colonists left New York to settle in Matagorda.
3	7:08	5:54		70	1793—Stephen F. Austin was born.
4	7:09	5:53		70	1916—Walter Cronkite was born.
5	7:10	5:52		70	1911—Roy Rogers was born.
6	7:11	5:51		70	1970—Ethan Hawke was born.
7	7:12	5:50		69	1835—A provisional government was established at San Felipe. 1995—The office of Treasurer of the State of Texas was abolished by constitutional amendment.
8	7:12	5:50		69	1835—The Grass Fight occurred near San Antonio. 1864—Lincoln started his second term as president.
9	7:13	5:49	New Moon	68	1924—Miriam Ferguson became first woman elected Governor of Texas.
10	7:14	5:48		68	1837—The Battle of Stone Houses was fought.
11	7:15	5:47		67	1918—WWI ended.
12	7:16	5:47		67	1860—Muleshoe Brand registered.
13	7:17	5:46		66	1974—Karen Silkwood died in an automobile accident.
14	7:18	5:45		66	1972—Former Congressman Martin died.
15	7:19	5:45		66	1906—John A. Brooks resigned commission as captain of Texas Rangers.

NOVEMBER 2007

November is the eleventh month of the year in the Gregorian Calendar and one of four Gregorian months with the length of 30 days.

Day of Month	Sunrise (AM)	Sunset (PM)	Moon Phase	Normal High Temp. (°F)	On This Date in History
16	7:20	5:44		65	1995—Bud Adams announced his plan to move the Houston Oilers to Tennessee.
17	7:21	5:44	First Quarter	65	1931—The Delta Drilling Company was founded in Longview.
18	7:22	5:43		65	1868—General Sheridan's Canadian River expedition was launched against the Cheyenne and Arapaho indians.
19	7:23	5:43		64	1845—First group of Mormon settlers arrived in Texas near Fredricksburg.
20	7:24	5:42		64	1945—Nuremberg trials began.
21	7:25	5:42		64	1945—Town of Thin Gravy changed its name to Truman.
22	7:25	5:41		63	1963—President John F. Kennedy was assassinated in Dallas.
23	7:26	5:41		63	1964—First successful heart bypass surgery.
24	7:27	5:41	Full	63	1835—The Texas Rangers organization was officially established by Texas's provisional government. 1892—Olea Forrest Kirkland, artist, was born.
25	7:28	5:40		63	1850—Texas gave up its claim to land that includes more than half of what is now New Mexico, about a third of Colorado, a corner of Oklahoma, and a small portion of Wyoming.
26	7:29	5:40		62	1930—H. L. Hunt acquired the Daisy Bradford oil well.
27	7:30	5:40		62	1908—Frank Hamer completed his first month as city marshal of Navasota.
28	7:31	5:40		62	1884—The Texas Confederate Home for Veterans was chartered.
29	7:32	5:40		62	1929—Admiral Byrd flew over South Pole.
30	7:33	5:39		62	1863—Confederate Troops vacated Fort Esperanza.

Day of Month	Sunrise (AM)	Sunset (PM)	Moon Phase	Normal High Temp. (°F)	On This Date in History
1	7:34	5:39	Last Quarter	61	1880—The Mission Pacific Railway entered Texas.
2	7:34	5:39		61	1907—Peck changed its name to Tomball.
3	7:35	5:39		61	1884—Outlaw Joseph Olney died.
4	7:36	5:39		60	1862—Confederate soldiers took back the Galveston.
5	7:37	5:39		60	1933—Prohibition ended.
6	7:38	5:39		60	1889—Jefferson Davis died.
7	7:38	5:39		60	1925—The West Texas Historical Society was formed.
8	7:39	5:39		60	1929—Buck Owens was born.
9	7:40	5:39	New Moon	59	1928—Dan Blocker was born.
10	7:41	5:40		59	1836—President Sam Houston approved the first national flag of the Republic of Texas.
11	7:42	5:40		59	1835—Mexicans surrendered San Antonio after the Siege of Béxar.
12	7:42	5:40		59	1910—The Toonerville Trolley streetcar began operating in Houston.
13	7:43	5:40		59	1777—A Spanish mapping crew sailed to Texas.
14	7:44	5:41		59	1918—The Leonard Brothers store opened in Fort Worth.
15	7:44	5:41		58	1887—The Fort Worth and Denver Railway train began operation.
16	7:45	5:41		58	1881—The Texas & Pacific Railway reached Sierra Blanca in West Texas, about 90 miles east of El Paso.
17	7:46	5:42	First Quarter	58	1951—The *John Henry Faulk Show* made its debut on WCBS.

December is the twelfth and last month of the year in the Gregorian Calendar and one of seven Gregorian months with the length of 31 days.

Day of Month	Sunrise (AM)	Sunset (PM)	Moon Phase	Normal High Temp. (°F)	On This Date in History
18	7:46	5:42	◑	58	1860—Cynthia Ann Parker was rescued.
19	7:47	5:42	◑	58	1890—Lubbock and Monterey consolidated.
20	7:47	5:43	◑	57	1835—The first Declaration of Texas Independence was signed.
21	7:48	5:43	◑	57	1861—Frontier Regiment
22	7:48	5:44	○	57	1996—Last game played by the Houston Oilers before they moved to Tennessee.
23	7:49	5:44	○	57	1986—*Voyager* completed global flight.
24	7:49	5:45	○ Full	57	1926—North Texas's only white Christmas of the 20th century occurred.
25	7:50	5:45	○	57	Christmas Day
26	7:50	5:46	○	57	1813—The Spanish government granted Moses Austin permission to establish a colony of Anglo-Americans in the Texas area. 1858—Twenty Anglos led by Peter Garland attacked a sleeping, innocent band of Brazos Reserve Indians and their leader Choctaw Tom on Ioni Creek. 1874—The first commercial buffalo hunt
27	7:50	5:47	○	57	1836—Stephen F. Austin, known as the "Father of Texas," died.
28	7:51	5:47	○	57	1976—Freddy King died.
29	7:51	5:48	◐	57	1845—Texas became a state.
30	7:51	5:49	◐	56	1938—San Antonio mayor indicted for misapplication of funds.
31	7:52	5:49	◐ Last Quarter	56	1937—Aransas National Refuge was established.

Texas Climatic Patterns

Texas cities have varying climatic conditions depending on their location within the state.

	Abilene	Amarillo	Austin	Brownsville	Corpus Christi	Dallas	Houston	Lubbock	San Antonio
Avg. High Temp. (°F)	76.2	70.5	78.9	80.7	81.0	76.3	78.7	73.5	79.5
Avg. Low Temp. (°F)	52.8	43.3	58.2	64.7	62.1	54.6	60.1	46.8	57.7
Avg. # of Days above 90°F (per year)	100	65	111	116	106	100	97	80	113
Avg. # of Days below 32°F (per year)	39	112	19	2	5	39	19	92	22
Highest Temp. Ever Recorded (°F)	113	108	112	107	103	113	109	114	111
Lowest Temp. Ever Recorded (°F)	-1	-14	-2	12	13	-8	7	-17	0
Avg. Date of First Fall Freeze	November 13	October 24	December 2	December 17	December 11	November 22	December 6	November 2	November 24
Avg. Date of Last Spring Freeze	March 22	April 13	February 26	January 31	February 16	March 13	February 18	April 5	March 2
Avg. Wind Speed (mph)	13.2	14.8	9.7	13.7	13.8	12.7	9.4	12.8	10.8
Avg. Rainfall (in. per year)	24.4	19.56	31.88	26.61	30.13	33.70	50.83	18.65	30.98
Avg. # of Thunderstorm Days (per year)	56	49	41	26	29	46	61	47	37
Avg. Snowfall (in. per year)	2.7	15.4	0.9	0	0	2.7	0.4	10.3	0.7

★★★ *Texas Sports* ★★★
HALL OF FAME

When sports fans think of Texas, they automatically think of football and baseball–or the Dallas Cowboy Cheerleaders, of course! But for the true sports fan, a trip to Texas must include a visit to the Texas Sports Hall of Fame, on the campus of Baylor University in Waco. Here you also find displays recognizing the men and women of golf, boxing, track and field, and auto racing.

The Texas Sport Writers Association originally established the Hall of Fame in Grand Prairie Texas in 1951. The Hall's goal was to recognize athletes who had brought fame and honor to Texas sports. The two-story structure covers 29,000 square feet and includes the Texas High School Football and Baseball Halls of Fame, and the Texas Tennis Fall of Fame.

Visitors can watch "Great Sports Headlines of Texas" in the Tom Landry Theater, view sports memorabilia on display, or participate in the many interactive exhibits for adults and children. *You can even compare your hand and shoe size to life-size replicas of NBA greats!*

YOU'LL ALSO SEE:

- *The jersey and cap* **Nolan Ryan** *wore when he pitched his fifth no-hitter as an Astro*
- *Silks and crop used by horse racing's most famous jockey,* **Willie Shoemaker**
- *The 1938 Heisman trophy won by* **Davey O'Brien**
- **Tom Landry's** *grey fedora*
- *A replica of the gold medal won by* **George Foreman** *in the 1968 Olympics*
- *A football from the* **first Cotton Bowl**
- **Rogers Hornsby's** *1928 St. Louis Cardinals uniform*
- *Boxing's 1966* **World Welterwelt belt**
  Harvey Pennick's *Little Red Book*

2005 Inductees—the latest inductees into the Hall on February 15, 2006

Bobby Bragan—baseball
Tim Brown—football
Augie Garrido—baseball
Zina Garrison—tennis
Bela Karolyi—gymnastics
Martha Karolyi—gymnastics
James Segrest—track
R.C. Slocum—football
Emmitt Smith—football

"The Top Ten Reasons to Visit the Texas Sports Hall of Fame."

10 We celebrate both seasons—fall football and spring football.

9 Darrell Royal says you should.

8 We've got the cleanest restrooms in Waco.

7 Home of the real "Babe"—Babe Didrikson Zaharias.

6 The place is full of horned frogs.

5 Staff does not use performance-enhancing drugs.

4 Mike Tyson is not a member.

3 No corked bats on exhibit.

2 Free George Foreman grill to the 1,000,000th visitor.

1 Texans are proud of their sports heritage.

The *Fastest* People in Texas
CARS

Carroll Shelby ··· *Racing for Life*

Carroll Shelby is one of the auto scene's most beloved icons. He has achieved racing wins around the world. *Sports Illustrated* named him "Driver of the Year" in 1956 and 1957, while the *New York Times* called him the "Driver of the Year" in 1957 and 1958. He's been inducted into the Automotive Hall of Fame and the International Motorsports Hall of Fame. Shelby worked with Ford on such legendary vehicles as the GT40 and the Shelby GT350 and

GT500 Mustangs. Perhaps most importantly, Shelby exemplified American ingenuity when he took an underpowered English AC Cars sports car, stuffed in a high-power Ford V8, and debuted his legendary Cobra, a car that went on to achieve racing fame and ultimately win the 24 Hours of Le Mans for the Shelby-American team.

Shelby Cobra

Carroll Hall Shelby was born on January 11, 1923, in Leesburg, Texas. After World War II, Shelby took an aptitude test that said he would be well suited to raising animals. Unafraid of new adventures, Carroll began a chicken farm. His chickens died of Limberneck disease, causing his farm to go bankrupt. While on the farm, racing was just a hobby, but it soon became his livelihood. Carroll often went straight from the farm to a race, and his attire of striped bib overalls quickly became his signature, representing his "down-home" personality and engaging charisma.

Shelby's smart business acumen has allowed him to succeed in many ventures. Chili making was one of his successful ventures, although there were some rocky paths to this success. The Original Texas Chili Company started after Carroll invested in hundreds of thousands of acres of land in Terlingua, Texas, and couldn't sell it. He and his partners hosted a chili cook-off and flew in a planeload of their friends to get things started. Many bowls of chili and bottles of beer later, the land was sold—the beginnings of the Texas Chili Company and the International Chili Society.

The Carroll Shelby Children's Foundation, a fund to help needy children with heart or kidney problems, was established after Shelby received a heart transplant in 1990 and a kidney transplant in 1996. Typical of Shelby, he continues to give back to the community with unwavering support.

A. J. Foyt ··· *And the Other Triple Crown*

One of the greatest racing drivers of the twentieth century, A. J. Foyt was born on January 16, 1935, in Houston. He won his first race, a midget race at Playland Park, when he was 18.

That victory in a reconditioned bullring launched one of the most exceptional careers in auto racing—one of dominance and longevity. For this Texan, the Indianapolis 500 was his kingdom. He is the only person to have driven in the race for 35 consecutive years. He drove 4,909 laps around the oval for a total of 12,272.5 miles (or about five trips from New York to San Francisco), earning $2,637,963 while competing in *just* the Indy 500. His seven national Indy car championships remain a record. So do his 67 Indy car victories, which are 15 more than Mario Andretti, the No. 2 driver. One year, Foyt won an astounding 10 of 13 races.

But the Indy 500 was not the only race he ruled. A. J. Foyt won 12 national titles and 172 major races, including a record 67 Indy races. He is the only driver to have won the "Triple Crown" of professional racing: the **Indianapolis 500** (1961, 1964, 1967, and 1977), the **NASCAR Daytona 500** (1972), and the **24-hour Le Mans** (1967, with Dan Gurney). Foyt has also won 6 other NASCAR events; 41 USAC stock car events; and 50 USAC sprint, midget, and dirt races.

C Y C L I N G

Lance Armstrong's ··· *Lucky Seven*

Lance Armstrong was born on September 18, 1971, in Plano, Texas. He is the American professional road-racing cyclist most famous for winning the Tour de France a record seven consecutive times from 1999 to 2005. Amazingly, he accomplished these victories after having brain and testicular surgery and extensive chemotherapy in 1996 to treat testicular cancer that had metastasized to his brain and lungs. He earned the *Sport Illustrated* Sportsman of the Year in 2002 and the *Associated Press* Male Athlete of the Year in 2002, 2003, 2004, and 2005.

After retirement, Armstrong started the Livestrong Foundation to support cancer research. A fashion phenomenon was born with the yellow Livestrong rubber bracelets. Each wristband sold for one dollar and as of January 2006, 58 million Livestrong bracelets had been sold. Lance currently works to support and campaign for cancer research funding. Find out more about the **Livestrong Foundation** at **www. livestrong.org.**

★ **Did You Know?**

Lance was born Lance Edward Gunderson, but took the last name Armstrong when his mother married her second husband, Terry Armstrong.

Republic of Texas Motorcycle Race

If you are looking for one of the best motorcycle rallies Texas has to offer, check out the Republic of Texas (ROT) rally in Austin. The official ROT site is at the Travis Expo Center just east of Austin, but there are many cool things to do beyond the rally grounds. Nighttime is a great time to be on downtown Austin's 6th Street with the motorcycle-lined streets that are closed to car traffic and filled with bikers. Since Austin is the Live Music Capital of the World, it's full of bands and a festive spirit. Held on the first weekend in June, the ROT is the largest motorcycle rally in Texas and one of the biggest in the United States.

Want to Play?

Match these Texas colleges with their team name.

COLLEGES	TEAMS
1. BAYLOR UNIVERSITY *(Waco)*	OWLS
2. MIDWESTERN STATE UNIVERSITY *(Wichita Falls)*	LONGHORNS
3. PRAIRIE VIEW A&M UNIVERSITY	RED RAIDERS
4. RICE UNIVERSITY *(Houston)*	RAMS
5. TEXAS STATE UNIVERSITY *(San Marcos)*	HORNED FROGS
6. TEXAS A&M UNIVERSITY *(College Station)*	AGGIES
7. TEXAS CHRISTIAN UNIVERSITY *(Fort Worth)*	MINERS
8. TEXAS SOUTHERN UNIVERSITY *(Houston)*	BEARS
9. TEXAS TECH *(Lubbock)*	INDIANS
10. TEXAS WESLEYAN UNIVERSITY *(Fort Worth)*	TIGERS
11. UNIVERSITY OF HOUSTON	BOBCATS
12. UNIVERSITY OF TEXAS *(Austin)*	PANTHERS
13. UNIVERSITY OF TEXAS *(El Paso)*	COUGARS

Early Texas Baseball

On April 21, 1867, the people celebrated something other than San Jacinto Day. The first recorded baseball game in Texas was played on that day, and the Houston Stonewalls crushed the Galveston Robert E. Lees, 35-2.

Cow pastures and fields served as baseball fields across the state of Texas. In 1872, a team from New Orleans traveled by stagecoach to play Texas teams in Dallas, Waco, and Austin. By 1884, a baseball rivalry existed between Texas A&M University and the University of Texas—a good twenty years before the rivalry in football began. In 1888, the Texas League became the first organized league in the Lone Star State and fielded six teams in Austin, Fort Worth, Houston, San Antonio, Galveston, and Dallas. Unfortunately, only two teams lasted the full season: Dallas and a combined team from Austin and San Antonio. Dallas won the league championship with a record of 55 wins and 27 losses for the season. The 1889 champions were from Houston, with a record of 54 wins and 44 losses.Fast-forward more than 100 years, and we have a team that is the National League baseball champion—the Houston Astros. Baseball has an enduring history in Texas. Who knows what may happen in the future? ⊕

MINOR LEAGUE
Baseball

The Minor Leagues celebrated their 100th anniversary in 2001. As part of this celebration, Bill Weiss and Marshall Wright researched the top teams over 100 years. As the chart will show you, Texas teams were included in 9 of the 100 rankings.

Top 100 Ranking	Team	Year	Record
4	Fort Worth Panthers	1924	109-41
14	Fort Worth Panthers	1920	108-40
17	Fort Worth Panthers	1922	109-46
25	Waco Pirates	1954	105-42
33	Fort Worth Panthers	1925	103-48
42	Houston Buffaloes	1931	108-51
46	Fort Worth Panthers	1921	107-51
65	Houston Buffaloes	1941	87-23
94	Abilene Blue Sox	1946	103-50

Baseball Cards Catch History

The production and collection of baseball cards has a rich history, and Texas has been a part of it.

Some of the earliest baseball cards depict players from the Texas League. Two early popular sets were issued in 1910: the Old Mill set and the Mello-Mint set. There were 640 cards in the Old Mill set, and each card in the set was 1.5 inches by 2.625 inches. At only 50 cards, the Mello-Mint set was produced by the Texas Gum Company in Temple, Texas. Each card was 2.75 inches by 1.5 inches, but there were no Texans in the set.

In 1910, Texas League teams were fielded by Dallas, Fort Worth, Galveston, Houston, San Antonio, and Waco; teams from Shreveport, Louisiana, and Oklahoma City, Oklahoma, were also in the Texas League. Players from each of these teams are represented in the Old Mill set.

The
Red River
RIVALRY

Texans know that the Cotton Bowl is both a stadium and a major college football game. The stadium located in Dallas opened in 1932 at the site of the Texas State Fair, originally built for the celebration of the Centennial of the Republic of Texas. Dallas oilman Curtis J. Sanford, believing Texas could host a game on par with the Rose Bowl, copyrighted the name "Cotton Bowl" and entered into an agreement with the State Fair to play the games at the stadium at Fair Park.

The Cotton Bowl Classic, first played in 1937, has become an American New Year's Day tradition, usually posting the first kickoff in a full day of college football. For years the deciding game for the championship of the now-defunct Southwestern Conference, the Cotton Bowl—now called the AT&T Cotton Bowl Classic—matches teams from the Big 12 and the Southeastern Conference.

For Texans, however, the real classic played each year at the Cotton Bowl Stadium is the "Red River Rivalry" between Texas and Oklahoma. The game, held during the State Fair of Texas, will continue to be played at the Cotton Bowl Stadium, rather than an on-campus site, at least until 2010, as a result of a plan to renovate the facilities.

Highlights of Cotton Bowl Games

At halftime in 1942, less than a month after the attacks on Pearl Harbor, 31 Texas, Oklahoma, and Alabama men enlisted in the Naval Air Corps.

In 1949, Southern Methodist's Doak Walker became the first Heisman winner to take the field in the Dallas Park.

Spectators at the 1954 Cotton Bowl recall the "bench tackle" made by Alabama's Tommy Lewis, who left the sidelines to tackle Dicky Maegle of Rice when none of his Crimson Tide teammates was in the area.

In 1979, Notre Dame quarterback Joe Montana led his team to a tie in the last play, after lagging behind 22 points in the fourth quarter. An extra point sealed their victory over Houston.

THE ASTRODOME
FACTS, HISTORY, AND STATISTICS

The Astrodome in Houston is the oldest stadium, having opened in 1965. Some people have called it the eighth wonder of the world. Why? It was the first ballpark to have a roof over the entire playing field!

Location: 8400 Kirby Drive; the South Loop Freeway/Interstate 610 parallels the first base side; Fannin Street parallels the third base side.

Dimensions: Foul lines: 340 ft (1965), 330 ft (1972), 340 ft (1977), 330 ft (1985), 325 ft (1992), 330 ft (1993), 325 ft (1994); power alleys: 375 ft (1965), 390 ft (1966), 378 ft (1972), 390 ft (1977), 378 ft (1985), 375 ft (1992), 380 ft (1993), 375 ft (1994); center field: 406 ft (1965), 400 ft (1972), 406 ft (1977), 400 ft (1985); apex of dome: 208 ft; backstop: 60.5 ft (1965), 67 ft (1990), 52 ft (1993).

★ Just the Facts

- Construction: H.A. Lott, Inc.
- Owner: Harris County
- Cost: $35 million (1965); $60 million (1989 expansion)
- Opened: April 12, 1965
- Former Tenants: Houston Astros (1965–1999); Houston Oilers (1965–1996)
- Surface: Tifway 419 Bermuda grass (1965); Astroturf (1966 to date)
- Capacity: 42,217 (1965); 46,000 (1966); 44,500 (1968); 45,000 (1975); 47,690 (1982); 54,816 (1990, baseball); 62,439 (football)
- Naming Rights: 2001—Reliant Energy paid $300 million for 32 years for the entire Astrodome complex
- Architects: Hermon Lloyd and W.B. Morgan teamed with Wilson, Morris, Crain, & Anderson

The Future of the Astrodome

At present, no major league team calls the Astrodome home; it is primarily used for citywide festivals and other events. There are plans in the works to convert the Astrodome into a resort. Although other fields and a stadium have replaced the Astrodome, there are no plans to tear the building down.

Why Teams No Longer Play at the Astrodome

Technology has changed since the construction of the Astrodome. About 20 years after its construction was completed, a retractable domed roof was developed. Retractable roofs allowed teams to enjoy beautiful weather, but when the temperature was too hot or it was raining, the roof could be closed. It was the best of both worlds.

Consequently, the Houston Astros left the Astrodome for Enron Field and played their last game in the Astrodome on October 9, 1999. The Houston Oilers completely jumped ship and moved to Nashville, Tennessee, eventually becoming the Tennessee Titans. The newest football team in Houston, the Houston Texans, plays at Reliant Stadium.

Did You Know?

1. When did Nolan Ryan pitch his fifth no-hitter in the Astrodome?

2. What was the original name of the Astrodome?

3. On what date was a game rained out because of flooding?

4. Who hit the home run that was really a single on June 10, 1974?

5. When was the first game on Astroturf played?

6. The Astrodome hosted the All-Star Game in what two years?

7. What unique use did the Astrodome serve in 2005?

8. Who was the original owner of the Astrodome?

9. On what date did Willie Mayes hit his 500th home run in the Astrodome?

10. Who broadcast a game from a gondola suspended from the apex of the dome on April 28, 1965?

Answers:

1. September 26, 1981; 2. Harris County Domed Stadium; 3. June 15, 1976; 4. Mike Schmidt of the Philadelphia Phillies; 5. April 8, 1966; 6. 1968 and 1986; 7. a temporary shelter for thousands of New Orleans residents displaced by Hurricane Katrina; 8. Judge Roy Hofheinz; 9. September 13, 1965; 10. Lindsey Nelson, the announcer for the New York Mets

FRIDAY NIGHT MADNESS & a National Championship

In Texas, football is not a sport. It's a religion. And, they start young. Here are some of the best-known youth organizations in the state.

The Texas Youth Football Association

(TYFA) was founded in 1995 to provide children an opportunity to participate in youth football and cheerleading regardless of their weight or skills. Although it is a competitive league, TYFA is open to all boys and girls. If the children work hard, they will be rewarded with an opportunity to play. Some objectives are to teach self-discipline, teach the fundamentals of the sport, and build healthy minds and bodies. TYFA is one of the fastest growing leagues in Texas and is the place where football dreams can sprout.

The North Texas Youth Football Association

has four age divisions (4–5, 6–7, 8–9, and 10–11), and each division (except 4–5) is divided into four conferences: National East, National West, American East, and American West. Children in the 4–5 category play only flag football. Tackle football begins with the 6–7 group. Each division competes in an eight-game season. The season ends with a multiweek playoff format to crown the North Texas State Champion.

The Mesquite Pee Wee Football Association,

hosted by the Mesquite Independent School District, is considered the Pee Wee Football Capital of the World because it has one of the largest participant groups in the United States. Nineteen teams in four age groups play both flag (ages 4–6 only) and tackle football (7–8, 9–10, and 11–12). Each coach is expected to give every player a reasonable chance at playing during the season.

Northern Zone Athletics is a nonprofit youth organization that aims to teach children sportsmanship, loyalty, courage, respect for authority, and honesty. There are five age groups: 5–6 (flag football), 7 (the midgets), 8–9 (the rookies), 10–11 (the juniors), and 12–13 (the seniors).

Carrollton Youth Football, Inc.

(CYF) is for children on the northern side of Dallas. It is a city-sanctioned football league in Carrollton, Texas, with four age divisions: 5–6 (flag football), 7–8 (freshman tackle division), 9–10 (junior varsity tackle division), and 11–12 (varsity tackle division). The rigorous rules of the NCAA are followed but modified for youth football. With CYF, every player on a team will play if they practice with the team every week.

Heart O' Texas Youth Football has over 700 participants this year and is the longest continually operating youth football league in the Waco, Texas, area. Founded in 1966 as Lake Air Pee Wee Football, it celebrates its fortieth anniversary this year. There are three age divisions that also have weight restrictions so that the participants are not exposed to serious injury. However, the flag football division has no weight restrictions. Teams are based on the school districts in the greater Waco area.

Central Texas Pop Warner

(CTPW), one of the larger Pop Warner programs in the United States, is made up of 17 associations, 110 separate football teams, and over 3500 youth participants. CTPW covers the greater Austin, Texas, area. Pop Warner

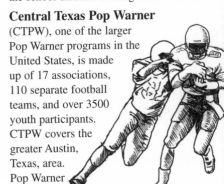

is dedicated to developing youth on and off the field. Scholastic aptitude is a requirement for participation because athletics and scholastics go hand in hand. Pop Warner affiliates are also located in Bryan/College Station (Brazos Valley Pop Warner), Tyler (East Texas Jr. Football League), Houston (Greater Houston Pop Warner), Nederland (Gulf Coast Pop Warner), Kingsville (Coastal Bend Pop Warner), Dallas (North Texas Pop Warner Football League), San Antonio (San Antonio Pop Warner Football Conference), Corpus Christi (South Texas Youth Football League), and Canyon Lake (West Comal–North Bexar Pop Warner Football).

The University of Texas Longhorns—National Champions

The University of Texas has claimed four national team football championships dating back to 1963. They rank fifth in schools for all-time best teams. Championships were earned under two coaches: Darrell Royal coached the 1963, 1969, and 1970 championship teams, while Mack Brown coached the 2005 championship team.

A Look at the 2005 Season

Date	Opponent	Result	Record (Conference Record)
September 3	La Lafayette	W, 60-3	1-0 (0-0)
September 10	at No. 4 Ohio State University	W, 25-22	2-0 (0-0)
September 17	Rice University	W, 51-10	3-0 (0-0)
October 1	at Missouri	W, 51-20	4-0 (1-0)
October 8	Oklahoma	W, 45-12	5-0 (2-0)
October 15	No. 24 Colorado	W, 42-17	6-0 (3-0)
October 22	No. 10 Texas Tech	W, 52-17	7-0 (4-0)
October 29	at Oklahoma State University	W, 47-28	8-0 (5-0)
November 5	at Baylor University	W, 62-0	9-0 (6-0)
November 12	Kansas	W, 66-14	10-0 (7-0)
November 25	at Texas A&M University	W, 40-29	11-0 (8-0)
December 3	at Colorado	W, 70-3	12-0 (8-0)
January 4	vs. No. 2 USC	W, 41-38	13-0 (8-0)

COLLEGE FOOTBALL AWARDS

WITH A TEXAS HERITAGE

The best college football players vie for a variety of awards of distinction. The most notable award is the Heisman Trophy, but there are other awards as well, including the Maxwell Award, the Walter Camp Award, the Fred Biletnikoff Award, the Churck Bednarik Award, and the Jim Thorpe Award. But do you know which awards have a Texas heritage?

The Heisman Trophy

The Heisman Trophy is awarded to the most outstanding college football player each season. The Heisman Trophy has been given to the following Texas college players:

- **Davey O'Brien (QB)**
  —**Texas Christian University (1938)**

- **Doak Walker (RB)**
  —**Southern Methodist University (1948)**

- **John David Crow (RB)**
  —**Texas A&M University (1957)**

- **Earl Campbell (RB)**
  —**University of Texas (1977)**

- **Andre Ware (QB)**
  —**University of Houston (1989)**

- **Ricky Williams (RB)**
  —**University of Texas (1998)**

The Davey O'Brien Award

Robert David (Davey) O'Brien, a quarterback at Texas Christian University, was born in Dallas, Texas, on June 22, 1917. O'Brien enrolled at TCU in 1935, but he did not start as quarterback until 1938, where he led the team in passing yards and only four interceptions and was named to the All-Southwest Conference first team. That season was topped off by a Sugar Bowl victory and a national championship. In addition to winning the Heisman Trophy, O'Brien was awarded the Maxwell and Walter Camp trophies as well. Davey O'Brien inspired greatness on and off the football field, and this award is a recognition of the college player who most emulates the great Davey O'Brien.

The Outland Trophy

Most college awards are awarded to running backs, quarterbacks, and receivers, but John Outland thought that interior lineman, both offense and defense, were due recognition because it was their work that helped others succeed on the field. John Outland is not a Texan, but his award has been won over the years by three University of Texas players:

- **Scott Appleton (1963)**
- **Tommy Nobis (1965)**
- **Brad Shearer (1977)**

Paul "Bear" Bryant Award

Coach Bryant was the coach at the University of Alabama for 25 years. He walked the sidelines of many a game and was one of the best-known coaches in college football. From 1953 to 1957, Bryant was the head football coach at Texas A&M. He achieved a mark of 25-14-2 during his four seasons with the Aggies.

The Touchdown Club of Houston has sponsored the Bear Bryant award since 1957, which is awarded to the coach of the year. Two renowned University of Texas coaches have won the award:

- **Darrell Royal (1961)**
- **Mack Brown (2005)**

The Manning Award

The newest award in college football, in honor of the quarterback accomplishments of Archie Manning and his sons Peyton and Eli, was awarded to a University of Texas player in 2005—**Vince Young**.

★ The "Bear"

Born in southern Arkansas on September 11, 1913

Led the Fordyce (Arkansas) Red Bugs (his high school) to a perfect season and the state championship

Attended the University of Alabama from 1931 to 1935

Served as an assistant coach at Alabama from 1936 to 1940

Served his country in World War II, based in North Africa

Returned after the war to coach Maryland for one year and then Kentucky until 1953 when he jumped ship for Texas A&M in 1953

Left College Station for the University of Alabama and a head coach position that spanned the next 25 years

Died in 1983

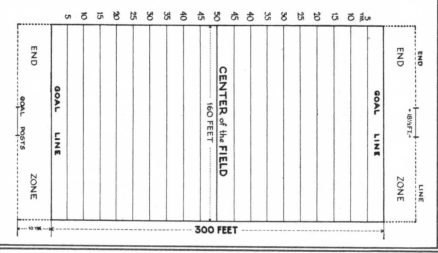

Quotes from
THE INCREDIBLE
GAME

TOM LANDRY

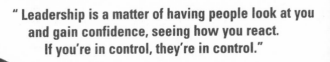

" A winner never stops trying."

" Football is an incredible game.
Sometimes it's so incredible,
it's unbelievable."

" I don't believe in team motivation. I believe in getting a team
prepared so it knows it will have the necessary confidence when it
steps on a field and will be prepared to play a good game."

" I've learned that something constructive comes from every defeat."

" Leadership is a matter of having people look at you
and gain confidence, seeing how you react.
If you're in control, they're in control."

" Setting a goal is not the main thing.
It is deciding how you will go about
achieving it and staying with that plan."

EARL CAMPBELL

" Somebody will always break your records.
It is how you live that counts."

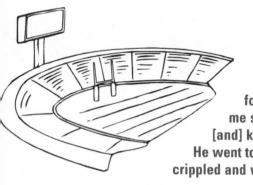

BOB LILLY

- - - - - - - - - - - - - - - -

" I attribute my entire
football career, as far as getting
me started, getting me interested,
[and] keeping me that way [to] my father.
He went to every game even though he was
crippled and wasn't real healthy."

DARRELL ROYAL

- - - - - - - - - - - - - - - -

" Luck is what happens when
   preparation meets opportunity."

" Winning coaches must treat
mistakes like copperheads in the bedclothes—
avoid them with all the energy you can muster."

" Football doesn't build character. It eliminates the weak."

VINCE YOUNG

- - - - - - - - - - - - - - - -

" I feel like I went out there and stayed relaxed,
   poised and had a good time. I was just being Vince,
   like y'all know."

" If they want me to show them more, I'll come work
   out for them."

DO YOU REALLY KNOW YOUR BASEBALL TEAMS?

1. Who holds the record for most at-bats as an Astro? How many did he have?

2. D. Knowles holds the lowest career ERA with the Rangers. What is that ERA?

3. The one millionth run in MLB history was hit by a Houston Astro. Who was that player? When did he do it?

4. Who was the first Houston Astro to throw 20 wins in a season?

5. What three players were elected into the Texas Rangers Hall of fame in 2004?

6. Who has the most stolen bases as a Texas Ranger?

7. Who was the very first manager for the Texas Rangers?

8. Who was the Ranger's first player to win the American League MVP award? When did he win it?

9. Who had 126 RBIs in the AL in 1970?

10. Who was the first Rangers player to have 1,000 career RBIs?

11. While I was a Texas Ranger, I struck out 1,452 batters. Who am I?

12. How many no-hitters did Nolan Ryan pitch while he was a pitcher for the Texas Rangers?

13. Who threw the most strikeouts in a single season while playing for the Astros?

14. Who had 660 at-bats in one season for the Astros? In what year did he achieve this feat?

15. What was the Astros former name?

16. When entering the 1986 NCLS, which Astro had an ERA of 2.22?

17. Leo Durocher was a manager of the Astros during what years?

18. Who was the first Major Leaguer to lose a nine-inning no-hitter on April 23, 1964?

Answers:

1. Craig Biggio, 9813; 2. 2.46; 3. Bob Watson, May 1975; 4. Larry Dierker; 5. Buddy Bell, Ferguson Jenkins, and Tom Vandergriff; 6. Bump Wills; 7. Ted Williams; 8. Jeff Burroughs, 1974; 9. Frank Howard; 10. Juan Gonzalez; 11. Charlie Hough; 12. two; 13. J. R. Richard; 14. Enos Cabell, 1978; 15. Colt 45s; 16. Mike Scott; 17. 1972–1973; 18. Ken Johnson

★ The President—A Baseball Fanatic

President George W. Bush became the general manager of the Texas Rangers in 1989. During his tenure, he oversaw the building of the new stadium in Arlington.

TEXAS HOOPS TRIVIA

Dallas Mavericks

Conference:	Western
Division:	Southwest
Founded:	1980
History:	1980 to present
Arena:	American Airlines Center
City:	Dallas
Team Colors:	Midnight blue, white, and silver
Head Coach:	Avery Johnson
Owner:	Mark Cuban
Championships:	None
Conference Titles:	0
Division Titles:	1 (1987)

San Antonio Spurs

Conference:	Western
Division:	Southwest
Founded:	1967 (joined NBA in 1976)

History: Dallas (Texas) Chaparrals (1967–1973); San Antonio Spurs (1973 to present)

Arena:	AT&T Center
City:	San Antonio
Team Colors:	Silver and black
Head Coach:	Gregg Popovich
Owner:	Peter Holt
Championships:	3 (1999, 2003, 2005)
Conference Titles:	3 (1999, 2003, 2005)
Division Titles:	14 (1978, 1979, 1981, 1982, 1983, 1990, 1991, 1995, 1996, 1999, 2001, 2002, 2003, 2005)

Houston Rockets

Conference:	Western
Division:	Southwest
Founded:	1967

History: San Diego Rockets (1967–1970); Houston Rockets (1970 to present)

Arena:	Toyota Center
City:	Houston
Team Colors:	Red, white, and silver
Head Coach:	Jeff Van Gundy
Owner:	Leslie Alexander
Championships:	2 (1994, 1995)
Conference Titles:	4 (1981, 1986, 1994, 1995)
Division Titles:	4 (1977, 1986, 1993, 1994)

Houston Comets

Conference:	Western
Division:	Southwest
Founded:	1997
Arena:	Toyota Center
City:	Houston
Team Colors:	Red, white, and blue
Head Coach:	Van Chancellor
Owner:	Leslie Alexander
Championships:	4 (1997–2000)
Conference Titles:	4 (1997–2000)
Division Titles:	4 (1977, 1986, 1993, 1994)

Golf in Texas?
It's a Matter of Course

NAME	NOTABLE	CITY
Barton Creek Golf Course	championship golf courses designed by Tom Fazio, Arnold Palmer, and Ben Crenshaw are a tribute to the game of golf and the unique terrain of the Hill Country in Austin; hosts the Barton Creek Austin Canadian Tour Pro-Am Classic for the benefit of golfers against cancer	Austin
Cedar Crest Golf Course	site of the 1927 PGA Championship	Dallas
Colonial Country Club	host of the MasterCard Colonial since 1938; a challenging course with lots of water hazards; high ratings in Golf Digest, Golf Magazine, and Golfweek	Fort Worth
Four Seasons Resort at Las Calinas	hosts the EDS Byron Nelson Championship; the most scenic hole is the seventeenth hole: it has an elevated tee box that faces southeast and offers a panoramic view of the resort, the grounds, and the eighteenth hole in the distance	Irving
Golf Club at Horseshoe Bay Resort	three courses designed by Robert Trent Jones, Sr.	Lake LBJ
Golf Club of Texas	a Lee Trevino-signature course; claims to be the "best golf experience in Texas"	San Antonio
Painted Dunes Golf Course	twenty-seven of the most scenic holes in the American southwest	El Paso
Palmer Course at La Cantera	the first Arnold Palmer-designed course in south Texas; hosts the Valero Texas Open	San Antonio
Redstone Golf Club	designed by Jim Hardy and Peter Jacobsen; opened in December 2002; a naturally wooded terrain is surrounded by wetlands; hosts the Shell Houston Open; the Dick Harmon School of Golf is located here	Humble
Quarry Golf Club	the back nine is located within the confines of a century-old rock quarry	San Antonio
South Padre Island Golf Course	located on Laguna Vista Cove and Laguna Madre	Laguna Vista
Tour 18	uniquely designed by using hole layouts from eighteen of America's top golf courses	Dallas and Houston
White Bluff Resort	designed by Bruce Lietzke	Lake Whitney
Whitestone Golf Club	a public-private venture designed by Jeff Brauer; the hilly, tree-covered property was carved out of 150 acres of rocky terrain and is resplendent in cacti, yucca, and native oak trees	Benbrook

The Two Bens

Two of the Best Golfers in the World

Ben Hogan

Ben Hogan was born in Dublin, Texas, on August 13, 1912. Hogan had a code of work, endurance, and study that never changed throughout his years of playing golf. He once said, "Work never bothered me like it bothers some people." That may have been his secret.

After several close matches in major championships, he won his first major at the 1946 PGA Championship. When he won the 1948 PGA Championship in May and the U.S. Open at Riviera three weeks later, Hogan felt he was at his peak.

Hogan's life changed on February 2, 1949, when a Greyhound bus crossed a center divider and crashed into the car carrying Hogan and his wife, Valerie. Hogan nearly died and suffered permanent leg injuries. Overcoming his injuries, Hogan won the 1950 U.S. Open at Merion in an 18-hole playoff with George Fazio and Lloyd Mangrum. "Merion meant the most," he would say later.

Hogan played only a few tournaments a year, but his best golf was ahead. In 1951, he won his first Masters and the U.S. Open at Oakland Hills. In 1953, he had his greatest year, winning his second Masters, his fourth U.S. Open, and his only British Open. He played his last official event in 1971, and he was inducted into the Texas Sports Hall of Fame in 1970.

Ben Crenshaw

Ben Crenshaw was born in Austin, Texas, on January 11, 1952. His father, a schoolteacher, introduced him to the game of golf. When Crenshaw was eight, his father put him under the guidance of Harvey Penick. "Having Harvey as a teacher had more effect on me than just as a teacher. He taught me so much about life."

After winning seventeen amateur events, including the NCAA title from 1971 to 1973 while an All-American at the University of Texas, Crenshaw had the strongest amateur résumé since Jack Nicklaus. He faced a difficult decision whether to stay in school another year, play the Walker Cup and the U.S. Amateur, or turn pro.

"Not winning a major for my first 11 years was difficult to accept given the number of good chances I had," Crenshaw ruefully concedes in his autobiography. "But in the end, the tough losses made my victories at Augusta even sweeter." Augusta holds many memories for him: "There's simply no place like Augusta. The feeling there is like no other place."

Wampus Cats
vs
Porcupines

Every grade school, high school, and college has a team nickname or mascot. Some names are common, ordinary names, for example: eagles, rams, cougars, tigers, cowboys, pirates, and mustangs. Others are unique. Of the hundreds of high schools in Texas, here are some of the unique school team mascots. (If the city name and school name differ, the city name is given in parentheses.)

Abernathy **Antelope**

Booker **Kiowas**

Brazosport (Freeport) **Exporters**

Breckenridge **Buckaroos**

Calhoun (Port Lavaca) **Sandcrabs**

Cameron Yoe **Yoemen**

Coleman **Bluecats**

Eastwood (El Paso) **Troopers**

Falfurrias **Jerseys**

Grapeland **Sandies**

Fredericksburg **Battlin Billies**

Hamlin **Pied Pipers**

Itasca **Wampus Cats**

Knippa **Rockcrushers**

Lincoln (Port Arthur) **Bumblebees**

Morris Academy (Houston) **Praying Hands**

Munday **Moguls**

Nazareth **Swifts**

Parkland (El Paso) **Matadors**

Port Isabel **Tarpons**

Robstown **Cottonpickers**

Roscoe **Plowboys**

Rotan **Yellow Hammers**

St. Michael Academy (Bryan) **Dragon Slayers**

Somerville **Yeguas**

Springtown **Porcupines**

Van **Vandals**

Winters **Blizzards**

It's Smokin'!

The history of Texas barbecue goes back to German butchers who settled in Central Texas during the mid-1800s. They took a hint from Mexican vaqueros and **emphasized beef**, not pork in their barbecue. Hand-rubbed meat with salt, pepper, and spices cooked at a distance of three to four feet from the fire in pits filled with available hardwoods, including oak, hickory, pecan, and mesquite. The taste was as distinctive as it was delicious.

In the history of barbeque cooking there are two methods: **direct**, where the heat directly cooks the meat grilling and **indirect**, where the heat does not directly sear and cook the meat.

In Texas, the usual preferred way to barbeque is the slow-cooked method.

★ Did You Know?

Texas chefs distinguish between the term barbeque and grilling. Grilling is a fast process over high heat, while barbequing is a very slow process. Most Texans will tell visitors if you are going to a barbeque restaurant and you don't see a pile of wood behind it, keep driving.

Sometimes a smoker will be used to draw smoke past the meat by convection for very slow cooking. This is essentially how barbecue is cooked in most genuine "barbecue" restaurants. Regardless of the method, the meat should be turned several times to ensure complete cooking.

When asked the secret to great barbecue, Bob Roberts, who was called the Dean of Barbeque answered honestly, "I wish I knew. It's the combination of a lot of things—cooking time, seasoning, sauce, and even atmosphere has a lot to do with it."

Associations and Clubs for Serious Barbeque Fans

International Barbeque Cookers Association IBCA

Lone Star Barbeque Society COOKING SCHOOL, McKinney, TX

214-544-2297 or E-mail: suebque@hotmail.com

The Lone Star Barbeque Society's
BARBEQUE CookOff Rules

In Texas, there is a barbeque cookoff contest almost every week.
Most cookoffs follow these rules written by The Lone Star Barbeque Society.

- -

Cookoffs are fair and honest with no one receiving an advantage. All trays are inspected by the Head Judge or his/her representative for conformity with turn-in requirements. A blind judging system is used to ensure anonymity of the cook.

- - - - - - - - - - - - - - - - -

❀ COOKED ON SITE ❯
All meat is brought to the site RAW. No pre-marinating, pre-soaking or pre-spicing. Promoters establish an official Start Time. Contest meat is always subject to inspection by Head Judge and/or promoter.

❀ TURN-IN TIMES ❯
These are posted on site and announced at the cook's meeting. Normal cookoffs usually use one-hour turn-in times. Cookoffs with 65 or more cooks will require hour-and-a-half turn-in times. All turn-in times have a 20 minute window.

❀ TURN IN QUANTITIES ❯
Normal requirements are: seven (7) slices of Brisket, approximately 1/4 to 3/8 inch thick (this is checked at turn-in); seven (7) pork spare ribs. One half of a non-disjointed chicken, skin on. In the case of pork shoulder/butt, 1 1/2 cups "pulled" pork. NOTE: Larger cookoffs may require additional quantities of meat that are determined at time of cookoff.

❀ MARKERS AND GARNISH ❯
Meat only! Absolutely NO garnish or sauce is allowed. The cook is provided with a styrofoam tray with one sheet of foil which is to be placed in the bottom of the tray. The meat is placed on the foil. Nothing may be "puddled" in the tray.

❀ SANITARY CONDITIONS ❯
The Head Judge may disqualify a contestant for unsanitary conditions or entries.

❀ WOOD FIRE ❯
All cooking is to be done on wood or wood products. NO gas or electric cooking heat! Gas or electric lighters, blowers, and/or rotisseries are permitted.

❀ WINDOW ❯
A "window" is an all-inclusive period of time! Therefore, a twenty (20) minute window means ten (10) minutes "before" the turn-in time until ten (10) minutes "after" the turn-in time. This allows for corrections to be made should someone have to return to their site for an additional rib or slice of brisket.

····· GOOD LUCK! ·····

BARBEQUE
Rubs and Marinades
Recipes for some of the best-kept secrets around the Lone Star State.

Hog Rub

1/2 cup ground black pepper
1/2 cup mild chili powder
1/2 cup sugar
1/4 cup coarse salt
4 teaspoons dry mustard
2 teaspoons cayenne

Mix together and store in an airtight container.

This rub is loaded with flavor. The combination of the hot chilies with the rich flavors of the allspice and cinnamon makes this seasoning very similar to a Jerk Rub.

Orange & Onion Marinade

1/3 cup orange marmalade
3 green onions, finely chopped
1/4 cup white wine
1 tablespoon olive oil
1 tablespoon cider vinegar
1 teaspoon Worcestershire sauce
1/2 teaspoon soy sauce

Place all ingredients in a medium saucepan. Allow to simmer on low heat until marmalade has thinned and all ingredients are combined. Allow to cool completely before using as a marinade.

Marinade for wood smoking bird, beef, or pork in an indirect heat smoker. Full wood smoke or partial wood and charcoal. This is especially good for beef brisket.

Lotsa Spice Rub

1/4 cup garlic powder
1/4 cup onion powder
2 tablespoons allspice
2 tablespoons brown sugar
1 tablespoon dried ground chipotle chili
1 tablespoon dried thyme
1 tablespoon cinnamon
2 teaspoons dried lemon zest
1 teaspoon cloves
1 teaspoon nutmeg
1/2 teaspoon hot chili powder

Combine all ingredients and store in an airtight container.

This is a flavorful marinade, which can be used on chicken, pork, and beef. Remember to let the marinade cool considerably before using it on raw meat.

Texas Marinade

1 cup brown sugar, not packed
1 1/2 cups teriyaki sauce
1/4 cup Worcestershire sauce
1/2 teaspoon liquid smoke flavoring
1/4 teaspoon meat tenderizer

In a medium bowl, mix together the brown sugar, teriyaki sauce, Worcestershire sauce, liquid smoke, and meat tenderizer. Pour over meat, and refrigerate in a sealed container. Shake container occasionally to cover meat. Take out of the refrigerator before cooking, and let come to room temperature while the smoker heats up. Never use prepared barbeque sauce with this marinade.

PIG OUT!

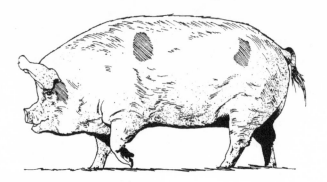

8 Easy Steps for Hog Roasting

1 Place 80 lbs. charcoal into the hog roaster, spreading evenly along the bottom.

2 Pour 1 quart of lighter fluid over the coals in the roaster.

3 Light the coals and let burn down until gray edges form.

4 Place the roaster pan into the roaster.

5 Place the pig on the pan in the roaster.

6 Close the lid and latch it. Opening the lid increases cooking time, so it is a good idea to lock the lid in place.

7 Cooking time is 12 hours. Nothing special is happening so remember, keep the lid closed.

8 After 12 hours begin slicing and serving your hog.

How to Build Your Own Roaster

Partially bury fourteen 8 x 8 x 16 inch cement blocks in a rectangle shape placing three blocks across each end and four blocks along the sides. (Adjust the pit according to the size of your pig.) Stack additional blocks three rows high on the sides of the pit and two rows high on the ends.

Next, construct a two-piece wire mesh rack to envelope a pig that is split down the middle and laid out flat (head and legs removed). This pig rack is a larger version of those that are used for grilling hamburgers.

Suggestion: Use 3/4 inch metal rod in constructing the frame for the rack. Extend two rods approximately 1 1/2 feet at each of the four corners. These extensions will allow the rack to rest on the blocks over the coals and will also be used as turning grips. By placing the turning grips on the end blocks, the pork is closer to the coals. When the heat is more intense, raise the rack by resting the grips on the higher side.

Start the fire in a small ring of rocks outside the pit. When the fire turns to coals, place a half-shovel full of coals inside the cooking pit at each corner.

Secure the carcass within the rack and lay it across the pit allowing the extensions to rest on the low end of the bricks. Turn the pig every 20 minutes and, using a new household mop, baste the meat with salt water each time you turn it. (Salt water will draw the fat from the pork.) Add a half-shovel full of coals to each of the four corner spots as needed. With the open pit method, a 200-pound pig will take up to 18 hours to cook.

★ **When is the Pork Done?**

The National Pork Producers Council now suggests that for medium doneness the internal temperature of pork need only reach 160° F or 170° F for well-done pork. According to Robin Kline, M.S. R.D., director of the Pork Information Bureau for the NPPC, these changes reflect new research based on the fact that pork products are leaner and more healthful today.

While 160° F is a safe temperature for roast pork, a temperature of 170° F for a whole pig will produce a product of superior acceptance.

Pig Roast Barbeque Sauce

INGREDIENTS:
1 qt prepared barbeque sauce
2 qts cider vinegar
4 tbsp salt
1 tbsp sugar
1 1/2 tbsp black pepper
1/4 sm bottle Worcestershire sauce
bay leaf

DIRECTIONS:
Combine all ingredients. Boil for 2 minutes and then simmer sauce for 15 minutes. Baste roasting pig.

Grilling

Rib   Short Loin   Sirloin   Round

Ground Beef | Chuck Roast, Blade Roast | Rib Roast, Rib Steaks: Rib Eye (Delmonico) | Club | T-Bone | Porterhouse | Pin Bone | Flat Bone | Wedge Bone | Rump Roast | Top Round

Arm Roast, Shoulder Roast | Short Ribs | Spare Ribs | Tip | Heel | Bottom Round

Brisket & Shank | Stew | Brisket | Short Ribs & Skirt Steak | Flank Steak, London Broil

Shank | Short Plate | Flank

Grilling is cooking directly over a heat source at a high temperature. For most meats, sear over high heat first, then move to lower heat to finish.

It's important to remember that the proper way to turn meat on a grill is with tongs or a spatula. Never stab the meat with a carving fork—unless you want to drain the flavor-rich juices onto the coals.

Keep yourself organized. Grilling is a relatively quick process, and you don't want to leave the grill to find an essential tool.

Give it a rest. Beef, steak, chicken—almost anything you grill—will improve its flavor if you let it stand for a few minutes before serving. This allows the meat juices, which have been driven to the center of a roast or steak by the searing heat, to return to the surface. The result is a juicier, tastier piece of meat.

• • •

Enjoy!

Choose the Right Cut

• •

Brisket: Cuts of beef from the chest region; these cuts are used to make corned beef or smoked for barbecue.

Chuck: Cuts of beef from the shoulder region or front end; usually used in cooking roasts and commonly referred to as pot roasts.

Round: Cuts of beef from the back end region; usually used in cooking roasts and commonly referred to as rump.

Top Loin Steak: The Beef Loin Top Loin Steak is the first type of steak cut from the beef loin. It is cut from the end of the beef loin that contains the last or 13th rib. The large eye muscle, the rib bone, and part of the backbone identify this steak.

T-Bone Steak: This steak has the characteristic "T" shaped vertebrae and the large eye muscle. The smaller muscle located below the T-bone is the tenderloin.

Porterhouse: The Porterhouse Steak is similar to the Beef Loin T-bone steak. However, the tenderloin muscle is much larger, and an extra muscle is located in the center of the Porterhouse Steak on the upper side.

Tenderloin: The tenderest retail cut from the entire beef carcass is the Beef Loin Tenderloin Steak. This steak has a fine texture, is circular in shape, and is usually about three inches in diameter.

Flank: Cuts of beef usually found as steaks; this is the cut most often used to make London Broil

Sirloin: Cuts of beef from the small back region; sirloin cuts are very versatile and can be found as steaks and roasts.

Sirloin, Pin Bone: The Beef Loin Sirloin Steak, Pin Bone is the first cut from the sirloin area of the Beef Loin. This steak looks much like the beef loin T-bone and porterhouse steaks in that it contains the T-bone, the large eye muscle, and the tenderloin muscle. However, it also contains an oval-shaped bone which you can see in the upper left corner of the steak. This bone is called the pin bone and is the tip portion of the hipbone.

Sirloin, Flat Bone: The Beef Loin Sirloin Steak, Flat Bone is the least valuable type of sirloin steak if both the flat hip and backbones are left in the steak.

Sirloin, Round Bone: The Sirloin Steak, Round Bone is located further back on the sirloin area of the beef loin. This particular sirloin steak has the greatest amount of lean and the least amount of bone.

• • • • • • • • • • • • • • • • • • • •

SOMETHING TO DRINK?

Iced Tea: Today, throughout the United States, there are two traditional iced teas. The only variation between them is sugar. Texans swear by their traditional sweet tea and drink it by the gallons. This tea is not restricted to a summer drink but is served year-round with every meal.

If you order iced tea in a Texas restaurant, you will receive sweet tea. Outside of Texas, in those other states, they serve iced tea unsweetened or "black."

Dr Pepper: The original homegrown soft drink. Dr Pepper is the oldest soft drink in America. Originally made in Morrison's Old Corner Drug Store in Waco, Texas, the drink was first sold to Texans in 1885. Since then it has become a worldwide sensation. If you are a true Pepper aficionado, you might be able to tell the difference in a Dr Pepper from the Dublin, Texas, plant. The Dublin Dr Pepper Bottling Company is the only Dr Pepper bottler that has always used pure cane sugar to sweeten the drink. So, unofficially, Dublin Dr Pepper would be THE Texas Soft Drink.

Coffee: The most indisputable nonalcoholic drink in Texas. Ardent coffee drinkers have been around since the early Texas Revolution years. When coffee was not available, a substitute was made of parched corn, wheat, or okra seeds.

Lone Star Beer: Named National Beer of Texas in 1940. It is a local beer that symbolizes the rich history of Texas. The Lone Star Brewing Company is based in San Antonio.

Metheglin: The name of this drink is derived from the Welsh word *meddyglym* meaning medicinal medicine. This mead with spices and sometimes a honey-based flavor is popular in parts of Texas with Scottish and German ancestry.

Big Red: Originally called Sun Tang Red soda, Big Red was invented in a Waco laboratory in 1937 by Grover C. Thomsen and R. H. Roark, 52 years after Dr Pepper's birth in the same city. The bubble-gum-flavored drink has a passionate following. It's also an essential ingredient for an authentic South Texas barbecue, the perfect quenching antidote to the spicy heat of the meat. The only beverage that consistently outsells Big Red in San Antonio is Coca-Cola. Any Texas kid will tell you, it tastes good.

Texas Wines: Texas wine country produces some of the best wine in the world. Choose a bottle from any local winery. Better yet, stop in during the harvest and choose a new favorite.

Be a **Master of Mixology**

POKER FACE

Ice cubes
1   measure tequila
1/2 measure triple sec or Cointreau
4   measures pineapple juice
1   lime wedge

Almost fill a highball glass with ice cubes. Pour on the pineapple juice, triple sec or Cointreau, and tequila. Stir well and garnish with the lime wedge.

PEPPER EATER

Ice cubes
Broken ice
1   measure tequila
1   measure triple sec or Cointreau
1   teaspoon pepper vodka*
1   measure orange juice
1   measure cranberry juice
1   hot red pepper

Half-fill a cocktail shaker with ice cubes. Pour in the tequila, triple sec or Cointreau, pepper vodka, orange juice, and cranberry juice. Shake well and strain into an old-fashioned glass three-quarters filled with crushed ice. Garnish with the red pepper. Take bets on who will eat their garnish!

*To make your own pepper vodka: steep a hot Mexican or Italian pepper in regular vodka for a few weeks.

TEXAS TEA

1 oz whiskey
1 oz cold tea
1 oz sherry

Shake and strain into a cocktail glass. Decorate with an olive.

MASSACRE

Ice cubes
2   measures tequila
1   teaspoon Campari
4   measures ginger ale

Almost fill a highball glass with ice cubes, add the tequila and Campari. Top with ginger ale, and stir well.

COWBOY COFFEE

4   quarts water
1 1/2 cups freshly ground coffee
1   eggshell
1/2   cup cold water

Bring water to a boil in a large saucepan or coffee pot. Add coffee grounds and eggshell to boiling water. Return to a boil, and then remove from heat and let stand for 2 minutes. Slowly add cold water to settle grounds to the bottom. Strain if desired.

Q. What did Teddy Roosevelt drink at the Menger Hotel when he was recruiting the Rough Riders?

A. A Boilermaker!
Made with a stein of beer and a shot of whiskey.

CHILI

The Official State Dish

"Chili concocted outside of Texas is usually a weak, apologetic imitation of the real thing. One of the first things I do when I get home to Texas is have a bowl of red. There is simply nothing better."

Former President Lyndon B. Johnson

The main differences between Texas chili recipes and those other chili recipes is that "real" Texas chili has no beans and the main ingredient, after the meat, is chili peppers - whether chopped, diced, powdered, or liquefied.

There are as many types of chili as there are regions of the state. A Texas "bowl of red" usually contains coarsely ground or small chunks of beef along with chile peppers, garlic, cumin, onions, and sometimes tomatoes.

The most important ingredient for the creation of great chili is sufficient time and energy for preparing the best name you can for your creation. Most chili recipes are quite similar unless, of course, you use something like turkey, buffalo, sausage, pork, or other exotic meat.

BEST CHILI NAMES (Heard at a chili cookoff): Blazing Saddles Chili, Dragon Fire Chili, Boiled Cigar Butts and Sheep Dip Chili, Triple XXX Chili, Brother Willy & Sister Lilly's Traveling Salvation Army Chili, Voodoo Chili, Chicken Lips Chili, Warlock Chili, Happy Heine Chili, Brimstone Broth, Hillbilly Chili, Scorpion Breath Chili, Wildfire Chili, Capital Punishment Chili, Terk's Tekil-Ya Chili, Vampire Chili, Buffalo Butt Chili, Werewolf Chili, Pineal Nectar Chili, Mephistophelean Chili, Satan's Soup Chili, Ragin' Cajun Chili, Bubba's Big Bang Recycled Chili.

After the chili is named, these are the characteristics that chili judges and consumers evaluate: **taste, consistency, aroma, color,** and **bite.**

TASTE

Taste, above all else, is the most important factor. The taste should combine the meat, peppers, spices, and other ingredients with no particular ingredient being dominant, but rather a blend of the flavors.

CONSISTENCY

Chili must have a good ratio between the sauce and the meat. Dry, grainy, greasy, lumpy and watery are not adjectives you want to describe your chili.

AROMA

Chili must smell great. This is the first step to a great bowl of chili. It indicates what is inside the bowl.

COLOR

Chili is a reddish-brown color. It is not yellow or green.

BITE

Bite or *aftertaste* is the heat created by the various type of chili peppers and chili spices.

Chili is named after the main ingredient, the chili pepper. Capsaicin is the oil in pepper that makes them hot.

Texas Chili Recipes

Real Texas chili does not have beans but if you must, add them when the water is added.

GRANDMA'S TEXAS CHILI

- - - - - - - - - - - - - - - -

2 lbs. lean chili meat
1 onion chopped
1 garlic clove chopped
Salt & pepper to taste
1 tbsp. oregano
1 tbsp. flour
Chili pepper or powder
1 sm. can tomato paste

Brown the meat with the onion and garlic.

Add the chili seasonings, salt and pepper, and oregano during the browning. Add enough chili seasoning until you think it is spicy enough.

Add flour to thicken after the meat is brown.

Add tomato paste to meat after it's brown.

Add enough water to make it soupy.

Let simmer on the stove over low to medium heat to let the flavor become enhanced.

TEXAS-STYLE CHILI

10 lbs. chuck blade steak

1 cup vegetable oil

3 large onions, chopped

9 medium green bell peppers, chopped

15 garlic cloves, minced

3 lbs. ripe tomatoes, peeled and chopped

18 oz. tomato paste

1 cup chili powder

1/4 cup sugar

2 tbsp. salt

2 tbsp. oregano (preferably Mexican oregano)

2 tbsp. ground black pepper

Cut steak into 1/2-inch cubes.

In a very large skillet or Dutch oven, brown the meat in oil, remove to a bowl and set aside.

Add onions, peppers, and garlic to drippings in pan over medium heat. Cook for 10 minutes, stirring occasionally. Add more oil if necessary.

Return the meat to the pan, and add tomatoes and their liquid and the remaining ingredients. Heat to boiling. Reduce heat to low, cover and simmer 1 1/2 hours or until meat is fork tender, stirring occasionally.

TEXAS RED CHILI (HOT)

3 lb. boneless beef round steak, cut into 1 inch cubes

1 lg. onion, finely chopped (about 1 c.)

4 cloves garlic, finely chopped

1/4 cup oil

2 cups tomato puree

2 to 3 tbsp. ground red chiles

1 tsp. cumin seed, ground

1 tsp. ground coriander

2 Anaheim chilies, seeded and chopped

4 Jalapeño chilies, seeded and chopped

Shredded cheddar cheese

Flour tortillas

Cooked pinto beans

Cook and stir beef, onion, and garlic in oil in 4-quart Dutch oven until beef is browned Stir in remaining ingredients except cheese, tortilla, and beans. Heat to boiling. Reduce heat, cover and simmer, stirring occasionally, until beef is tender, about 2 hours. Serve with cheese, tortillas, and beans.

Texas Chili Parlor serves its legendary chili with an adult rating. From "X" for beginner, moving on to "XX" or even "XXX" (sample at your own risk). They even make you sign a release. It's the traditional Lone Star chili.

XXX THAT'S HOT

Texas Chili Parlor 512-472-2828
1409 Lavaca Street • Austin, TX 78701

JON'S REAL TEXAS CHILI

1/4 cup oil

4 lbs. top round, cubed

6 cloves garlic, chopped

2 lg. onions, chopped

2 lg. green peppers, chopped

3/4 oz. cumin

1/4 cup oregano

2 bay leaves

2 tbsp. dried chilies

3 tbsp. flour

1 qt. beef stock

2/3 cup tomato paste

Tabasco

Salt

Heat oil over medium heat. Add beef and sear well. Remove meat and set aside. Add garlic, peppers, and onions and sauté over medium heat 10 minutes. Add cumin, oregano, bay leaves, and chilies. Stir and mix well. Add flour and mix well. Cook 10 minutes over medium low heat until smooth paste is golden brown. Add beef and stir in beef stock, tomato paste and Tabasco to taste. Bring to boil, reduce heat and simmer covered 30 to 45 minutes or until meat is done.

TEXAS JAILHOUSE CHILI

3 lbs. coarse ground beef

1/4 cup olive oil

1 qt. water

3 1/2 tbsp. chili powder

10 cloves finely chopped garlic

1 tsp. ground cumin

1 tsp. oregano or marjoram

3/4 tsp. cayenne pepper

3 tbsp. paprika

1 tbsp. sugar

1 tbsp. salt

3 tbsp. flour

6 tbsp. yellow cornmeal

1 cup water

Brown beef in olive oil. Add 1 quart water; simmer 1 to 1 1/2 hours; drain fat. Add chili powder, garlic, cumin, oregano or marjoram, pepper, paprika, sugar, and salt. Simmer an additional 1/2 hour. Mix flour, cornmeal, and 1 cup water together and add to above mixture. Cook (stirring to prevent sticking) about 5 minutes more to see if additional liquid is needed. **Can be doubled. Freezes well.**

Did You Know?

A molcajete is a mortar and pestle cooking tool that dates as far back as the Aztecs in Mexico, who used it to grind corn into meal.

Pan De Campo
COWBOY BREAD

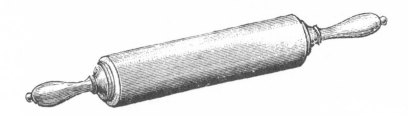

THE OFFICIAL STATE BREAD OF TEXAS

Texas Governor Rick Perry signed a bill into law designating Pan de Campo the official State Bread of Texas. The translation for *pan de campo* is "camp bread." More often, it is called cowboy bread or poncha bread. The simple baking powder bread was a staple of the early Texans. It is still very popular today, and there are quite a few pan de campo cookoffs in South Texas every year.

Classic pan de campo is baked in a Dutch oven. It comes out as a round loaf of bread, about an inch to two inches thick, golden brown on the edges.

The main ingredient in all pan de campo variations is flour. The shortening for the bread is a debated subject in Texas. Original recipes would have used hog lard. The lard imparts little flavor to the bread, but it will make for a moister bread at the end. Other recipes use canola, corn oil, or Crisco as the shortening.

Baking powder is what makes pan de campo dough rise. The reason cowboys made this bread is that baking powder was easy to carry in a saddlebag. The only thing the cowboy needed to worry about was keeping it dry.

As for water verses milk, the recipe will define which to use. It is difficult to tell the difference in the final bread.

SPINDLE TOP *PAN DE CAMPO*

8 cups unbleached all-purpose flour
8 teaspoons baking powder
4 teaspoons salt
4 teaspoons sugar
3 cups milk
1 1/2 cups canola oil

*Mix the dry ingredients in a large bowl.
Mix in the oil as best you can. (After the
initial mix of oil, a pastry cutter was the
best way to proceed.)*

*Add enough milk to make a stiff dough.
Divide into four portions, form into
rounds, and bake.*

RAVEN'S *PAN DE CAMPO*

2 cups unbleached all-purpose flour
1 heaping teaspoon baking powder
1 teaspoon salt
1/3 cup butter-flavored shortening
Water

*Mix the dry ingredients in a large bowl.
Cut in the shortening with pastry cutter
until a cornmeal-like texture results.*

*Add just enough water to get a thick dough
that comes away from the sides of the bowl.
Turn out on a floured surface and knead
just until it comes together smoothly.*

*This recipe will make about a dozen
biscuit-size portions, or you can form the
dough into one round no more than one
inch thick. In a conventional oven, bake
at 400°F until golden brown.*

VALLEY-STYLE *PAN DE CAMPO*

4 cups unbleached all-purpose flour
2 tsp. salt
1/4-1/2 teaspoon baking powder
1/2 cup shortening
Hot water

*Mix the dry ingredients in a large bowl.
Cut in the shortening. Add just enough
hot water to make a thick dough.
Turn the dough out on a floured surface
and knead two to three minutes or until
smooth. Do not overwork it.*

*Divide the dough into two portions.
Let it rest covered with a damp cloth
for 15 to 20 minutes.*

*Form into rounds and bake.
(Here it is up to you as to the form
of baking used, Dutch oven or
conventional oven.) Conventional oven
should be about 350°F. Bake until
golden brown.*

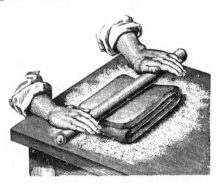

Cock-A-Doodle-Moo, Chicken Fried Steak

It is hard to get more Texan than chicken fried steak. Chicken fried steak or country fried steak is associated with soul food and southern cuisine, and particularly with Texas.

The quality of the beef will define how good this dish will be. This recipe calls for cube steaks, but good round steak that you have asked the butcher to run through the tenderizer or that you have tenderized yourself with a mallet (no big deal and can be a real stress reliever) can be even better. Rarely would a high quality cut of meat be used for this dish.

Chicken fried steak, or CFS as it is affectionately known, is the reigning queen of comfort food in Texas. Every city, town, and village in Texas takes pride in their CFS. Some, admittedly, are better than others. Texans have a unique way of rating restaurants that serve CFS. The restaurants are rated by the number of pickup trucks that are parked out in front. Never stop at a one-pickup place, as the steak will have been frozen and factory breaded. A two-and-three, pickup restaurant is not much better. A four-and-five pickup place is a must-stop restaurant, as the CFS will be fresh and tender with good sopping gravy.

If you want to try to make this in your own kitchen, here is the recipe.

TEXAS-CHICKEN FRIED STEAK

4 tenderized beef cutlets ("cube steaks")
OR 1 round steak, with fat removed,
that you've tenderized yourself

1 egg
1/4 cup milk
all-purpose flour

cooking oil or melted Crisco
1/2 teaspoon salt
1/4 teaspoon ground black pepper
1/4 teaspoon paprika
1/4 teaspoon white pepper

Beat the combined egg and milk and set aside. Mix the salt, black pepper, paprika, and white pepper and sprinkle on both sides of beef cutlets.

Dredge the cutlets in the flour, shaking off the excess. Then dip each cutlet in the egg/milk mixture, then back in the flour. (You are going to get your hands messy here, so take your rings off.) Set cutlets aside on a piece of waxed paper.

Heat the cooking oil in a large cast-iron or other heavy skillet over medium-high heat for a few minutes. Oil should be about a half-inch deep in the pan. Check the temperature with a drop of water; if it pops and spits back at you, it's ready.

With a long-handled fork, carefully place each cutlet into the hot oil. Protect yourself (and your kitchen) from the popping grease that results. Fry cutlets on both sides, turning once, until golden brown. Reduce heat to low, cover and cook 4 or 5 minutes until cutlets are done through. Drain cutlets on paper towels.

Need Gravy?
We've Got You Covered

*T*exas has gravy to go with every meal. At breakfast, there is Sawmill gravy, to eat with biscuits, pan gravy to eat with dinner, and cream gravy or pot roast gravy at supper. There is even giblet gravy to cover Thanksgiving. If you're lost without your mama's recipes, here are the basics to get you through a normal day.

Cream Gravy

Recommended for Chicken Fried Steak

After the cutlets are removed from the pan, pour off all but about 2 tablespoons of oil, keeping as many as possible of the browned bits in the pan. Heat the oil over medium heat until hot.

Sprinkle 3 tablespoons flour (use the leftover flour from the chicken fried steak recipe—waste not, want not) in the hot oil. Stir with a wooden spoon, quickly, to brown the flour.

Gradually stir in 3/4 cup milk and 3/4 cup water, mixed together, stirring constantly with the wooden spoon and mashing out any lumps. Lower heat, and gravy will begin to thicken. Continue cooking and stirring a few minutes until gravy reaches desired thickness. Check seasonings and add more salt and pepper according to your taste.

Note to Cream Gravy novices: Gravy-making is an inexact science. Cream gravy is supposed to be thick, but if you think it is too thick, add more liquid until you are satisfied with it.

Sawmill Gravy

Sausage, Biscuits, and Sawmill Gravy the Perfect Breakfast

1 pound pork sausage (can be less, but you need at least enough to make 2 tablespoons of drippings)

3 tablespoons all-purpose flour

2 cup milk

Pepper to taste

Crumble the sausage and fry it until it is brown. Remove it from the skillet to drain on paper towels. Reserve 2 tablespoons of drippings in the skillet.

Over low to medium heat, add the flour to the pan drippings, stirring constantly so that the flour "cooks" for about a minute. Gradually add the milk, stirring constantly until smooth and thickened. Stir in the pepper and cooked, crumbled sausage, and cook until mixture is hot. Serve over biscuits.

Basic Pan Gravy

2 tablespoons meat drippings

2 tablespoons all-purpose flour

1 cup liquid-broth, water or meat juices

Salt and pepper to taste

After the meat is removed from the pan and put in a warm place, pour off all but 2 tablespoons of the pan juices in the skillet. If you're not sure about how much is left in the pan, pour off all the drippings and measure 2 tablespoons back into the skillet. Heat up the drippings over medium-low heat.

Sprinkle the flour over the heated drippings, and stir it constantly so that the flour "cooks" for about a minute. Then gradually add the liquid, stirring constantly, until the gravy begins to thicken and bubble. Add the salt and pepper. Remove the skillet from the heat, pour the gravy into your prettiest gravy boat, and you're done.

The 6-pound
STEAK DARE

Many Try, Few Succeed

In Texas, there are restaurants where they offer you a challenge. **The 6-pound steak dare: eat it in 75 minutes and it is free.** That is 96 ounces of meat consumed in a one hour and 15 minute period. Many try to finish, however few succeed. Keep in mind that the USDA food guide pyramid recommends 3 ounces as a serving size for beef.

⇒ Tips for Cooking Any Steak ⇐

✻ To test for doneness, press the meat with your finger. Rare meat will be soft and wobbly, medium will have a springy firmness and well-done will feel very firm and unyielding.

✻ A steak will cook a little after you remove it from the grill or oven, so stop broiling when the steak tests slightly less done than desired.

✻ For great results every time, use an instant-read kitchen thermometer. Insert the thermometer in the thickest part of your steak, hamburger, or chops away from any bone or marbling. Thermometer readings should be 120°F to 125°F for rare, 130°F to 135°F for medium-rare, and 140°F to 145°F for medium.

✻ Although steaks are optimum in flavor and texture when cooked to no more than medium doneness, some people prefer their steaks well-done. The internal temperature for medium-well steak is 155°F and well-done 160°F.

✻ Keep in mind that overcooking causes greater shrinkage and decreased tenderness.

✻ Turn your steak when the meat juices start to bubble up through the meat to the top of the steak.

What is marbling?

Marbling is white flecks of fat within the meat muscle. The greater amount of marbling in beef, the higher the grade because marbling makes beef more tender, flavorful, and juicy.

How do you want it cooked?

RARE

A rare steak is red inside. Its center is warm, but not much more. If vegetarians are offended by the sight your rare steak, you got it right. Press on your forearm near the elbow to simulate the springiness of a rare steak.

MEDIUM-RARE

A medium-rare steak is red in the center but completely heated. The outer rim is pink instead of red. Press on your forearm a little farther from the elbow to feel the resistance of a medium-rare steak.

MEDIUM

The center of a medium steak has red in the center, but the most of the steak is pink. Press on the middle of your forearm to simulate the resistance of a steak cooked to medium.

MEDIUM-WELL

A medium-well steak has the slightest trace of red in the center. It is almost all pink but not quite dried out. The resistance most of the way down your arm resembles the resistance of a medium-well steak.

WELL-DONE

A well-done steak has no red and some would like little or no pink inside. It has very little springiness to it.

Make Your Own Beef Jerky

You will need a one-pound beef flank or round steak, soy sauce, garlic salt, and pepper. Trim all visible fat from the steak. Slice with the grain into 1/8-inch thick strips. Dip strips into soy sauce and place them on a wire rack over a shallow pan. Season with garlic salt and pepper. Bake in 350° F oven until internal temperature reaches 160° F. Reduce oven temperature to 140 to 150° F and continue to cook for 8 to 10 hours or until dry and chewy. If using a food dehydrator, roast in oven until internal temperature is 160° F, and then follow directions for your dehydrator.

Another method is to slice and then marinate the beef for 3 to 4 hours in the following marinade: 1 tsp. liquid smoke, 3 tsp. soy sauce, 2 tsp. Worcestershire sauce, 2 tsp. water, 2 tsp. salt, coarsely ground pepper to taste, 1/4 tsp. hot pepper sauce. Then follow the above directions for baking.

Tips

1 Put beef in freezer for 15 minutes prior to preparation to make it easier to slice.

2 When baking, keep oven door slightly ajar so the jerky will dry and not cook.

3 Store jerky in a sealed container in the refrigerator for food safety purposes.

★ Think Beef

LEAN BEEF HAS ONLY ONE MORE GRAM OF SATURATED FAT THAN A SKINLESS CHICKEN BREAST. AND IT HAS SIX TIMES MORE ZINC, THREE TIMES MORE IRON, AND EIGHT TIMES MORE VITAMIN B12. SO YOU CAN EAT HEALTHY, AND **IT DOESN'T TASTE LIKE IT.**

• • • ❀ • • •

www.BeefItsWhatsForDinner.com

Natíve Foreign Food

Tex-Mex is the fusion of native Texan food and Mexican food into an entirely new cuisine. This popular cuisine is neither Texan nor Mexican. It is the original "Native Foreign Food." When traditional Mexican food crossed the border into Texas restaurants and became "Americanized," a food frenzy followed.

Why not? The food is filling, vibrant, tasty, and usually inexpensive. Tex-Mex restaurants are popular because they combine the familiar Wild West of movies with the romantic Latin setting of a local cantina. Combination platters allow the guest to try many different entrees while sipping on their favorite flavored margarita.

Navigating through a Tex-Mex menu can be confusing. Here are a few Tex-Mex terms for your next night out.

ANCHO CHILE
The dried version of the popular POBLANO chilies. The sweetest of all the dried chilies with a slightly fruity flavor. Ancho has a mild paprika flavor, with sweet to moderate heat. Mostly used for making sauces.

BURRITO
A large (10") flour tortilla filled with ingredients such as beef, beans, chicken, or pork. The ends are tucked under to seal it. They are eaten plain or topped with cheese, salsa, lettuce, tomatoes, and guacamole. If fried, they are now called CHIMICHANGAS.

COMAL
Cast iron, round, flat griddle used in making TORTILLAS.

FLAUTA
Translates literally to "flute." This is a corn tortilla that has been stuffed with beef, chicken, pork, or even beans—then rolled and pinned, then deep-fried until crisp. It looks like a tube when finished. They are usually served two or three to a plate with lettuce, cheese, and guacamole.

FRIJOLES
Beans, southern-grown pinto beans. Assume they are refried unless listed as BORRACHO or RANCHERO style.

HUEVOS
Simply, eggs.

PUERCO
Spanish, Tex-Mex, and Mexican for PORK. Used extensively in Tex-Mex cooking, the most common use of puerco is in TAMALES.

QUESO

Cheese. In Tex-Mex cooking, any type of cheddar is the first choice. This is the primary difference between Mexican Food and Tex-Mex food. Mexican food uses goat cheese; Tex-Mex uses chedder.

SALSA

Sauce, refers generally to a tomato based condiment. Uncooked salsa as in "pico de gallo" is called "salsa CRUDA" or "salsa FRESCA."

SERRANO CHILE

A small (1 1/2 inches) fresh HOT, pepper. As it matures, it will turn red, then yellow. Some Texans pop them in their mouths like candy.

TACO

A Mexican or Tex-Mex "sandwich" eaten as an entree or snack. They are made with corn or flour tortillas folded over. Any filling can be used.

TORTA

Mexican "sub" sandwich that is made on a "BOLILLO" which is a white or wheat roll.

TOSTADA

Tostada means "toasted chip." They are served as an appetizer, snack, or meal. Many restaurants put beans, meats, cheeses, and whatever else they can think of on top of them.

Try This

Deep-Fried Ice Cream

20 ounces chocolate chip ice cream
2 cups 4-grain flake cereal
(or Corn Flakes), crushed
1 1/2 tablespoons sugar
3 1/2 teaspoons ground cinnamon
2 eggs
1 teaspoon water
Oil for deep-frying
Cinnamon mixed with sugar

Form ice cream into 4 balls. Place in baking pan and freeze solid, 2 hours or longer. Mix cereal, sugar, and cinnamon. Divide equally between 2 pie plates or other shallow containers. Beat eggs with water.

Roll each ice cream ball in cereal mixture and press coating into ice cream. Dip coated ball in egg wash, then roll in second container of cereal mixture. Again press coating onto ice cream. Freeze coated ice cream balls solid, 4 to 6 hours.

Deep-fry frozen, coated ice cream balls 30 to 45 seconds. Drain on towel and place in decorative bowl. Top with dollop of whipped cream and decorate with cherry.

Yield: Makes 4 servings. Enjoy!

WE LOVE OUR
Hard-Shelled Nuts

The only native commercially grown nut in Texas is the pecan. It grows in most of the state's river valleys and is found in 152 counties. The word pecan is from the Algonquian *peccan* for **"hard-shelled nut,"** The pecan tree has been the state tree since 1919. Eighty percent of the world's pecans are produced in the United States. Last year that equaled 400 million pounds. The top producing states are-number-one ranked Georgia, followed by Texas. Occasionally Texas ranks first with an average crop of 60 million pounds. The following are recipes offered by the Texas Pecan Growers; of course, they are best served with Texas pecans.

EASY MICROWAVE PECAN BRITTLE

1   cup sugar
1/2 cup light corn syrup
1   cup pecans
1   teaspoon butter or margarine
1   teaspoon vanilla extract
1   teaspoon baking soda

Combine sugar and corn syrup in 1 1/2 quart glass mixing bowl, stirring well. Microwave on high for 4 minutes. Stir in pecans. Microwave on high 5 to 7 minutes, until lightly browned. Stir in butter and vanilla. Microwave 1 more minute. Stir in soda. Pour mixture onto a lightly greased baking sheet. Cool. Break into pieces and store in airtight container. Makes about 3/4 pound.

HONEY PECAN PORK CHOPS

1 1/4 lbs. boneless pork loin, pounded thin and sliced into cutlets
1/2   cup all-purpose flour
      Salt, pepper to taste
2-3   tablespoons butter or margarine
1/4   cup honey
1/2   cup chopped pecans

In a shallow dish, mix together flour, salt, and pepper. Dredge cutlets in flour, shaking off excess flour. In a large skillet, melt butter over medium heat. Add cutlets and cook 3 to 4 minutes per side or until brown. Transfer to a warm plate. Add honey and pecans to dripping in pan. Heat over medium heat, stirring constantly, until pecans are lightly browned. To serve: place cutlets on a serving platter and top with sauce. Yield: 4-6 servings.

TRADITIONAL PECAN PIE

4   **eggs, beaten slightly**

1   **cup pecan halves or pieces**

2/3 **cup sugar**

1/3 **cup melted butter**

1   **dash cinnamon**

1   **dash salt**

1   **cup light corn syrup**
     Unbaked pie crust

Beat eggs. Add remaining ingredients including pecans. Pour into 9-inch unbaked pie shell. Bake at 350° for 50 to 60 minutes or until knife inserted halfway between center and edge comes out clean.

Did You Know?

The Texas Pie Supper is an ingenious spin on the fundraiser called a pie supper. The local group, whether it be the PTA, church social, or volunteer fire department, hold a pie supper to raise funds. They bake enough pies to feed the city of Dallas and then they invite politicians to come to the event and speak and bid on the pies. The highest bidder is then allowed to speak to the group for a longer period of time. The system works extremely well in years with hotly contended close races. East Texas is credited with the birth of the idea of how to get money from a politician's pocket.

The Pecan Sheller's Strike of 1938

On January 31, 1938, 12,000 San Antonio pecan shellers went on strike to protest a wage cut and terrible working conditions. Before the strike, a typical wage ranged between two and three dollars a week. Beyond health concerns at the plant, 148 deaths from Tuberculosis for each 100,000 persons in San Antonio were blamed at least partially on the fine dust that was released from the 400 shelling plants in that city alone. Soon after the strike ended, Congress passed the Fair Labor Standards Act, establishing a minimum wage of twenty-five cents an hour. Despite efforts to protect shellers' jobs, cracking machines replaced more than 10,000 shellers in San Antonio shops in a three-year period.

The **Fritos** Bandwagon

*E*lmer Doolin ate at a San Antonio restaurant in 1932, and what he ate changed the face of snacking. Elmer was so taken with the corn chips served with his lunch that he paid $100 for the recipe. That same year, armed with the recipe and thirty-nine retail accounts, Doolin began to manufacture the corn chips under his new company's name, The Frito Corporation.

The first company newsletter, the Frito Bandwagon, and a research and development laboratory followed in the next few years. Frito diversified, made potato chips, and bought a chili company out of Dallas. In 1961, Frito merged with the Lay Company and in 1965 became part of the Pepsico Corporation. During the 1990s, the company was number one in the world in salted snack foods.

Frito Pie has been a popular dish in Texas for generations. There are two versions, one quick and easy and one baked. The first version has three steps. Split open the top of a bag of Fritos. Pour in hot chili, onions and cheese. Shake and eat it. This version is not as effective since the packaging has changed from the insulated bags of yesteryear. Another version requires baking.

INGREDIENTS: 3 cups Fritos corn chips, 3/4 cup chopped onion, 1 cup grated cheddar cheese, and 2-1/2 cups chili. Spread the Fritos in a baking dish and layer the rest of the ingredients over the chips. Bake in a 350° oven until bubbly. Eat and enjoy.

How well do you know Fritos? Take this Quiz

1 Who is the Frito Bandito?

2 Who was the famous voice actor we heard when the Frito Bandito sang, before the end of his reign?

3 Can you name all the types of Fritos?

ANSWERS: 1. The cartoon mascot for Fritos corn chips from 1967 to 1971. 2. Mel Blanc 3. Original, Chili Cheese, Flamin' Hot, Barbeque, Sabrositas (lime & chile), King Size, Scoops (Wider chips intended for dipping) and Hoops (Go snacks).

The Ultimate Progressive Dinner
VISIT THESE TEXAS FOOD CAPITALS

Athens - *Blackeyed peas*

Alvord - *Annual Watermelon Festival since 1922, now replaced by Pioneer Days*

Balmorhea - *World Championship Frijole Cookoff*

Barstow - *Won a silver medal for grapes at the 1904 World's Fair*

Caldwell - *"Kolache Capital of Texas"*

Centerville - *Blackeyed Pea Festival from 1937 until WWII*

Crystal City - *"Spinach Capital of the World"*

Commerce - *Crawfish Festival in May*

Conroe - *Cajun Catfish Festival in October*

Cotulla - *"The Mother of All Sweet Onions": The Texas Grano 50*

Elgin - *"Hot Guts"*

Flatonia - *Chili*

Floresville - *"Peanut Capital of Texas"*

Fredericksburg - *Peaches*

Gilmer - *Yams. The Yamboree is perhaps the oldest food festival in the state.*

Golden - *Sweet Potato Festival on the fourth Saturday of October*

Gorman - *Gorman Peanut Festival*

Floyd County - *Punkin Festival*

Hempstead - *Watermelon*

Jacksonville - *"Tomato capital of the world" early 1900's*

Iago - *Cane*

La Grange, Monument Hill - *The Black Bean Episode*

Lockhart - *Barbecue Capital of Texas*

Lufkin - *Annual Southern Hushpuppy Cookoffs*

Luling - *Watermelon*

Malakoff - *Cornbread*

McDade - *Watermelon*

Medina - *Apples*

Mission - *Texas Citrus Fiesta, an annual celebration in January*

Mykawa - *Rice*

Oatmeal - *Oatmeal*

Pasadena - *Strawberry Capital, annual Strawberry Festival*

Pearsall - *"Home of the Potato Fest"*

Pecos - *Cantaloupes*

Poteet - *Strawberries*

Putnam - *The source of the Burkett Papershell Pecan*

San Benito - *Cabbage Day*

San Saba - *Pecan*

Seagraves - *"The Caged Egg Production Center of the World" – 1950s*

Sheridan - *Fig Capital*

Terlingua - *Chili Cookoff*

Weslaco - *Onions*

Weslaco - *Weslaco's fruit, vegetable, and flower show*

South Texas - *Citrus*

169

TEXAS is for  FOOD LOVERS

Annual Events Throughout Texas

Epicurean Evening

Houston

Join the Clear Lake Chamber of Commerce for a "Taste of Space" and sample from dozens of area restaurants and clubs.

Jalapeño Festival

Laredo

The Jalapeño Festival features the famous waiter's race, wherein waiters from both Texas and Mexico see who can reach the finish line first carrying a tray with a glass of champagne and an open bottle. There is also a jalapeño-eating contest.

Savor Dallas

Dallas

An international experience of wine, food, spirits, cooking seminars, and the arts. Featuring star chefs of Dallas and renowned friends.

Houston Livestock & Rodeo Show

Houston

The largest livestock exposition and biggest rodeo in the world. Includes the World's Championship Bar-B-Que Contest. Three days of cooking and competition, luring 140,036 guests.

Oysterfest

Fulton

The first weekend in March, Oysterfest features carnival rides, games, food, men's and women's raw oyster eating contests, live music, decorated oyster contest, oyster-shucking contest.

World's Largest Rattlesnake Round-Up

Sweetwater

Snake hunts, Miss Snake Charmer, snake handling shows, fried rattlesnake meat, Brisket & Chili Cook-off, Rattlesnake Meat Eating Contest.

Annual Crawfish Crawl and Festival

Clear Lake

Crawfish Crawl, Gumbo Cook-Off, crawfish eating contests, entertainment.

Texas Hill Country Wine & Food Festival

Austin

Established in 1986, this is the oldest and largest wine and food festival in the Lone Star State and is distinctively defined by its connection to Texas culture, tradition, flavors, and hospitality. Every April there is a four day-long celebration of food and wine throughout Austin and the scenic Hill Country.

Poteet Strawberry Festival
Poteet

The Poteet Strawberry Festival® is one of the oldest, most popular events in the state, and is recognized as the largest agricultural festival in Texas as well as one of the most exciting, most dynamic festivals in the Greater Southwest.

The Grand Wine & Food Affair
Houston

A festival to provide knowledge, enjoyment, and exposure to fine wines and foods. Highlights the great chefs of the world and the culinary traditions that have been enhanced by the rich ethnic diversity of our region. Enjoy a variety of entertaining events from winemaker dinners, an elegant grand tasting, casual sip & stroll, cooking demonstrations, and wine seminars.

Annual Pasadena Strawberry Festival
Pasadena

Strawberry Festival Parade (May 13), Largest Strawberry Shortcake, Carnival, Bar-B-Q Cookoff, Washer Pitch Contest, Mud Volleyball Tournament.

Gumbo Cookoff & Cajun Music
Anhalt

Gumbo Cookoff, fresh boiled crawfish and shrimp from Louisiana, Cajun food, and three Cajun bands.

Luling Watermelon Thump
Luling

Watermelon seed spitting contest, melon eating contests, music, midway, food, arts & crafts, car show, etc.

Annual Cajun Festival
Grand Prairie

The food will be Cajun-style all the way, featuring traditional South Louisiana favorites such as spicy, boiled crawfish, jambalaya, red beans & rice, gumbo, and more.

Wine Week in The Woodlands
The Woodlands

Events feature renowned local, regional and national chefs as well as respected winemakers and experts from around the globe.

Annual Houston Hot Sauce Festival
Houston

This sizzling festival draws over 20,000 Chiliheads to the area. Hot sauce, salsa, spices, marinades, chips, dips, jam, jellies, pickles, peppers, bloody mary mix, condments, gourmet food, recipes, etc.

Dallas Wine & Food Festival
Dallas

Award-winning wines from around the world, food tastings, informative seminars, chef demonstrations, and author book signings. Experience the latest trends in home entertaining and dining out; rub elbows with vintners, chefs, and culinary experts.

TAILGATING TEXAS Style

Understand the Rules
★ ★ ★ ★ ★ ★ ★ ★ ★ ★ ★ ★ ★ ★ ★

Dress in team colors.

Plan your menu.

Make a list of the items you want to take along.

Plan to arrive three to four hours early and stay one to two hours after the game.

Find a good spot to park.

Fly a flag on a very high pole so friends can find you.

Decorate your tailgate site with team pennants and other team stuff.

Meet your tailgate neighbors, throw the football with friends, read the Sunday paper, and have a good time.

Food should be ready 1 1/2 hours before the game starts.

Leave area clean.

TOP 10 MUST HAVES AT A TAILGATE PARTY
★ ★ ★ ★ ★ ★ ★ ★ ★ ★ ★ ★ ★ ★ ★ ★

10 Jumper cables—After a great tailgate party, some would love to stay in the parking lot forever...but not everyone.

9 Toilet paper—The MVP (most valuable product) of the parking lot. Don't get caught with your pants down in a Port-A-Potty with no TP.

8 Plastic trash bags—A dedicated tailgater always respects their surroundings and leaves it clean.

7 Extra ice—There is no excuse to ever run out of ice. Just bring a full extra ice chest and enjoy.

6 Rain gear—When everybody else is in their car or truck, you'll be cookin'!

5 First aid kit—Just in case that football hits you in the head.

4 Sun block—You might burn the food, but there's no excuse for cooking yourself.

3 A friend—Change the life of a loved one. Bring them to their first tailgate party.

2 Comfortable shoes—Sometimes we forget how much we visit, and with the right shoes, you can walk to your stomach's content.

1 Antacid—With all the foods consumed at the tailgate, we need some help. Remember defense wins championships.

Ooh! Aah!
The Natural Wonders of Texas

Adventure-seeking naturalists will have lots of fun in the Lone Star State.

The Lighthouse,
Palo Duro State Park

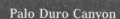

Palo Duro Canyon

Palo Duro Canyon is in the Texas Panhandle, southeast of Amarillo. The state park opened in 1934, and the northern 18,000+ acres are accessible to the public. At 120 miles long, 20 miles wide at some points, and a maximum depth of 800 feet, Palo Duro has been called the **Grand Canyon of Texas**.

The canyon was formed from erosion of the Prairie Dog Town Fork of the Red River. Wind and water erosion over thousands of years created remarkable formations, including

Hoodoo You Know?

A hoodoo is a tall column, pillar, or pinnacle formed naturally from the erosion of soft sedimentary rock. It is known for its distinct and sometimes grotesque shape.

the **Lighthouse** hoodoo, a natural column of rock in the shape of a lighthouse. Caves and other hoodoos are abundant throughout the canyon.

The Palo Duro Canyon is the site of the oldest cattle ranch in the Texas Panhandle, the **JA Ranch**. This ranch was originally established as a partnership between Irish landowner John Adair, his wife Cornelia, and Charles Goodnight. Goodnight had served as the Adairs' guide during a buffalo hunt on the Colorado plains in 1874, and had told the Adairs of the canyon's benefits, such as plains for cattle's summer grazing and shelter for wintering.

In 1877, they formed a five-year partnership with Goodnight providing the ranching know-how, and Adair the capital for purchasing the land. Goodnight suggested using John Adair's initials for the ranch's name, and thus the brand "JA" was formed. In 1934, the State

173

of Texas bought the upper section, now the Palo Duro Canyon State Park.

CANYON FACTS

Palo Duro Canyon State Park, 11450 Park Road 5, Canyon, TX 79015

Activities: camping, horseback riding, hiking, nature study, bird-watching, mountain biking, scenic drives

Camping reservations: 512-389-8900

Park information: 806-488-2227; 800-792-1112; pdc@palodurocanyon.com

Pioneer Amphitheatre box office: 806-655-2181

Chuckwagon Restaurant: 806-488-2152

Old West Stables (an ideal way to explore the canyon is on horseback): 806-488-2180

Heard Natural Science Museum and Wildlife Sanctuary

Located in McKinney, a few miles north of Dallas, the Heard Wildlife Sanctuary provides habitats for native and endemic wildlife, trains naturalists and land stewards in good land management, and preserves the ecosystems of Collin County. There are over four miles of public-access trails among the 289 acres. You'll encounter different sights, sounds, colors, textures, and patterns, along with birds, insects, animals, prairie grass, and flowers.

One of the most spectacular features is the native plant garden. The garden has a huge and glorious display of trees, shrubs, grasses, vines, and other plants that are native to Texas. In early spring, exotic and spicy fragrances fill the air.

The indoor exhibits in the museum provide interac-tive opportunities to learn about Texas's natural environment. A few of the exhibits include rocks, minerals, and fossils of Texas; North Texas ecosystems; and venomous snakes.

Heard Natural Science Museum and Wildlife Sanctuary, 1 Nature Place, McKinney, TX 75069

General information: 972-562-5566; info@heardmuseum.org
A great place for school field trips—over 20,000 students visit every year.

The Colorado River Trail

When most people think of the Colorado River, they think of Colorado, Arizona, and the Grand Canyon. Well, there is a Colorado River in Texas, and it stretches some 600 miles from San Saba (in central Texas, northwest of Austin) to the Gulf of Mexico.

The back roads of the Colorado River Trail are breathtaking. Peer out the window at the gorgeous water and lake views. You might want to charter a boat to float down the river trail. There are docks located in many towns along the trail. Big ranches and towering cliffs surround the river trail, and wildflowers frame the picturesque countryside.

Get a free guide to the river by sending your name and address to the Lower Colorado River Authority (LCRA)
P. O. Box 220, Austin, TX 78767

Nacogdoches Trail

The Nacogdoches Azalea Trail in the oldest city in Texas is a tour for all your senses. Fix your eyes on a kaleidoscope of colors, hear the sound of birds singing, and smell the journey of exploration. The region is famous for birding trails, historic sites, and some of Texas's largest lakes.

Nacogdoches Convention and Visitors Bureau 200 East Main, Nacogdoches, TX 75961

Information: 888-OLDEST-TOWN; info@visitnacogdoches.org

East Texas Wildflower Trail

A colorful tradition resumes every spring as the wildflowers bloom. It is a living Technicolor tapestry, full of wonder and surprise. The Lady Bird Johnson Wildflower Center is the ideal starting point. Towns and communities throughout the area, including Early, Johnson City, Blanco, San Sabo, Brady, Llano, Mason, Burnet, Lampasas, and Fredericksburg, to name a few, host a variety of events during the wildflower season.

The diversity of East Texas, from almost impenetrable forest and bramble to manmade lakes, makes the scenery breathtaking. In addition, the Alabama-Coushatta Indian Reservation near Livingston gives visitors an opportunity to learn about the culture of the Native Americans in the area.

Lady Bird Johnson was an advocate of maintaining the natural landscape: "The environment is where we all meet: where we all have a mutual interest; it is the one thing all of us share. It is not only a mirror of ourselves. It is a focusing lens on what we can become."

Lady Bird Johnson Wildflower Center
4801 La Crosse Avenue, Austin, TX 78739

Information: 512-292-4100

Aransas Wildlife Refuge

Established in 1937, the Aransas Wildlife Refuge protects wildlife along the coastal regions of Texas. The land is constantly being reshaped by storms and tidal surges from the Gulf of Mexico. The refuge consists of over 70,000 acres, mostly on the Blackjack Peninsula. The refuge is home to cranes, alligators, deer, and many other species. Whooping cranes live in the refuge from late October to mid April. The peninsula has scattered blackjack oaks, grasslands, and thickets over deep, sandy soils.

Aransas National Wildlife Refuge, P.O. Box 100, Austwell, TX 77950; the actual refuge is located about 35 miles northeast of Rockport.

Information: 361-286-3559

Facilities: paved tour road, wildlife interpretive center museum, 40-foot observation tower, miles of walking trails, picnic area

Stephen Austin Interpretive Trail

Southwest of Nacogdoches in the Angelina National Forest is the Stephen F. Austin Experimental Forest Interpretive Trail System. The U.S. Forest Service has developed this area into a wildlife habitat and silviculture (forest) laboratory. The primary objective is wildlife and timber management research. The trail was developed in 1997 and takes visitors into some of the most dynamic and scenic areas of the 2,560-acre forest. There are two trails: The Jack Creek Loop is a 0.8-mile trail among the forest and Jack Creek. The Management Loop is a 2-mile loop that shows forest management practices at various stages. Wildlife viewing abounds on both trails, including 80 species of butterflies and 150 species of birds. There are also approximately 30 indigenous mammals to the forest.

USDA Forest Service, Wildlife Habitat and Silviculture Lab, 506 Hayter, Nacogdoches, TX 75961
Information: 936-569-7981

Fisherman's Wharf

Port Aransas is the home of Fisherman's Wharf Deep Sea Fishing. Two deep-sea vessels, the Wharf Cat and the Scat Cat, offer a variety of seasonal migrations in the Gulf of Mexico. Trips aboard the Wharf Cat include expeditions for king mackerel, dolphin, and shark, while trips on the Scat Cat include expeditions for red snapper, grouper, and other highly prized bottom dwellers. Each vessel is equipped with full hot and cold concessions, helpful crews, and a smooth ride. There is also a passenger ferry (Jetty Boat) to St. Jo Island where visitors can fish, surf, shell, and beachcomb. The Jetty Boat also offers dolphin watches every day in the late afternoon.

Information: 800-605-5448

Reservations are recommended, although walk-ons are permitted when space is available.

High Island Sanctuary

High Island is a salt dome on Bolivar Peninsula in Galveston County. Although only 38 feet above sea level, it is the highest point along the Gulf of Mexico between the Yucatán Peninsula and Mobile, Alabama. The marshes near the salt dome are an oil-rich area. But the most notable fact of the island is the Smith Oaks Bird Sanctuary.

The earliest family on the island was Charlotte and George Smith, first purchasing the land in 1879 and living there permanently in 1899. Charlotte was a flower lover, and crepe myrtle, camellias, and banana shrubs greet visitors at the entrance to the sanctuary. Birds were attracted to the area because of the oaks and flowers growing there. The family homestead remained until 1985. In 1988 and 1993, the Houston Audobon Society bought controlling interest of the land from the Smith family descendants.

Coleto Creek Park

The Guadalupe-Blanco River Authority operates the 3,100-acre reservoir for Central Power and Light Company as cooling water for a coal-powered generator. The park was opened in 1981 for outdoor recreation opportunities, including camping, fishing, water skiing, hiking, and wildlife viewing. Of the 190 acres in the park, 40 acres have been developed. Coleto Creek is also a designated birding trail.

Coleto Creek Park and Reservoir,
365 Coleto Park Road,
Victoria, TX 77905
Information:
361-575-6366;
jrobisheaux@gbra.org

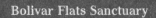

Bolivar Flats Sanctuary

Bolivar Flats Sanctuary, in Port Bolivar, Texas, is an active area of tidal mud flats, salt marsh, brackish marsh, and upland roosting. This area is home to some 140,000 shorebirds. Thirty-seven species use the Flats for feeding and roosting. Gulls, terns, herons, egrets, the American white pelican, brown pelican, and the peregrine falcon are among some of the birds that live here year-round. The flats are constantly changing due to wind and sea storms in the Gulf of Mexico.

When is the best time to see your favorite bird species? The following chart shows some of the many species inhabiting the Bolivar Flats.

SPECIES	Spring	Summer	Fall	Winter
American White Pelican	✔	✔	✔	✔
Brown Pelican	✔	✔	✔	✔
Snowy Egret	✔	✔	✔	✔
Great Blue Heron	✔	✔	✔	✔
Snow Goose				✔
Wilson's Plover	✔	✔	✔	✔
Spotted Sandpiper				✔
Short-Eared Owl			✔	✔
Barn Swallow		✔		
Marsh Wren	✔		✔	
Red-Winged Blackbird	✔	✔		
House Sparrow		✔		
Northern Cardinal				✔
Peregrine Falcon	✔			✔

Bandera Ranches

Bandera is the Cowboy Capital of the World, so what better place could there be to explore Texas ranches? Bandera is about 45 miles northwest of San Antonio. Rodeos are held twice weekly from Memorial Day through Labor Day. Hop on horseback and ride the trails of the Hill Country of Texas. Go fishing or hunting for turkey and white-tailed deer (in season). Visit a honky-tonk (nightclub) and then spend the night at one of the many area ranches.

Running-R Ranch

The Running-R Ranch specializes in the perfect horseback ride. Daily rides range from one to five hours, and the skill level of the trails varies from easy to challenging. Every ride is accompanied by a knowledgeable cowgirl or cowboy.

Running-R Guest Ranch, Inc., 9059 Bandera Creek Road, Bandera, TX 78003-3866

Information: 830-796-3984; runningr@texas.net

Mayan Dude Ranch

The Medina River cascades through the ranch. Trails provide panoramic views of the hills and valleys.

Mayan Dude Ranch, P.O. Box 577, Bandera, TX 78003

Information: 830-796-3312; mayan@mayanranch.com

Dixie Dude Ranch

Immerse yourself in a real-life working ranch, established in 1937, where longhorn cattle, goats, and pigs are raised; where cowboys compete in rodeos; and where every meal is home cooked.

Dixie Dude Ranch, P.O. Box 548, Bandera, TX 78003

Information: 830-796-4481, 800-375-YALL (800-375-9255)

Silver Spur Ranch

Are you looking for the peace of a western sunset and a real western experience? Then tie on your red bandana and put on your blue jeans, for you are going ranching!

Silver Spur Ranch, 9266 Bandera Creek Road, Bandera, TX 78003

Information: 830-796-3037

Twin Elm Guest Ranch

Ride scenic trails, fish in the cypress-shaded Medina River, swim in a private pool, laze around in the shade of an oak tree. This and more await you at Twin Elm Guest Ranch.

Twin Elm Ranch, P.O. Box 117, Bandera, TX 78003

Information: 830-796-3628; 888-567-3049; twinelm@indian-creek.net

Living Desert Trail
and Guadalupe Mountains

The Living Desert Trail, an enhanced nature trail, has plants native to the Chihuahuan Desert. Each plant is labeled with its scientific and common names. The trail begins at the historic Fort Stockton guardhouse. The Chihuahuan Desert is home to the largest living collection of desert cacti and succulents. The surrounding Guadalupe Mountains National Park is part of a steep, rugged mountain range with deep canyons and diverse ecosystems. Thousands of species thrive in the canyon and adapt to the extremes of the tough terrain and changing climate. Eighty miles of trails and backcountry are in this region of the park. It is one of America's best-kept secrets.

The Visitor Center at Pine Springs is accessed via U.S. Hwy 62/180 between Carlsbad, New Mexico, and El Paso, Texas.

Information: 915-828-3251

Natural Bridge Caverns

Stalagmites, stalactites, flowstones, chandeliers, and soda straws—where would you find these? Texas's largest natural landmark, that's where, with a half mile of underground caverns. On March 27, 1960, four spelunkers stumbled upon the largest known cavern in Texas. The cavern is 99 percent active and growing, so new formations crop up continually. The largest "room" is the Hall of the Mountain Kings, 350 feet long, 100 feet wide, and 100 feet high. The temperature in the cave is a comfortable 70°F year-round.

How did it get its name? At the entrance is a 60-foot natural limestone bridge. When a sinkhole collapsed beneath the limestone slab, the bridge remained. The bridge now spans the amphitheater setting.

Natural Bridge Caverns®, 26495 Natural Bridge Caverns Road, Natural Bridge Caverns, TX 78266

Information: 210-651-6101; nabrcavern@aol.com

Big Bend National Park

Big Bend National Park is a hiker's paradise with over 150 miles of trails to explore (permits required). Elevations in the park vary from 1800 feet at the end of Bosquillas Canyon to the 7825-foot Emory Peak in the Chisos Mountains. Some of the trails include Panther Path, Lost Mine Trail, the Castolon Historic Compound, and the Santa Elena Historic Trail.

After hiking, you may want to try rafting the Santa Elena Canyon—the last true deserted wilderness in Texas. This two-day trip also includes camping. The first day is a lazy, relaxing journey of amazing vistas and conversations with a local guide (all trips are escorted). The second day is nonstop adrenaline rushes with a short hike around the nonnavigable river around Rock Slide.

Big Bend National Park is so named because of the Rio Grande and the monstrous turn it takes in the middle of the valley. Regardless of the season, it is well worth repeated visits.

If you plan your visit the first weekend in November, you must go to the International Chili Cook-Off in nearby Terlingua, Texas. The world's greatest chili is at your fingertips! The event draws championship chili cookers from throughout North America, as well as people who associate with these championships.

Big Bend National Park headquarters are on Highway 118, 70 miles south of Marathon, Texas, and 108 miles from Alpine, Texas.

Big Bend National Park, P.O. Box 129, Big Bend National Park, TX 79834

Information: 432-477-2251

Did You Know?

Almost 10% of Texas is covered by forest, which includes four national forests and five state forests.

Guadalupe Peak is the highest peak in Texas at 8,749 feet. (There are over 90 mountain peaks that are at least a mile high.)

The geographic center of Texas is about 15 miles northeast of Brady in northern McCulloch County.

An oak tree near Fulton is estimated to be 1,500 years old.

There are 23,292 farms with 1,000 acres or more, totaling 132 million acres, or 80% of the state's land area.

The King Ranch near Corpus Christi is larger than the state of Rhode Island.

The land area of Texas is 267,339 square miles, which is 7.4% of the land area in the United States.

The name Texas comes from the Hasini Indian word *tejas*, meaning "friends."

Texas rivers and tributaries empty into the Gulf of Mexico.

Find a State Park Near You

Big Bend Country

Balmorhea State Park	Fort Stockton, Pecos	Guadalupe River State Park	Van Horn
Davis Mountains State Park	Fort Davis	Monahans Sandhills State Park	Monahans
Franklin Mountains State Park	El Paso	Ranch State Park	Presidio

Gulf Coast

Brazos Bend State Park	Needville	Lake Texana State Park	Edna
Galveston Island State Park	Galveston	Matagorda Island State Park Port	O'Connor, Port Lavaca
Goose Island State Park	Rockport, Aransas Pass, Corpus Christi	Mustang Island State Park	Port Aransas
		Sea Rim State Park	Sabine Pass
Lake Corpus Christi State Park	Corpus Christi	Sheldon Lake State Park	Houston
Lake Houston State Park	New Caney, Houston		

Hill Country

Colorado Bend State Park	Lampasas	Lockhart State Park	Lockhart
Garner State Park	Uvalde	Longhorn Cavern State Park	Burnet
Kerrville-Shreiner State Park	Kerrville	McKinney Falls State Park	Austin
Kickapoo Cavern State Park	Brackettville	South Llano River State Park	Junction
Lake Brownwood State Park	Brownwood		

Panhandle Plains

Abilene State Park	Abilene	Lake Arrowhead State Park	Wichita Falls
Big Spring State Park	Big Spring	Lake Colorado City State Park	Colorado City
Copper Breaks State Park	Crowell	Palo Duro Canyon State Park	Canyon, Amarillo
Fort Griffin State Park	Albany	San Angelo State Park	San Angelo

Piney Woods

Atlanta State Park	Texarkana	Martin Dies, Jr., State Park	Jasper
Caddo Lake State Park	Marshall, Jefferson	Mission Tejas State Park	Crockett
Daingerfield State Park	Daingerfield	Rusk/Palestine State Parks	Rusk, Palestine
Jim Hogg State Park	Rusk	Sabine Pass Battleground State Park	San Augustine, Center
Lake Bob Sandlin State Park	Pittsburg, Mount Pleasant		
Lake Livingston State Park	Livingston	Stephen F. Austin State Park	Independence, San Felipe
Martin Creek Lake State Park	Longview, Carthage		

Prairies and Lakes

Bastrop State Park	Bastrop	Fort Richardson State Park	Fort Worth, Graham
Bonham State Park	Bonham	Huntsville State Park	Huntsville
Cedar Hill State Park	Cedar Hill	Lake Mineral Wells State Park	Mineral Wells
Cleburne State Park	Cleburne	Lake Tawakoni State Park	Wills Point
Cooper Lake State Park	Cooper, Sulphur Springs	Lake Whitney State Park	Hillsboro, Meridian, Clifton
Dinosaur Valley State Park	Glen Rose	Meridian State Park	Meridian
Eisenhower State Park	Denison	Possum Kingdom State Park	Mineral Wells
Fairfield Lake State Park	Fairfield	Purtis Creek State Park	Athens
Fort Boggy State Park	Centerville	Ray Roberts Lake State Park	Pilot Point, Valley View
Fort Parker State Park	Mexia	Tyler State Park	Tyler

South Texas Plains

Bentsen-Rio Grande Valley State Park	McAllen	Lake Somerville State Park	Somerville, Ledbetter
Blanco State Park	Fredericksburg, San Antonio	Lyndon B. Johnson State Park	Johnson City
Buescher State Park	Smithville	Mother Neff State Park	
Choke Canyon State Park	Three Rivers, George West	Moody	South Texas Plains
Falcon State Park	Falcon Heights, Roma	Palmetto State Park	Gonzales, Luling, Shiner
Inks Lake State Park	Johnson City, Fredericksburg	Pedernales Falls State Park	Johnson City
Lake Casa Blanca International State Park	Laredo	Fredericksburg	South Texas Plains

Texas Wildflowers

Wildflower	Color	Where Typically Found
Agaves	yellow	Chihuahuan Desert
American lotus	white	South and East Texas
Basket flower	red	throughout state
Beach morning glory	white	coastal beaches
Black-eyed Susan	yellow	throughout state
Blackfoot daisy	white	West and North Texas
Bluebells	blue	North and South Texas
Bougainvillea	varies	Rio Grand Valley
Butterfly weed	red	East and Central Texas
Cacti	varies	Panhandle
Cardinal flower	red	throughout state
Cedar sage	red	Central Texas
Cenizo	blue	West Texas
Chocolate flower	yellow	Central and West Texas
Coreopsis	yellow	East Texas
Dogwood	white	East Texas
Fleabane	white	East Texas
Foxglove	blue	roadsides, rocky areas
Gayfeather	red	throughout state
Goldenrod	yellow	throughout state
Grass pink	red	Southeast Texas
Huisache daisy	yellow	Central and South Texas
Indian blanket	red	throughout state
Indian paintbrush	red	throughout state
Lantana	red	throughout state
Lemonmint	blue	throughout state
Magnolia	white	East Texas
Mexican hat	yellow	throughout state

Wildflower	Color	Where Typically Found
Mountain pink	red	Central and West Texas
Ocotillo	red	West Texas
Obedient plant	red	East Texas
Pink evening primroses	red	North Texas
Pitcher plant	yellow	East Texas
Prickly pear cactus	red	throughout state
Rain lilies	white	East Texas
Sand verbena	pink	West Texas
Sleepy daisy	yellow	Central Texas
Spider lilies	white	coastal prairies
Spiderwort	blue	throughout state
Standing cypress	red	East Texas
Swamp mallow	red	Gulf Coast
Tahoka daisy	purple	West Texas and Panhandle
Texas bluebonnets	blue	throughout state
Texas dandelion	yellow	eastern half of state
Texas mountain laurel	purple	Central and Southwest Texas
Texas thistle	blue	all areas except Panhandle
Verbena	blue	all areas except Piney Woods
White prickly poppy	white	Central and South Texas
Wild azaleas	white	East Texas
Wild phlox	red	South Central Texas
Winecups	magenta	all areas except West Texas
Yucca	white	throughout state; most prominent in West Texas

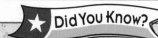

Did You Know?

DeWitt County is the Wildflower
Capital of Texas.

Roses Love Texas

*E*veryone loves the timeless rose. Often our best memories of roses come from the gardens of our grandmothers. It's easy to continue that tradition yourself, and doing so offers great rewards. New roses are always being cultivated, but many older types (some older than your grandmother) are still available. Most Texans know that Tyler, Texas, is the Rose Capital of the World, but why should they have all the fun? The rose categories below contain many selections that will grow well in Texas. Use the descriptions below to find roses that best fit your gardening style, then check out the many selections at your local garden center.

Climbing Roses

Blooms in white, yellow, pink, and red. These can grow quite tall (up to 15 feet or more), and like to lean and arch. They grow best tied to structures such as a fence or post, but come in handy for softening a barrier or defining an outdoor space.

Floribunda Roses

Offering lovely shades and mixes of red, orange, yellow, pink, and white, the beautiful Floribunda rose is created from the crossing of hybrid teas and polyantha roses. These plants grow robust clusters of blooms, making them ideal for quick bouquets.

Grandiflora Roses

A cross between the hybrid tea and the floribunda, grandifloras bloom in white, pink, orange, red, yellow, and blends. Utilizing the best features of its parents, the grandiflora offers long stems and many blooms. These are a terrific choice as background plants, and can be beautifully paired with shorter rose types for an interesting effect.

Heirloom Roses

Blooming in white, pink, and red, these are ideal focal points in the landscape. Heirloom roses may be planted alone or among companions such as a bed of perennials. Their beauty comes with a price, however. Watch out for what can be rather large thorns!

Miniature Roses

The small roses with the big heart, these little beauties are tougher than they look. They offer several color choices and can even be grown indoors in the proper environment. Try these for added color in your landscape, or plant in a container to add life to a patio. If you're gardening in a small space, miniature roses are an ideal choice.

Polyantha Roses

A good choice for a limited space, polyanthas are low-growing and offer blooms from spring through fall. Colors include orange, pink, yellow, white, and red. Its beautifully shaped blooms are scented or unscented, depending on your selection. If you don't like saying goodbye to fading blooms, this one will give you a long season of happiness.

Species Roses

These roses grow in the wild and need plenty of room. Species roses are the oldest rose classification—over 100 different species can be found growing all over the world. They can grow as shrubs, or climbing or trailing, and need minimal care. There are a large variety of colors available. If you want to try a country-cottage-style garden, these may be the choice for you.

CAPTIVATE Your Wild Side

TEXAS ZOOS AND AQUARIUMS

Visiting a zoo is a grand way to spend a day. Animals, particularly animals that are unfamiliar, awe children and adults alike. Texas's biggest cities are home to some of the best zoos in the United States. Here is our rundown of the best zoos in the Lone Star State.

San Antonio Zoo

3903 North St. Mary's Street, San Antonio, TX 78212
Information: 210-734-7184; information@sazoo-aq.org

3800 animals, representing 750 species

Current exhibits: Africa Live, African Plains, Amazonia, Lory Landing, Gibbon Forest, Prairie Chickens, Richard Friedrich Aquarium, Reptile House, Hixon Bird House, Rift Valley, Cranes of the World, Kronskosky's Tiny Tot Nature Spot, Prairie Dogs; Butterflies! Caterpillar Flight School is a visitor favorite.

Fort Worth Zoo

1989 Colonial Parkway, Fort Worth, TX 76110
Information: 817-759-7555

**435 species represented, including
35 endangered species**

Current exhibits: World of Primates, Asian Falls, Raptor Canyons, Chee·tos Cheetahs, African Savannah, Komodo Dragon, Meerkat Mounds, Thundering Plains, Herpetarium, Texas Wild!

The only zoo in the United States to house all four great ape species: gorilla, orangutan, bonobo, and chimpanzee.

Caldwell Zoo

2203 Martin Luther King Blvd., Tyler, TX 75702
Information: 903-593-0121; info@caldwellzoo.org

Over 2000 animals, many of which are endangered

Features scavenger hunts for school field trips: Bird Search!, Conservation Corps!, Habitat Hunt!, Mammal Mania!, Sensational Senses!, Who am I?, Zoo to Do!

Dallas Zoo

650 South R. L. Thornton Freeway, Dallas, TX 75203
Information: 214-670-6826

8000 animals

Current exhibits: Chimpanzee Forest, ZooNorth, Endangered Tiger Habitat, Wilds of Africa, Monorail Safari, Elephant Experience, Keeper Connection

Houston Zoo

1513 N. MacGregor, Houston, TX 77030
Information: 713-533-6500

3500 animals, representing 700 species

Best time to visit: fall and winter

Popular attractions: the Natural Encounters Building, which houses many exhibits and animals; Children's Zoo, Wildlife Carousel

The Texas Zoo

110 Memorial Drive, Victoria, TX 77901
Information: 361-573-7681; texaszoo@texaszoo.org

Primary residents: ocelots, otters, lemurs, spoonbills, pelicans, coatis, wolves, snakes

Capital of Texas Zoo

376A Jenkins Road, Cedar Creek, TX 78612
Information: 512-303-6675; info@capitaloftexaszoo.org

Cameron Park Zoo

1701 N. Fourth Street, Waco, TX, 76707
Information: 254-750-8400

Newest exhibit: Brazos River Country

Paso Zoo

4001 E. Paisano, El Paso, TX 79905-4223

Information: 915-521-1850;
elpasozoo@elpasotexas.gov

270 species, *including 442 mammals, reptiles, amphibians, and birds; 959 fish; and 415 invertebrates. Natural habitat exhibits: Reptile House, South American Pavilion, America's Aviary, Cisneros Paraje, Birds of Prey, American Biome, Forest Atrium, Asian Grasslands, Asian Endangered Walk, Elephant Complex*

Gladys Porter Zoo

500 Ringgold Street, Brownsville, TX 78520
Information: 956-546-2177

377 species of animals, 225 species of plants

Four zoogeographic areas: Africa, Asia, Tropical America, Indo-Australia

Other exhibits: Herpetarium, Aquatic Wing, Free-Flight Aviary, Macaw Canyon, Bear Grottos, California Sea Lions, Small World

Ellen Trout Zoo

402 Zoo Circle, Lufkin, TX 75904
Information: 936-633-0399

700 reptiles, birds, and mammals from around the world

Exhibits: Maasai giraffe, the white rhinoceros, and the Nile hippopotamus

Abilene Zoological Gardens

2070 Zoo Lane, Nelson Park, Abilene, TX 79602
Information: 325-673-WILD (325-673-9453);
abilene.zoo@abilenetx.com

800 animals, representing some 200 species

Tiger Creek Wildlife Refuge

Tiger Creek Wildlife Refuge (TCWR)
17552 FM 14 Tyler, TX 75706
903-858-1008 - Office

Tiger Creek Wildlife Refuge (TCWR) is a big cat sanctuary that was developed in 1997, founded in 1998 (The Year of the Tiger), and officially opened to

the public on May 15, 1999. Brian and Terri Werner started the refuge. Tiger Creek is nestled in the gentle, rolling hills and valleys of the piney woods of East Texas. The site is heavily wooded with oaks, hickory, pines, and dogwood trees and is divided by a spring-fed creek named Tiger Creek. Four employees, a small staff of volunteers, and its board members run the facility. Tiger Creek currently is in the growth stage working toward creating larger, more natural habitats for the resident cats.

The Texas State Aquarium

2710 Shoreline Blvd., Corpus Christi, TX 78402
Information: 361-881-1200; 800-477-GULF (800-477-4853)

Popular attractions:

Discover the creatures of cartilage at Stingray flats. Otter Space highlights the frisky North American River Otter. Turtle Bend gives a close-up look at the endangered species, while Texas Trails gives a peek at the local Texas animals. Don't miss the Outdoor Marsh. The Observation Deck at the Texas State Aquarium is a great place to view Corpus Christi Beach and Downtown.

Moody Gardens Galveston Island Aquarium Pyramid

One Hope Boulevard, Galveston, TX 77554
Information: 409-744-4673; 800-582-4673

Popular attractions:

The Aquarium Pyramid at Moody Gardens is a blue glass pyramid more than 12 stories high. Built on two viewing levels, you can visit the largest bodies of water in the world—North Pacific, South Pacific, South Atlantic, and Caribbean—and take in the beauty and marine life without leaving Texas. The aquarium includes large touch tanks and jewel tanks to enhance the vivid beauty of the ocean world.

Get in Touch with Your inner COWBOY

Whatever your camping style—tents, cabins, RV parks, or a combination—Texas's geographic features and climate make it ideal for various preferences.

Below are some of the larger and more popular campgrounds in Texas.

Abilene State Park

Tuscola, Texas (southwest of Abilene)

Information: 915-572-3204

Over 500 acres in a low range of hills called the Callahan Divide

Activities: Swimming, hiking, nature study, picnicking, fishing, biking, interpretive programs

Facilities: Sewer, electric and water hookups; screened shelters, individual site parking, developed sites with table and grill; restrooms with showers; swimming pool and wading pool; playgrounds and courts

Nearby attractions: A portion of the official Texas longhorn herd and one buffalo live here; Fort Griffin State Park and Historic Site; Abilene Zoological Gardens; Dyess Air Force Base's vintage aircraft; Buffalo Gap Historic Village

Atlanta State Park

Atlanta, Texas (a few miles southwest of Texarkana)

Information: 903-796-6476

1475 acres with 170 miles of shoreline on a 20,300-acre reservoir

Activities: Swimming, nature study, hiking, water-skiing, boating, fishing, camping, picnicking, biking

Facilities: Sewer, electric and water hookups; fishing and boating; restrooms with showers; all campsites have tent pad, picnic table, water, fire pit, and grill; group picnic pavilion; concrete boat-launching ramps; covered fish-cleaning shelter; playgrounds, courts, and trails

Nearby attractions: Caddo Lake State Park, Daingerfield State Park, Starr Family Home

State Historic Site (Marshall, Texas), Sulphur River State Wildlife Management Area

Balmorhea State Park

Toyahvale, Texas (Jeff Davis County; 4 miles southwest of the town of Balmorhea)

Information: 915-375-2370

About 46 acres

Won a 1998 Texas Quality Initiative Award for innovation from the Texas Department of Transportation

The 77,053 sq. ft. San Solomon Spring in the center of the park feeds a 25 feet deep, spring-fed swimming pool that is 1.75 acres in size and a constant temperature of 72–76°F.

Activities: Swimming, picnicking, camping, scuba diving

Facilities: Sewer, electric, water, and cable TV hookups; hotel-like lodging; restrooms with showers; sheltered campsites

Nearby attractions: Davis Mountains State Park, Fort Davis National Historic Site, McDonald Observatory, Chihuahuan Desert Research Institute, Museum of the Big Bend, the Mystery Marfa Lights, Ste. Genevieve Vineyard/Winery

Bastrop State Park

Bastrop, Texas (30 miles southeast of Austin)

Information: 512-321-2101

A forested region of loblolly pine and hardwoods with rolling hills

Activities: Backpacking, camping, picnicking, canoeing, swimming, golfing, wildlife viewing, hiking, interpretive programs, biking, fishing, scenic drives

Facilities: Sewer, electric, and water hook-ups; rustic cabins; restrooms with showers; dining hall; lodges and group barracks

Nearby attractions: Lake Bastrop, Buescher State Park, Lake Somerville State Park & Trailway, McKinney Falls State Park

Caddo Lake State Park

Karnack, Texas (15 miles northeast of Marshall)

Information: 903-679-3351

Activities: Camping, hiking, swimming, picnicking, nature study, fishing, boating, canoeing, pontoon boat tours, hunting (per regulations)

Facilities: Water and electric hookups; some cabins; campsites have table, fire ring, and grill (maximum 8 people per campsite); screened shelters

Nearby attractions: Starr Family State Historic Site; childhood home of Mrs. Lyndon B. Johnson; Soda Lake State Wildlife Management Area

Cleburne State Park

Cleburne, Texas (southwest of Fort Worth in Johnson County)

Information: 817-645-4215

528 acres encompassing a picturesque 116-acre lake

Activities: mountain biking, fishing, boating (no personal watercraft allowed), paddle-boats, camping

Facilities: Water and electric hookups; campsites with table, grill, and fire ring; restrooms with showers; group barracks

Nearby attractions: Dinosaur Valley State Park, Meridian State Park, Lake Whitney State Park, Acton State Historic Site; Fossil Rim Wildlife Center; Texas Amphitheater, Six Flags over Texas

Galveston Island State Park

Galveston, Texas

Information: 409-737-1222

Over 2,000 acres

Activities: Beach camping, swimming, camping, bird-watching, nature study, hiking, mountain bike riding, fishing, educational tours (by appointment only)

Facilities: Water and electric hookups; screened shelters; restrooms with showers; fish-cleaning shelter; interpretive center

Nearby attractions: San Jacinto Battleground State Historic Site, the Battleship Texas, Brazos Bend State Park, Varner-Hogg Plantation State Historic Site, Brazoria National Wildlife Refuge

Lake Bob Sandlin State Park

Pittsburg, Texas (Titus County)

Information: 903-572-5531

About 640 acres on the forested north shores of the 9,400-acre Lake Bob Sandlin

The original site of the Fort Sherman Stockade

Activities: Picnicking, hiking, swimming, mountain biking, in-line skating, fishing, bird-watching, wildlife viewing, interpretive tours, nature walks

Facilities: Electric and water hookups; limited-use cabins; restrooms with showers; screened shelters; lighted fishing pier; fish cleaning facility; two-lane boat ramp

Nearby attractions: Governor Hogg Shrine, Daingerfield State Park, Lake Monticello, Lake Cypress Springs, and Tankersley Gardens (Mt. Pleasant, Texas)

Monahans Sandhills State Park

Monahans, Texas (half hour west of Odessa)

Information: 915-943-2092

3,840 acres

Activities: Camping, hiking, picnicking, horseback riding, bird and wildlife viewing, sand surfing on 70-foot high sand dunes, Texas Camel Treks

Facilities: Water, electric, and sewer dumping hookups; Dunagan Visitor Center; group dining hall

Nearby attractions: Balmorhea State Park, Million Barrel Museum, the Odessa Meteor Crater

Palmetto State Park

Gonzales, Texas
(abuts the San Marcos River)

Information: 210-672-3266

Named for the tropical dwarf palmetto plants that abound in the park

Activities: Camping, picnicking, hiking, fishing, birding, nature study, canoeing, pedal boats, swimming, tubing, educational programs

Facilities: Water and electric hookups; one campsite also has a sewer hookup; group camping area; restrooms with showers and baby changing stations; playgrounds

Nearby attractions: Pioneer Village Living History Center, the Gonzales Memorial Museum, the Central Texas Oil Patch Museum, Lockhart State Park, Sebastopol State Historic Site

Stephen F. Austin State Park and San Felipe State Historic Site

San Felipe, Texas

Information: 409-885-3613

Over 600 acres, with 12 acres adjacent to the Brazos River. This is the setting to which Stephen Austin first brought the 297 families to colonize Texas. Rich bottomland, wildlife, hiking, and history all make this a great camping site.

Take a natural and historic tour while you are here.

Activities: Picnicking, swimming, camping, fishing, hiking, golfing, and nature and historical tours

Facilities: Water, electric, and sewer hookups; picnic sites; screened shelters; restrooms with showers; tent camping; group dining hall for day use; playground; laundry tubs

Nearby attractions: San Jacinto Battleground, San Jacinto Monument, and the battleship *Texas*; Houston-area attractions: Hermann Park Zoo, the Museum of Natural Science, AstroWorld, major league baseball, NASA

South Llano River State Park

Junction, Texas

Information: 915-446-3994

Over 500 acres with 1.5 miles of river frontage

Adjoins the Walter Buck Wildlife Management Area with multitudes of deer and wild turkey

Closed six months of the year to protect wild turkey roosting

Activities: Camping, picnicking, canoeing, tubing, swimming, fishing, hiking, mountain bike riding, bird and nature study

Facilities: Sewer dump stations; water and electric hookups; restrooms with showers; walk-in sites (four people per site) with tables and fire rings; drinking water for every four campsites

Nearby attractions: Kerrville-Schreiner Park, Fort McKavett State Historic Site, Admiral Nimitz Museum State Historic Site (National Museum of the Pacific War), Enchanted Rock State Natural Area

Lake Mineral Wells State Park and Trailway

Mineral Wells, Texas

State Park appreciated most by rock climbers. Located at Rock Creek, a tributary of the Brazos River, the park is the site of the "medicinal" Mineral Wells Lake.

Activities: Camping, swimming, and boating

Facilities: Water and electric

Area Attractions: Fort Richardson State Park, Historic Site and the Lost Creek Reservoir State Trailway, Possum Kingdom State Park, Cleburne State Park, Dinosaur Valley State Park, Clark Gardens, the Brazos River, and Possum Kingdom Lake

Lost Maples State Natural Area

Vanderpool, Texas

A 2,174-acre forest makes this the number one campground in the fall. Place your reservations early to secure a prime campsite.

Facilities: Water and electric

Area Attractions: Garner State Park, Hill Country State Natural Area, Kerrville-

Schreiner Park, Camp Verde, Lake Medina, and the towns of Utopia and Bandera

Monahans Sandhills State Park

Monahans, Texas

70-foot high sand dunes make for incredible sand tobogganing and great camping. Equestrian trails, hiking and wildlife watching round out the experience. Camel Treks are held in the park, also.

Facilities: Water and electricity

Area Attractions: Balmorhea State Park; Million Barrel Museum in Monahans and the Odessa Meteor Crater

Palmetto State Park

Gonzales, Texas

Named for the tropical dwarf palmetto plants that abound in the parkland, this state park is an educational and canoeing Mecca. The two water sources, the San Marcos River and the local oxbow lake provide ample water activities.

Facilities: Water and electric, one campsite with water electric and sewage

Area Attractions: Pioneer Village Living History Center, the Gonzales Memorial Museum, the Central Texas Oil Patch Museum, Lockhart State Park; and the Sebastopol State Historic Site

Sea Rim State Park

Sabine Pass, Texas

This park was temporarily closed after Hurricane Rita. Wildlife observation, birding and beach combing changed after the hurricane and it is an educational experience to see this area rebuild. Historical surroundings and a seasonal bird list are all you need for this park.

Facilities: Water and electric

Area Attraction: Sabine Pass Battleground State Historic Site, Village Creek State Park, McFadden National Wildlife Refuge, Pleasure Island, Sabine Woods, Big Thicket National Preserve, and the J. D. Murphree Wildlife Management Area

South Llano River State Park

Junction, Texas

This park adjoins to the Walter Buck Wildlife Management Area and is home to multitudes of deer and wild turkey.

New to the State Park system, South Llano River State Park offers swimming and floating in the river. Six months of the year, part of the park is closed to protect the wild turkey roosting. This park offers a wildlife and camping interaction not rivaled by many nationwide.

Facilities: Sewer (dump stations), water and electric

Area Attractions: Kerrville-Schreiner Park; Fort McKavett State Historic Site; Admiral Nimitz Museum State Historic Site - National Museum of the Pacific War; Enchanted Rock State Natural Area

Devils River State Natural Area

Del Rio, Texas

Hike, bike, or boat into this primitive campsite. This is a true what you bring in—you take out camping site. There is no water, so you must bring your own. However the archeological treasure trove of pictographs is well worth the additional planning and reservations.

A series of springs in the river provide 80 percent of its water supply. The river is long, with deep pools, wide shallows, and relatively rough, deep turbulent rapids. There are large, dense areas of trees and the area is free of pollution and the other trappings of civilization. It is easy to slip back in time in this camping destination.

Camping: Primitive

Area Attractions: Seminole Canyon State Park and Historic Site, Kickapoo Cavern State Park, and Amistad National Recreation Area

For a listing of all of the campgrounds in the state, visit http://www.recreation.usa.com/camptin/texas.html or http://www.allcampgrounds.com/tx.html.

Bird Watching

With 613 documented bird species in Texas, bird-watching in Texas is both fun and educational. Approximately 75 percent of all American birds are represented in the Texas wild, not counting zoos and other preserves in the state.

Grab a field guide, a pair of binoculars, and as much time as you can spare, and spend it ogling the avian population. The birds don't mind your peeping, and there are countless spots throughout the state to view them.

The American Bald Eagle

Texas (and Oklahoma) are wintering grounds for the bald eagle. Thousands of eagles migrate to the region every year, living wherever there is bountiful food and open water.

Escorted tours along the Red River in January and February guarantee sightings of this national icon. Call 866-PRO-GUIDE (866-776-48433) for more information.

The Texas State Bird

The northern mockingbird was officially adopted as the state bird of Texas on January 31, 1927. The mockingbird is found in all parts of the state, in winter and in summer.

South Padre Island

Birding on South Padre will provide lasting memories. Watch the belted kingfisher,

★ Audubon Societies in Texas

Bastrop County Audubon Society

Golden Triangle Audubon Society

Llano Estacado Audubon Society (south plains of West Texas)

Bexar Audubon Society (San Antonio)

Dallas County Audubon Society

El Paso/Trans Pecos Audubon Society

Fort Worth Audubon Society

Houston Audubon Society

Huntsville Audubon Society

Panhandle Bird Club (Canyon, Texas)

Prairie and Timbers Audubon Society (McKinney, Texas)

Rio Brazos Audubon Society (the Central Brazos Valley area)

Travis Audubon Society (Austin)

Tyler Audubon Society

oystercatcher, egrets, herons, plovers, terns, clapper rails, and more. Colley's Fins to Feathers offers three-hour boat tours for up-close watching of shore birds.

- -

P.O. Box 2611, S. Padre Island, TX 78597
956-761-7178; fin2feather@aol.com
Great Texas Coastal Birding Trail

- -

Running 500 miles along the Texas coastline from Beaumont to the Rio Grande Valley, the Great Texas Coastal Birding Trail encompasses a variety of birding sites. What will you see? Whooping cranes, hummingbirds, frigate birds, royal terns, ducks, hawks, piping plovers, and much, much more.

The Great Texas Coastal Birding Trail consists of 43 separate loops. Each loop encompasses an array of associated sites and birds. A detailed trail map provides information about the birds usually found in the vicinity. Observation platforms abound.

A Checklist of Some of the Birds Found in Texas

WHAT HAVE YOU SEEN?

Blackbird	Grebe	Roadrunner
Bluebird	Grosbeak	Robin
Bobwhite	Gull	Sandpiper
Bunting	Harrier hawk	Skimmer
Cardinal	Heron	Sparrow
Catbird	Hummingbird	Spoonbill
Chickadee	Kingfisher	Starling
Clapper rail	Kite	Swallow
Cormorant	Lark	Tanager
Cowbird	Loon	Tern
Crane	Meadowlark	Thrasher
Cuckoo	Mockingbird	Thrush
Dove	Oriole	Titmouse
Eagle	Osprey	Turkey
Falcon	Oystercatcher	Verdin
Finch	Parakeet	Vulture
Flycatcher	Parrot	Warbler
Frigate bird	Pelican	Whistling duck
Gannet	Plover	Woodpecker
Goldfinch	Quail	Wren
Goose	Raven	

Leave No Trace

Outdoor Ethics for Everyone

What does it mean to "leave no trace?" Whenever you are enjoying the outdoors, such as a state park or a wilderness and refuge area, you should leave the area in the same condition as it was when you arrived.

Leave No Trace is an international organization dedicated to preserving the outdoors and limiting the impact of hikers, campers, picnickers, bikers, horseback riders, and the like. Although based in Colorado, this organization strives for outdoor preservation across the United States.

Leave No Trace Center for Outdoor Ethics P.O. Box 997, Boulder, CO 80306 303-442-8222; 800-332-4100

The following principles from the Leave No Trace Center for Outdoor Ethics will make your outdoor adventure more enjoyable.

Plan Ahead and Prepare

✔ Know the regulations and special concerns for the area you will visit.

✔ Prepare for extreme weather, hazards, and emergencies.

✔ Schedule your trip to avoid times of high use.

✔ Repackage food to minimize waste.

✔ Use a map and compass to eliminate the use of marking paint, rock cairns, or flagging.

✔ Travel and camp on durable surfaces.

✔ Follow established trails and use already developed campsites. Camp at least 200 feet from lakes and streams.

✔ Keep campsites small.

✔ Walk single file in the middle of the trail.

✔ Dispose of waste properly.

✔ Inspect your campsite and rest areas for trash or spilled foods. Dispose of all trash in park receptacles. Secure trash if it must be transported.

✔ Deposit solid human waste in holes dug 6–8 inches deep at least 200 feet from water, camp, and trails. Cover and disguise when finished.

✔ Use small amounts of biodegradable soap for washing and scatter the used water.

✔ Leave what you find.

✔ Preserve the past: examine, but do not touch, cultural or historic structures and artifacts.

✔ Leave rocks, plants, and other natural objects as you find them.

✔ Minimize campfire impacts.

✔ Use a lightweight stove for cooking and enjoy a candle lantern for light at night.

✔ Where fires are permitted, use established fire rings, fire pans, or mound fires.

✔ Keep fires small. Use only sticks from the ground that can be broken by hand.

✔ Burn all wood and coals to ash, put out campfires completely, and then scatter the cool ashes.

✔ Respect wildlife.

✔ Observe wildlife from a distance. Do not follow or approach them.

✔ Never feed animals.

✔ Avoid wildlife during sensitive times: mating, nesting, raising young, or winter.

✔ Be considerate of other visitors.

✔ Be courteous. Yield to other users on the trail.

✔ Take breaks and camp away from trails and other visitors.

✔ Let nature's sounds prevail. Avoid loud voices and noises.